The Ultras

Over the last 50 years, the ultras have become the most widespread, outspoken and spectacular form of football fandom across the globe. Whilst the ultras phenomenon began in Italy, then spread across Southern Europe into Northern Europe, it is now the dominant style of fandom in North Africa, South East Asia and East Asia and is spreading into North America and Australia. This spectacular style of fandom has been spread through global media, social media and increased travel, where fans can view, engage and interact with a range of fans from across the globe and bring various local dimensions to their fandom. This volume brings together a range of articles about the ultras' style of football fandom. It is designed to be an introduction: a first account of ultras for the uninitiated. What follows are analyses and accounts of ultras in Italy, France, Germany, Poland, Turkey, Israel, North America, Australia, Indonesia and Croatia. Not only does this volume demonstrate the prevalence of the ultras' style of fandom across the globe, it shows how football becomes an important cultural arena to see the intersections of globalization and localism.

This book was originally published as a special issue of *Sport in Society*.

Mark Doidge is Senior Research Fellow at the University of Brighton, UK. His research focuses on political activism among football fans across Europe, particularly anti-racism and supporting refugees, and the broader political identities associated with football fandom. He is the author of *Ultras: The Passion and Performance of Contemporary Football Fandom* (2020), *Collective Action and Football Fandom* (2018) and *Football Italia* (2015).

Martin Lieser is an independent scholar and Senior Concept Manager at a Munich-based sports marketing agency. Before transitioning into business, he pursued a PhD in Japanese Studies from the University of Vienna, Austria. Throughout his studies his research has focused on sports culture and more particularly on the social and cultural dimensions of football fandom in Japan.

Sport in the Global Society: Contemporary Perspectives
Series Editor: Boria Majumdar, *University of Central Lancashire, UK*

The social, cultural (including media) and political study of sport is an expanding area of scholarship and related research. While this area has been well served by the *Sport in the Global Society* series, the surge in quality scholarship over the last few years has necessitated the creation of *Sport in the Global Society: Contemporary Perspectives*. The series will publish the work of leading scholars in fields as diverse as sociology, cultural studies, media studies, gender studies, cultural geography and history, political science and political economy. If the social and cultural study of sport is to receive the scholarly attention and readership it warrants, a cross-disciplinary series dedicated to taking sport beyond the narrow confines of physical education and sport science academic domains is necessary. *Sport in the Global Society: Contemporary Perspectives* will answer this need.

For a complete list of titles in this series, please visit www.routledge.com/series/ SGSC

Recent titles in the series include:

Youth Sport and Social Capital
Bleachers and Boardrooms
By Sean F. Brown

Being Disabled, Becoming a Champion
Edited by Nicholas Bancel, Julie Cornaton and Anne Marcellini

Christianity and Social Scientific Perspectives on Sport
Edited by Tom Gibbons and Stuart Braye

Sport, Outdoor Life and the Nordic World
Edited by Nils Asle Bergsgard, Solfrid Bratland-Sanda, Richard Giulianotti and Jan Ove Tangen

The Ultras
A Global Football Fan Phenomenon
Edited by Mark Doidge and Martin Lieser

The Ultras
A Global Football Fan Phenomenon

Edited by
Mark Doidge and Martin Lieser

First published 2021
by Routledge
2 Park Square, Milton Park, Abingdon, Oxon OX14 4RN

and by Routledge
52 Vanderbilt Avenue, New York, NY 10017

Routledge is an imprint of the Taylor & Francis Group, an informa business

© 2021 Taylor & Francis

All rights reserved. No part of this book may be reprinted or reproduced or utilised in any form or by any electronic, mechanical, or other means, now known or hereafter invented, including photocopying and recording, or in any information storage or retrieval system, without permission in writing from the publishers.

Trademark notice: Product or corporate names may be trademarks or registered trademarks, and are used only for identification and explanation without intent to infringe.

British Library Cataloguing in Publication Data
A catalogue record for this book is available from the British Library

ISBN 13: 978-0-367-61600-7

Typeset in Minion Pro
by Newgen Publishing UK

Publisher's Note
The publisher accepts responsibility for any inconsistencies that may have arisen during the conversion of this book from journal articles to book chapters, namely the inclusion of journal terminology.

Disclaimer
Every effort has been made to contact copyright holders for their permission to reprint material in this book. The publishers would be grateful to hear from any copyright holder who is not here acknowledged and will undertake to rectify any errors or omissions in future editions of this book.

Contents

Citation Information	vii
Notes on Contributors	ix

Introduction   1
Mark Doidge and Martin Lieser

1   Openers, witnesses, followers, and 'good guys'. A sociological study of the different roles of female and male ultra fans in confrontational situations   9
Bérangère Ginhoux translated by Jessie Dubief

2   Polish ultras in the post-socialist transformation   22
Radosław Kossakowski, Tomasz Szlendak and Dominik Antonowicz

3   Ultras in Turkey: othering, agency, and culture as a political domain   38
Yağmur Nuhrat

4   'The East' strikes back. *Ultras Dynamo*, hyper-stylization, and regimes of truth   51
Daniel Ziesche

5   The (Re)Constitution of football fandom: Hapoel Katamon Jerusalem and its supporters   70
Netta Ha-Ilan

6   Ultras in Indonesia: conflict, diversification, activism   87
Andy Fuller and Fajar Junaedi

7   'Supporters, not consumers.' Grassroots supporters' culture and sports entertainment in the US   100
Markus Gerke

8   Social agency and football fandom: the cultural pedagogies of the Western Sydney ultras   114
Jorge Knijnik

9 Carnival supporters, hooligans, and the 'Against Modern Football'
   movement: life within the ultras subculture in the Croatian context   128
   Benjamin Perasović and Marko Mustapić

10 Ethnography and the Italian Ultrà   145
    Matthew Guschwan

    Index   161

Citation Information

The chapters in this book were originally published in *Sport in Society*, volume 21, issue 6 (June 2018). When citing this material, please use the original page numbering for each article, as follows:

Introduction
Mark Doidge and Martin Lieser
Sport in Society, volume 21, issue 6 (June 2018), pp. 833–840

Chapter 1
Openers, witnesses, followers, and 'good guys'. A sociological study of the different roles of female and male ultra fans in confrontational situations
Bérangère Ginhoux translated by Jessie Dubief
Sport in Society, volume 21, issue 6 (June 2018), pp. 841–853

Chapter 2
Polish ultras in the post-socialist transformation
Radosław Kossakowski, Tomasz Szlendak and Dominik Antonowicz
Sport in Society, volume 21, issue 6 (June 2018), pp. 854–869

Chapter 3
Ultras in Turkey: othering, agency, and culture as a political domain
Yağmur Nuhrat
Sport in Society, volume 21, issue 6 (June 2018), pp. 870–882

Chapter 4
'The East' strikes back. Ultras Dynamo, hyper-stylization, and regimes of truth
Daniel Ziesche
Sport in Society, volume 21, issue 6 (June 2018), pp. 883–901

Chapter 5
The (Re)Constitution of football fandom: Hapoel Katamon Jerusalem and its supporters
Netta Ha-Ilan
Sport in Society, volume 21, issue 6 (June 2018), pp. 902–918

Chapter 6

Ultras in Indonesia: conflict, diversification, activism
Andy Fuller and Fajar Junaedi
Sport in Society, volume 21, issue 6 (June 2018), pp. 919–931

Chapter 7

'Supporters, not consumers.' Grassroots supporters' culture and sports entertainment in the US
Markus Gerke
Sport in Society, volume 21, issue 6 (June 2018), pp. 932–945

Chapter 8

Social agency and football fandom: the cultural pedagogies of the Western Sydney ultras
Jorge Knijnik
Sport in Society, volume 21, issue 6 (June 2018), pp. 946–959

Chapter 9

Carnival supporters, hooligans, and the 'Against Modern Football' movement: life within the ultras subculture in the Croatian context
Benjamin Perasović and Marko Mustapić
Sport in Society, volume 21, issue 6 (June 2018), pp. 960–976

Chapter 10

Ethnography and the Italian Ultrà
Matthew Guschwan
Sport in Society, volume 21, issue 6 (June 2018), pp. 977–992

For any permission-related enquiries please visit:
www.tandfonline.com/page/help/permissions

Notes on Contributors

Dominik Antonowicz, Nicolaus Copernicus University, Poland.

Mark Doidge, School of Sport and Service Management, University of Brighton, UK.

Jessie Dubief, University of Lille 1 USTL, Lille, France.

Andy Fuller, Asia Institute, The University of Melbourne, Australia.

Markus Gerke, Department of Sociology, State University of New York at Stony Brook, USA.

Bérangère Ginhoux, Centre Max Weber, University of Jean Monnet, France.

Matthew Guschwan, independent scholar, Bloomington, IN, USA.

Netta Ha-Ilan, Department of Sociology and Communication, The Open University of Israel, Israel.

Fajar Junaedi, Communications Studies Department, Universitas Muhammadiyah Yogyakarta, Indonesia.

Jorge Knijnik, School of Education and Institute for Culture and Society, Western Sydney University, Australia.

Radosław Kossakowski, Institute of Philosophy, Sociology and Journalism, The University of Gdańsk, Poland.

Martin Lieser, independent scholar, Hamburg, Germany.

Marko Mustapić, Ivo Pilar Institute of Social Sciences, Croatia.

Yağmur Nuhrat, Department of Sociology, Istanbul Bilgi University, Turkey.

Benjamin Perasović, Ivo Pilar Institute of Social Sciences, Croatia.

Tomasz Szlendak, Nicolaus Copernicus University, Poland.

Daniel Ziesche, English Department, Technische Universität Chemnitz, Germany.

Introduction

Mark Doidge and Martin Lieser

ABSTRACT

The ultras have become the most spectacular form of football fandom in the early twenty-first century. Thanks to global media, social media and increased travel, fans view, engage and interact with a range of fans from across the globe and bring various local dimensions to their fandom. This volume brings together a range of articles into the ultras style of football fandom. Whilst the ultras phenomenon began in Italy, then spread across Southern Europe into Northern Europe, it has now become truly global. This volume is designed to be an introduction; a first account of ultras for the uninitiated. What follows are analyses and accounts of ultras in Italy, France, Germany, Poland, Turkey, Israel, North America, Australia, Indonesia and Croatia. Not only does this demonstrate the prevalence of the ultras style of fandom across the globe, it shows how football becomes an important cultural arena to see the intersections of globalisation and localism.

Ultras frequently make the news for their actions inside and outside the stadium. Often this is for their disruptive and antisocial activities. The 2014 Coppa Italia final was disrupted after some Roma ultras attacked and shot Napoli fans prior to the match. In order to disrupt the kick off, Napoli ultras threw flares onto the pitch and order was only restored when the capo, or head, of the Napoli ultras, Genny 'a Carogna, negotiated with Napoli's captain Marek Hamsik that the game could go ahead. Genny 'a Carogna was banned for five years, not for the disturbance, but for wearing a 'Speziale Libero' t-shirt that called for the release of Antonio Speziale, an ultra from Catania who was imprisoned for the death of a policeman during a riot between police and ultras of Palermo and Catania in the Sicilian Derby seven years earlier. In 2015, Standard Liege ultras were criticized for displaying a large banner of the serial killer Jason Voorhees from *Friday the 13th* holding the severed head of Steven Dufour, the player who had played for Liege but was now playing for their rivals Anderlecht. Alongside the graphic picture was written in English 'Red or Dead'. The Liege fans got their wish as Dufour saw red after he was sent off for kicking the ball into the fans in frustration at the abuse he received. Whilst these are examples of some of the more antisocial aspects of fan culture, ultras were also prominent in displaying banners declaring 'Refugees Welcome', in Germany, Greece and some Italian clubs in particular.

Other ultras groups have shown support for earthquake victims or expressed solidarity and love for players and managers, such as Borussia Dortmund ultras displaying a large choreography of their departing manager, Jürgen Klopp, with an image of the coach and the words 'danke Jürgen'.

Violence, rivalry, politics and powerful displays of fandom are some of the unifying themes that describe the ultras form of fandom and are explored within this volume. What unites ultras is their passionate and unwavering support of their club. The ultras originated in Italy in the late 1960s (Roversi 1992; Podaliri and Balestri 1998; Testa and Armstrong 2010; Doidge 2015a). Originally they were political as the groups took the political banners, flags and chants of the protests into the stadium. By the 1980s, new groups were less ideologically political and focused on violence as they took their influence from British hooliganism. By the 1990s, Italian ultras maintained their rigorous support of their clubs, but were willing to unite with their rivals in order to challenge state repression (Podaliri and Balestri 1998; Contucci and Francesio 2013; Doidge 2015a). The ultras style spread across south-eastern Europe, into the former Yugoslavia, southern France, Greece and Turkey during the 1990s. Part of this was geographical proximity, but it was also influenced by the popularity of Serie A on television and fans could see what Italian ultras were doing. Television and social media have helped the ultras style spread in the twenty-first Century into Northern and Eastern Europe, particularly Germany, Austria, Czech Republic and Poland. Ultras in Cairo played an instrumental role in the Arab Spring (Tuastad 2014). They used their experience of challenging the police in the political arena and effectively became the armed wing of the revolution. Ultras have also spread worldwide, as this volume shows. Social media, television and migration have helped the phenomenon emerge in North America, Australia and South East Asia. For this reason, this style of football fandom is worthy of a further investigation.

This volume came about through a series of conversations at conferences and (of course) football matches. It became apparent that many people across Europe, in particular, were researching different aspects of fan culture. The ultras have become the dominant form of fandom in Europe and scholarship was reflecting this. Case studies have been undertaken in a variety of European settings including Italy (Testa and Armstrong 2010; Contucci and Francesio 2013; Doidge 2013, 2015a, 2015b), Germany (Merkel 2012; Gabler 2013), Poland (Antonowicz, Kossakowski, and Szlendak 2015, 2016; Kossakowski 2015), 'Croatia (Hodges 2014, 2016), Turkey (McManus 2013; Nuhrat 2013), France (Ginhoux 2015a, 2015b) and Denmark (Mintert and Pfister 2014a, 2014b). Yet there had not been a single edited volume or special issue that brought ultras scholarship together. Whilst no special issue can hope to cover the range and depth of scholarship, we hope to provide an introduction to this fascinating form of football fandom.

The range of articles in this volume demonstrates how prevalent the ultras style of fandom has become across the globe. We were inundated with requests to be part of this volume, even after the deadline had passed. This shows how ultras are a popular and fascinating topic of study. The intention of this volume was to be inclusive and provide an overview of ultras across the world. In the future there is the potential for themed special issues around violence, media representations, gender and methods to name a few. This volume is designed to be an introduction; a first account of ultras for the uninitiated. What follows are analyses and accounts of ultras in Italy, France, Germany, Poland, Turkey, Israel, North America, Australia, Indonesia and Croatia. Whilst the ultras phenomenon began in Italy, then spread across Southern Europe into Northern Europe, it has now become truly global. Thanks to social media and television, fans from around the world can watch what other fans are doing and incorporate their style into their own repertoire. The beauty of studying football fans is that they give us insights into how global and local cultures intersect.

Ultras: global–local conflict and influence

Each of the articles in this volume draws out their own conclusions and locally specific issues. Yet certain themes emerge throughout. Readers may spot their own themes, but we have identified a small number of recurring topics. These relate to the global influence and style of ultras, and their incorporation of different global influences. Many authors have identified how the groups take their influences from the Italian ultras and British hooligans and casuals. This occurs in forms of clothing and the brands that are worn. Kossakowski, Szlendak and Antonowicz emphasize the performance of ultras in Poland. These performances are rooted in class-based religious traditions. Much of this is directed towards a rebellious, anti-authority form of activity. As elsewhere in this volume, localized traditions are incorporated into wider global trends of ultras being 'against modern football', commercialism and regulation. Yet in Poland, most of the focus is on regulation of the ultras' way of life, rather than commercialism as the latter has not occurred to the same extent as in other nations. Performance is central to the presentation of the group and delimits who 'we' are in relation to the weaker 'other'. Like the Dresden ultras in Ziesche's article, many fan groups in Poland revel in their rebellious, dangerous image. In order to do this, Polish ultras draw on various historical, anti-Communist and nationalist slogans and images that reinforce a particular historical and political narrative and emphasize the ultras as being at the vanguard of unpopular views.

Whilst we can see the influence of Italian and more general ultras culture, it still adapts to local influences. In the case of Ultras Dynamo, Ziesche shows how a specific club identity based within the former GDR can combine with ultras culture to form a specific localized identity. This identity is rooted in being seen as outsiders – chaotic, dangerous, potentially violent and ironically East German. This self identity is carefully presented. Banners are stylized to look threatening and group names refer to hooliganism and violence. It is also presented through social media as the group uses videos to directly address members and attempt to control some of the extreme elements of the group. Social media can act as a way of disciplining ultras, as well as of self-expression away from the match.

Knijnik locates the ultras of Western Sydney Wanderers in the cultural milieu of Western Sydney. Playing and supporting football signified the players and fans as outsiders and immigrants to the older Australians who preferred rugby, cricket and Aussie Rules football. Significantly, Knijnik argues that ultras provide one of the few spaces for a critical engagement with civil and commercial society. This cultural pedagogy ensures members understand and locate themselves in the broader social world. Being an ultras member is a communal and social event which helps to determine who 'we' are compared to others. The group is constituted through the physical performance in the stadium. The collective effervescence of emotional energy in the stadium helps produce social cohesion and collective identity, not only for the Red and Black Bloc, but also for the region as a whole. This helps reduce ethnic difference within the group, whilst emphasizing the regional difference to Sydney and the rest of Australia.

The ultras presentation of self also relates to the way that ultras present themselves in the stadiums. Rhythmic clapping, chanting, pyrotechnics, banners and choreographies are all incorporated into the ultras repertoire. This approach is demonstrated in Fuller and Junaedi's beautifully written insight into ultras culture outside of Europe. Through their anthropological account of Indonesian football, they take the reader on a familiar journey in a potentially unfamiliar terrain. What can be seen from their account of ultras at Persis Solo and Bonek are many recognizable patterns of ultras culture. There is the passionate devotion to the football club using a variety of chants, flags, flares and gestures, all led by a capo. This broadly masculine group expects loyalty and solidarity. They are politically active and actively protest against the Indonesian Football Federation, FIFA and 'Modern Football'. Their account also shows how global culture is appropriated. Football, music and fashion are all incorporated into this style.

Conflict is another recurring theme. Ultras have become synonymous with violence, particularly as they became influenced by British hooliganism. The role of conflict helps account for the ways in which ultras differentiate themselves from others. The performance in the stadium helps to separate them from their rivals, both local and political. The antisocial elements of ultras culture have provoked the ire of those in authority – clubs, football federations and police. Although many ultras groups consider themselves to be ideologically apolitical, they frequently engage in 'football politics'. This means that groups will protest and campaign against laws and regulations that are affecting their enjoyment of the game. This is coming from two perspectives. The first is the economic transformation of football over the last 30 years that has seen unprecedented levels of sponsorship and television deals that have resulted in changes to player recruitment and many more global supporters of global teams.

Ginhoux's excellent exploration of violence and masculinity within the ultras of St Etienne gives an insight into the hierarchy and roles within a group. The 'openers' look for targets, with 'witnesses' looking on. In the 'background', the gendered aspect of the group sees female ultras on the periphery of violence and adopting 'feminine' roles, such as caring for the injured. The violence is predominantly done by the 'first line' of 'good guys'. Not only are these the most skilled fighters, they embody a specific masculinity exhibited in their clothing, comportment and demeanour. There are unwritten rules within the ultras groups. They may fight for pride, to hurt, but not to maim. Groups who don't play by the rules are not respected. There is no honour in using weapons. Trans-cultural confrontations can cause confusion as different 'rules' are used. Drawing on the work of Randall Collins, Ginhoux identifies how much of the confrontation is about emotional domination of the situation. There have to be significant numbers to retain honour. But most of the confrontation is a performance that attempts to minimize the potential of violence.

Nuhrat's insightful account of çArşı, the most prominent fan group of Beşiktaş in Istanbul, demonstrates the paradox at the heart of ultras fandom. In the globalized corporate world of contemporary football, ultras provide a vital part of the mediatized spectacle. Their colourful choreographies and passionate support help create an enhanced televisual product. Silvio Berlusconi, the owner of AC Milan, who suggested that fans should be admitted into the stadium for free to improve the media product, observed this (Doidge 2015a). Ultras add a touch of edginess to the spectacle – the threat of violence, the aggression and rivalry. This 'fear and fascination', as Nuhrat calls it, ensures that ultras are tolerated by clubs. In spite of, or maybe because of this, there is an intrinsic suspicion of authority, especially the police, football federations and a dislike of 'modern football'. As Nuhrat argues, 'Wishing to be in total control of football as a spectacle, administrators praise or rather tolerate fervour and passion so long as they have the final say in relation to how they can be packaged – in a way that can generate profit for the club'. The capitalist consumption of football will permit those aspects of fandom that facilitate profit, whilst criminalizing behaviour that does not.

The desire to differentiate themselves from rivals helps sharpen each group's identity. Ziesche also reiterates the way Ultras Dynamo attempt to distance themselves from the influence of the Far Right. In doing so, they argue that they are apolitical and their capo, Lehmi, explicitly said that 'all political chants can be left out of the stadium'. Within this call to be apolitical, anti-discriminatory positions are seen as being left wing and therefore have also been pushed out of the stadium. Whilst racism and anti-Semitism have been pushed out by the ultras, sexism and homophobic chants continue and attempts to challenge this are seen as 'political'. Despite this, the Dynamo ultras are active in 'football politics'. Yet this is not done in a leftish, anti-consumerist approach, but in an antisocial aggressive manner.

The stylistic mélange of the US is reflected in the reflexive discussion and utilization of various cultural forms of fandom. Influences from Europe, particularly Britain and Italy, and South America are adopted and adapted in the football stadiums of North America. The 'rebellious' aspect of ultras culture permits a different form of sports' consumption. Gerke observes how it sits in 'stark contrast to the unilaterally regulated space of American Football, basketball, baseball and hockey stadiums in the US and Canada'. Like their counterparts elsewhere in the world, the ultras at New York Red Bull have a complicated relationship with their owners. There has been open protest at the way the club is run by the energy drink manufacturer. Forms of protest taken from ultras traditions help reinforce the fans' identity. For some, they protest by only wearing clothing and colours of the Metros era, before Red Bull took over and changed the name, badge and colours. Ultras use consumption as a form of resistance to global corporate football. But this resistance is tapered by the ownership structure of football. The fans only have so much power and this leads to a more pragmatic approach.

Perasović and Mustapić's insightful ethnographic study observes the presence of an ultras' subculture and highlights how it incorporates certain uniform aspects of style, whilst being a heterogeneous group. They discuss the growth and role of Torcida from Hajduk Split, the oldest fan group in Europe, and how it has adapted to the changing political-economic development of Croatian football. Unlike many ultras groups across Europe, Torcida has not fragmented and remains resolutely strong when protesting. The 'against modern football' slogan is often used by Torcida to encapsulate many different aspects of contemporary football including politics, regulation, ownership and commercialism. 'Against modern football' is also involved in images within the subculture, such as flags and t-shirts. Images like old leather footballs and retro images invoke a 'golden age' of football before police surveillance and commercialism. This is all celebrated in the carnivalesque atmosphere around the stadium.

The inspiration of ultras culture is not the only cultural influence on ultras groups. Hooliganism has influenced over the years and the 'No To Modern Football' movement continues to exert a powerful attraction. Another contemporary form of fandom is supporter democracy and this is covered in the case study of Hapoel Katamon Jerusalem. Once again, football politics is a key factor of HKJ. The fans grew disillusioned with the owners of Hapoel Jerusalem and established their own club with democratic structures. This allows the fans a voice to discuss their traditions and strategies. The group is explicitly anti-discriminatory and runs projects with local Jewish and Arab communities. This political identity is reflexive and rooted in local social relations, yet it is performed through the global culture of ultras fandom. This style helps to create an 'authentic' and 'dedicated' group of fans. Yet this is debated and discussed through various forms of social media that seeks to have an inclusive voice, which in itself, reinforces the political traditions of the fans.

Last but not least, Guschwan provides the only methodological article in this volume. The volume finishes with an article about the ultras where the phenomenon began: Italy. Gushwan gives the reader a practical, reflective journey about being an outsider within the ultras. So much of the ultras is about clearly stating who 'we' are, and dividing from outsiders – rivals, non-ultras, police and authorities. As an ethnographer, Gushwan was not simply an outsider to the group, but to the whole sporting culture. As the dominant methodology in studies of ultras, Gushwan's reflections constitute an important consideration for those interested in the study of ultras. Whilst also highlighting some of the pitfalls associated with this method, he provides an outline of some areas of consideration that will be useful to future ethnographies and hopefully allow others to get a sense of what ethnographic studies of ultras can do.

The future of ultras scholarship

This collection of articles demonstrates the vitality and range of scholarship being undertaken into ultras culture. They allow us to compare and contrast different case studies and see how a global ultras culture, a *mentalita ultras*, is emerging (Doidge 2015a). Yet this is adapting to local circumstances. Like other forms of football scholarship, there is a wealth of opportunities to explore. Perhaps it is the nature of football fandom that encourages a certain commonality in methodology. Ethnographic and participatory methods provide colour and depth to groups. Interviews and focus groups help unpick some of the contestations, paradoxes and conflicts within football fan culture. Yet these are not the only methods that can be used, particularly, as these methods will be influenced by the gender and ethnicity of the researcher. Moving forward, academics need to move on from the predominantly ethnographic approach to fandom and explore other ways of accessing football fans and presenting their world. Social media was a recurring theme amongst the articles in this volume. Discourse analysis of forums and twitter can provide an insight into public debates. The visual performance captured through videos and photos lends itself to visual methods where we can understand the aesthetics of choreographies and protests. Meanwhile, analyses of political and media discourses can provide some critical reflections on the growing criminalization and repression of ultras. Finally, much scholarship into football fandom in general, and ultras in particular, is sociological or anthropological. We need to embrace other disciplinary approaches, such as history, political science, criminology, media studies and gender studies. This will deepen our understanding of ultras and develop football studies as a discipline.

Despite the popularity and importance of research into the *ultras*, it will not escape the notice of many readers of this special edition that many of the contributors are male. The editors were aware that this could have been an issue and expressly invited contributions from female academics. Some of these were unable to contribute, for a variety of reasons. But what this shows is that there is a clear gender gap in the study of *ultras*. This is particularly true of football fandom in general (Cere 2002; Dunn 2014, 2016; with Welford 2015; Pope 2014, 2015) but seems more acute when looking into a global phenomenon like the *ultras*. Undoubtedly, some *ultras* groups are predominantly masculine. Researchers should be aware of this aspect and acknowledge the gendered dynamic. Masculine fan groups will generate specific forms of interactions, emotions and cultures that arise from their masculine assumptions of fandom. These need to be analysed in order to fully understand and articulate the *ultras* way of life.

The fascination with the ultras ensures a rich and colourful fan culture. This volume captures a small number of the great research undertaken and gives an insight into groups from around the world. Despite the local differences, certain recurring themes emerge, particularly politics, both ideological and 'football politics' within the 'No To Modern Football' movement. Other aspects emerge including violence, performances, rivalries with other groups and challenging authorities. We hope you enjoy these accounts and that they stimulate readers to do their own research into this fascinating phenomenon.

Acknowledgements

The editors would like to thank the various reviewers for their time and support in peer-reviewing the articles contained within this volume.

Disclosure statement

No potential conflict of interest was reported by the authors.

References

Antonowicz, Dominik, Radosław Kossakowski, and Tomasz Szlendak. 2015. *Aborygeni i konsumenci. O kibicowskiej wspólnocie, komercjalizacji futbolu i stadionowym apartheidzie* [Aborigines and consumers. About the Jewish community, the commercialization of football and stadium apartheid]. Warszawa: IFiS PAN.

Antonowicz, Dominik, Radosław Kossakowski, and Tomasz Szlendak. 2016. "Flaming Flares, Football Fanatics and Political Rebellion: Resistant Youth Cultures in Late Capitalism." In *Eastern European Youth Cultures in a Global Context*, edited by Matthias Schwartz and Heike Winkel, 131–144. Basingstoke: Palgrave Macmillan.

Cere, Rinella. 2002. "'Witches of Our Age': Women Ultras, Football and the Media." *Culture, Sport, Society* 5 (3): 166–188.

Contucci, L., and G. Francesio. 2013. *A Porte Chiuse: gli ultimi giorni del calcio italiano*. Milano: Sperling and Kupfer.

Doidge, Mark. 2013. "'The Birthplace of Italian Communism': Political Identity and Action Amongst Livorno Fans." *Soccer & Society* 14: 246–261.

Doidge, Mark. 2015a. *Football Italia: Italian Football in an Age of Globalization*. London: Bloomsbury.

Doidge, Mark. 2015b. "'If You Jump Up and Down, Balotelli dies': Racism and Player Abuse in Italian Football." *International Review for the Sociology of Sport* 50 (3): 249–264.

Dunn, Carrie. 2014. *Female Football Fans: Community, Identity and Sexism*. London: Palgrave.

Dunn, Carrie. 2016. *Football and the Women's World Cup*. London: Palgrave.

Dunn, Carrie, and Jo Welford. 2015. *Football and the FA Women's Super League: Structure, Governance and Impact*. London: Palgrave.

Gabler, J. 2013. *Die Ultras: Fußballfans und Fußballkulturen in Deutschland*. Köln: Papyrossa.

Ginhoux, B. 2015a. "Comment devient-on un « gars du groupe » quand on est une fille? Carrière et combines des supportrices ultras." *Agora débats/jeunesses* 71: 7–21.

Ginhoux, B. 2015b. "En dehors du stade: l'inscription des supporters « ultras » dans l'espace urbain." *Métropolitiques*. http://www.metropolitiques.eu/En-dehors-du-stade-l-inscription.html.

Hodges, A. 2014. "The Hooligan as 'Internal' Other? Football Fans, Ultras Culture and Nesting Intra-orientalisms." *International Review for the Sociology of Sport* 51 (4): 410–427.

Hodges, A. 2016. "Violence and Masculinity Amongst Left-wing Ultras in Post-Yugoslav Space." *Sport in Society* 19 (2): 174–186.

Kossakowski, R. 2015. "'Where are the Hooligans? Dimensions of Football Fandom in Poland" *International Review for the Sociology of Sport*. doi:10.1177/1012690215612458.

McManus, John. 2013. "Been There, Done That, Bought the T-shirt: Beşiktaş Fans and the Commodification of Football in Turkey." *International Journal of Middle East Studies* 45: 3–24.

Merkel, Udo. 2012. "Football Fans and Clubs in Germany: Conflicts, Crises and Compromises." *Soccer & Society* 13 (3): 359–376.

Mintert, S., and G. Pfister. 2014a. "The Female Vikings, a Women's Fan Group in Denmark: Formation and Development in the Context of Football and Fan Histories." *The International Journal of the History of Sport* 31 (13): 1639–1655.

Mintert, S., and G. Pfister. 2014b. "The FREE Project and the Feminization of Football: The Role of Women in the European Fan Community." *Soccer & Society* 16 (2–3): 405–421.

Nuhrat, Y. 2013. "Fans at the Forefront of Occupy Gezi." *Ballesterer*, July 20. Accessed February 26, 2016. http://ballesterer.at/aktuell/football-fans-at-the-forefront-of-occupy-gezi.html

Podaliri, C., and C. Balestri. 1998. "The Ultras, Racism, and Football Culture in Italy." In *Fanatics! Power, Identity and Fandom in Football*, edited by A. Brown, 88–100. London: Routledge.

Pope, S. 2014. "'There are Some Daft People Out There!': Exploring Female Sport and Media Fandoms." *Sport in Society* 17 (2): 254–269.

Pope, S. 2015. "'It's Just Such a Class Thing': Rivalry and Class Distinction Between Female Fans of Men's Football and Rugby Union." *Sociological Research Online* 20 (2): 11.

Roversi, A. 1992. *Calcio, Tifo e Violenza: Il Teppismo Calcistico in Italia*. Milan: Mulino.

Testa, A., and G. Armstrong. 2010. *Football, Fascism and Fandom: The UltraS of Italian Football*. London: A&C Black.

Tuastad, D. 2014. "From Football Riot to Revolution. The Political Role of Football in the Arab World." *Soccer & Society* 15 (3): 376–388.

Openers, witnesses, followers, and 'good guys'. A sociological study of the different roles of female and male ultra fans in confrontational situations

Bérangère Ginhoux, translated by Jessie Dubief

ABSTRACT
This paper proposes to deal with the masculine and aggressive culture of ultra football fans. We are particularly interested in analysing violence in the social world of ultras thanks to Randall Collins's theory that considers 'violence as situational process'. What happens during situations of tension? This article will particularly insist on a description of what each actor of these situations does: ultras, 'opposing' fans and policemen. How do they adapt their way of doing things in situation and in interaction? We will describe different figures of ultras who participate in confrontational situations: the openers, the followers, the witnesses, and the 'good guys' who are the notorious and hardest fighters. The world of ultras is based on an 'aggressive masculinity' encouraging fight skills. Nevertheless, women are also involved in ultras' groups and take part in confrontational situations. How do they participate in violence? We will describe and analyse the specific role of female ultras in violent situations.

Introduction

In France, ultras are members of hierarchical groups that are mostly organized in a formal structure (usually associations with a management board composed of a president, a treasurer and a secretary[1]). Representatives are in charge of decision taking and of relationships with the directors of the Football Club they support, security actors, leaders of other groups or journalists. These groups claim to belong to the Ultra Movement born in Italy in the 1960s (Louis 2006). They 'consider that they belong to the same world that has its own practices, values, rules, networks' (Hourcade 2004, 37). They share a common cultural background (codes, rules, principles, languages) and activities that distinguishes them from traditional fan clubs (officially affiliated to the Football Club), spectators and classical fans but also hooligans (Dunning, Murphy, and Williams 1988; Bufford 1999). Their main activity is to perform displays in the terraces[2] using vocal support and choreographies (agitating and raising arms, jumping, holding shoulders) but also drums, flags or banners that are often used during *tifos*.[3] In addition, the main ultra groups write fanzines[4] and make *matos*[5] – support material – that they sell during football games. Members who take an active part in the group are mostly aged from fifteen to thirty years old. In France, ultra movements appeared in the 1980s when groups were formed in Marseille (Commando ultra in 1984), Paris (Boulogne Boys in 1985), Nice (Brigade Sud Nice 1985) or Bordeaux (ultramarines 1987) and have been very active since then. Currently, in every stadium of clubs playing in Ligue 1 there are ultra groups who share a similar culture and a particular mode of being fan (Bromberger 1995; Hourcade 1998; Mignon 1998b).

All these groups are competing in different situations: during terrace displays by using their vocal qualities (power and variety of songs) as well as their artistic and organizational qualities (*tifos*); during away games where they go *en masse*; during fights in which the group demonstrates its physical strength and its courage in order to defend the group and its emblems, mainly the *bâche*[6] – the ban. Ultra groups also share a 'confrontational culture' (Ginhoux 2013) based on a logic of permanent confrontation and of evaluation of the groups and their identity. Indeed, the social world of ultras is based on a 'rude culture' and an 'aggressive masculinity' (Elias and Dunning 1986) that encourage fight skills. For the ultras, it's about learning how to confront other groups, symbolically or physically, in order to defend one's 'group identity' (members, emblems) and one's local identity (the attachment to one's town and its territory (Ginhoux 2015b)).

In this article, the world of ultras will be considered as a 'fighters' school', a space where fans develop both moral and physical abilities to fight. Concretely, who participates in those situations and what is the role of each member? What about the 'guys' who are more skilful than others in those situations? How do other leaders appear in a situation? Finally, we will question the role of female members in those situations and their relation to violence.

This article is mainly based on ethnographic data, gathered during a Ph.D. in sociology (2007–2013)[7] which mainly consisted in participant observations within two ultra fan groups of Saint-Etienne (the *Magic Fans*[8] and the *Green Angels*[9]) and in semi-structured interviews with female and male members of those two groups as well as with actors of security forces (policemen, stewards).

A fighters' school

'Ultras, it's violence and support' (Lucas, male, 30[10]). Violence is part of the ultra world. However, every group does not have the same relation to violence. For most of them, violence emerges during particular situations while others premeditate and organize it. It is the case for *casuals*, ie fans described as independent who favour an engagement in which violence and *fights* are predominant. Here, *fights*[11] mainly refers to scheduled brawls – between two groups who agree on the number of participants, the place and the hour – taking place in specific locations (wastelands, fields, forests). Thus, compared to other ultras, casuals are closer to the figure of the hooligan with whom they share a taste for fight. But it is not the case of the '*Magic Fans* or of the *Green Angels*, [they] don't smack each other around, it's not the aim of the game' (Mateo, policeman).

> We've never been into setting up encounters to fight. We're not hooligans. But we happen to be violent to defend our group, our colors. We know very well that during away games we go into cities where we are expected. It's the same at home, we won't accept that a group peacefully gets around in Saint-Etienne. (Quentin, male, 30)

Thus, ultras from Saint-Etienne mainly resort to violence in the framework of the 'defense' of their territory but they do not organize *fights*. Yet, some members are more attracted by fights than others and like to go to away games as casuals – *en indépendant*, by their own means – in order not to be surrounded by the police and to have more possibilities to confront opposing fans. In this framework, violence mainly emerges with situations: it can be researched but it is more spontaneous and linked to situational opportunities. It is all about emotions and tension emerging from interactional situations: 'It is the immediate situational confrontation that brings up an overwhelming tension; for face-to-face violence to occur there must be some situational way around this emotional field' (Collins 2008, 27). We will consider these violent situations through an interactionist perspective. These situations will also be viewed as 'moral experiences' (Goffman 1968), events which have consequences on how ultras are in their group.

The world of ultras is based on a 'confrontational culture' and encourages situations of confrontational tensions in which the goal is to dominate the other group – morally or physically. Symbolic confrontations (songs, animations, gestures) and real confrontations (fights, throwing projectiles, etc.) can build or tarnish the reputation of the groups and of their members. Events, like fighting situations, shape the status of the groups: some enhance their reputation while others don't (Spaaij 2008). Those events influence the interactions between ultras by reinforcing or depreciating their status. That is why they have to be prepared for these 'confrontational tensions' (Collins 2008) and to know how not to lose one's face (Goffman 1973). Thus, ultras learn to master the codes and the requirements of the 'confrontational culture': respect of the group's internal hierarchy; playful aggressiveness; resistance to confrontation; protection of the group's reputation and honour; symbolic and physical defence of the group's emblems, members and territory; ability to fight physically and verbally (Lepoutre 1997). The world of the ultras is a universe where the use of physical strength and a 'fighter' identity are highly valued: 'The use of physical strength is considered as a perfectly legitimate means to exert power [in the meaning of the domination of others] as well as to manage and resolve conflicts' (Bouton 2011). But it seems that, in this world, learning to fight is mainly learning to be respected, learning to respond to affronts, learning how to not be a pushover and to defend one's scarf as well as the *bâche* and the *matos* of the group (drums, banners, flags, etc.). Finally, learning to fight would favour moral qualities over physical qualities: a form of 'learning to suffer and to control pain' (Bujon 2009) similar to boxers. This very hierarchical world submits ultras to situations of confrontational tension in which, according to their positions, they have to show courage and tenacity (moral qualities): young members endure hazing from the oldest ones, women are mistreated or harassed (Ginhoux 2015a), members who are at fault are severely called to order, etc. Generally speaking, the ability of ultras to prove their combativeness (never back off, never show one's fear nor run away or look down) and to physically defend themselves is regularly challenged during confrontations or face to face fights with opposing fans, in the stadium as well as in urban public space and during trips to away games. Throughout those situations, ultras build strength of character and abilities to face moral, psychological and physical attacks.

But the social world of ultras is also a world that emphasizes 'the possession of this rare quality that is the ability to exert an emotional domination' (Bouton 2011). Thus, the ability to defend oneself is as appreciated as the possession of attack skills: aggressiveness, harsh words, nervousness, impulsiveness, even a certain madness that favours excess more than temperance in the eagerness to confront and in the strength of the punch.

Most of the time, those abilities are acquired in a practical way, on the ground – at the stadium or in the bus trips to away games. Through stories of confrontations or through experienced situations, young members learn, for example, that they should protect the *bâche* before all and, at an individual level, their scarf. It's not rare for established members to provoke hand-to-hand fights, or fights with PVC tubes, inside the group. They can also provoke pogoes in order to test the physical strength and the resistance of young members: 'when it is about initiating evilness […] the relationship is the same as between a persecutor and its victim. […] The challenges or provocations are […] an invariant aspect of initiation' (Strauss 1992, 118, 120). Those fights between 'guys of the group' look like what Randall Collins calls 'mock fights', which are simulated fights. They 'are often accompanied by laughter, joking, or squeals of delight; although this may occur more on one side than another, and one side can have much more fun' (Collins 2008, 277). Even if these relatively common fights are 'for fun' because they don't aim at inflicting real injuries, young members are not having as much fun as the oldest who 'show them up' and laugh much more. Finally, there is something serious about these fights because they are useful for selecting young members and training some of them. But this initiation to fight can also take place through some sort of more organized 'trainings'. Some young ultras happened to be invited to fights with other 'guys', down town or in nightclubs, in order to learn to fight. Those excursions also aimed at creating strong solidarity and cohesion within this young generation. The targets were often groups of young men from the neighbourhood who are known for their ability to fight, thus ensuring a confrontation.

> The targets, however, cannot be too easy. […] Getting into the highest levels of the hierarchy involves taking on persons who are themselves known to be extremely tough: because they are especially ready to fight, because they win their fights, and because they are willing to escalate the amount of violence by using weapons. (Collins 2008, 357)

Those mock fights, trainings or confrontational situations between ultras always aim at spotting the young members with a potential 'fight charisma' (Liam, male, 27), ie those who have the most abilities and thirst for fight. However, if some ultras can seem more competent that others, it does not mean that they have more predispositions to be violent. Field work with ultras from Saint-Etienne rather showed that, as Randall Collins asserts it, violence is more linked to situations than to individuals. Because 'to use violence, being motivated is absolutely not enough. [What enables a violent act] is a combination of situational opportunities and sometimes a question of interactional techniques that one should have acquired' (Collins 2010, 243).

A new hierarchy

During a confrontational situation, ultras develop involvements and roles which are different from those that are officially assigned by the group (leader, representative, etc). And yet, during violent moments, hierarchy and role distribution do not disappear. 'The group which is willing to fight is stratified: there are those who are 'particularly aggressive', which are members who are famous for their 'fight charisma', the experienced leaders, but also others [who] follow and join the fight while other members Stay aside" (Collins 2008, 317).

We will describe several roles: the openers, the witnesses, the followers and the 'good guys' who are the notorious and hardest fighters.

The openers

The role of the 'openers' refers to two practices: one consisting in keeping watch over the street; and another one consisting in informing, watching and alerting. This role is often assumed by young members or women, who are used as 'scouts' (Elena, female, 28). They are sent on reconnaissance and are responsible for making contact with opponents and indicating their position to the rest of the group. For instance, Nino (male, 25) explained how, when he was younger, he and two other members had been in charge of going to a pub close to Lyon's stadium and known as the 'hideout' where fans from Lyon gathered before the game. They walked into the bar and quickly checked that the 'targets' – fans from Lyon – were there. Then, they informed the members of their group who came as casuals so that these ones could, within a minute, go out from the nearby subway station. It allowed them to rely on the element of surprise and have the upper hand on the fans from Lyon and policemen. In fact, policemen are never very far away in order to avoid a real physical 'contact' between ultras. That is why the strategy of rapidity and surprise is relevant during confrontational situations. 'There's so much security that the only way for something to happen is for you to surprise the opposite guys and cops to dodge them' (Laurent, male, 30).

The openers are also those who, during home games, 'hang around' in town and are particularly careful about spaces considered as potential 'action places' (Goffman 2003): some pubs, specific squares, train stations and surroundings of the stadium. They are often prowling the streets by groups of two or three people, but can also walk alone, going on foot, by car or by scooter. Their role is to inform the rest of the group of the presence of opposing fans. As part of this mission, women can be very efficient because they are 'less easily identifiable so guys will be less careful and they are easier to catch' (Elena, female, 30). As they are not considered as a serious target, guys are less eager to lash out at them: 'guys won't hit a woman!' (Elena).

The witnesses

If every ultra who is present during confrontational situations is a witness, some of them assume the role of witnesses as they do not take part in the fight. Lucas (male, 30) explains: 'we took two or three good young guys with us so that they can relate and say we were there'. Witnesses have a crucial role given that only those who were there are allowed to tell what happened. An eyewitness 'enjoys a presumption of sincerity, of plausibility from its audience' (Guilhaumou 1999, 138). The phrase 'only those who were there know', often used in the ultra world, can be considered as a kind of ultra motto. The function of eyewitnesses, of 'those who were there', is critical because the stories of fights become founding stories for the group, even more if the outcome of the fight was a theft of *bâche* or of *matos*. Among those witnesses, there can be a fan in charge of filming or photographing. In some groups, this task usually falls to a female fan. Moreover, the presence of an audience favours the situations of physical violence: it is an occasion for ultras with a 'fight charisma' to dramatize their aggressiveness and their abilities to exert an 'emotional domination', which means taking the upper hand on the tension exerted on the interaction (aggressive look, determined posture, invectives and firm gestures). The other one, the opponent, is emotionally dominated when he seems scared, doubtful or hesitates to fight. The ability to impose one's emotional domination is not always correlated to real physical abilities to fight: 'sometimes, during parties or in the street, I won face-to-face fights just by showing off because I was more determined, the guy in front of me thinks he came across a weirdo and throws in the towel' (Nino, male, 25). Therefore, when members are not considered a 'good guy', being an ultra may also consist in 'playing the tough guy' in a world that mainly relies on a symbolic competition (banners, *tifos*, songs) and on the dramatization of confrontations through gestures (miming the gesture to cut a throat, invitations to fight, giving opponents the finger, etc.), insults and aggressive attitudes indicating that they are ready to fight. 'A usual attitude [...] is to "seem savage" [...], to frighten rather than be frightened, to play the tough guy, to be impressive' (Rostaing 2010, 89, 90[12]).

In the background: beginners and women

Among those who stay in the background, it is clear that some of them do not like to fight. For others, like beginners and women, outposts are often forbidden. Every female ultra fans met during interviews insisted on the fact that they 'stay aside and don't actively get involved in the fight, of course!' The systematic use of the term 'of course' suggests that this side-lining goes without saying. In fact, it is clearly the result of an interdiction from the male members who do not only judge that 'physically, girls will never be equal' (Elena, female, 30; quoting one of the group's representatives). They also consider women as 'a burden for the guys who have to watch after them and to protect them' (Gaëlle, female, 27). However, some women affirm to have 'the same adrenaline as the guys, sometime the same hate towards opposing fans' (Elena, female, 30).

There are two main scenarios among these women. First, there are those who are not attracted by violence and who take advantage of the fact that they are women in order not to participate to fights: 'if I can avoid being in the middle of a fight, I can deal with it because I'm not someone who likes it, I don't have a fighter's soul' (Gaëlle, 27). On the other side, there are those who have a taste for violence and who, for some of them, have aptitudes to fight and who did already fight, sometimes with other female fans. Fights between female fans are extremely rare. However, given that guys do not confront women, when female fans offend the group, women usually answer. Elena (female, 30) says:

> we arrived at the stadium and one of my girl friends said 'fuck I know these girls, they look like X (female members of an opposing group)!' And actually, our supervisors came by and recognized them and they felt it so they started to leave. And we followed them because there was no way that we let them leave this way, they don't have to hang out peacefully nearby our stadium. We catch them and we started to ask them who they were, what they were doing here and we asked them to show us their tickets and we took them, until one of the guys stuck his nose into it and a girl friend of mine said 'they're ours! You, you take care of the guys and we take care of the girls.' And she punched one of them with a bloody straight right, her girl friends wanted to interpose themselves and after that, like in every fight, someone gives a punch and one, two, three of them get involved and it ends more or less in an exchange of punches. Then the cops came very quickly because they were nearby and they separated us.

Women never take part in the training situations above-cited because in the ultra world only young men are prepared to fight. Thus, most of the time, women lack the physical abilities needed to confront opposing fans. Those who fight are often women who have already experienced fighting outside the ultra world. 'That's mainly when we go out, girls set us about and we are not, me and my friends, women who let things happen' (Elena, female, 30). Some of them even have the same 'impulsive temperament as guys. In these moments, adrenaline guides you. If I come to blows it's that I'm in a state in which I don't control myself anymore, so I no longer have that feeling of fear!' (Elena, female, 30).

However, given that they rarely participate to fights, female ultra fans often have other roles: opener, photographer or they are in charge of repatriating and 'taking care of guys who can be in a bad way after a fight' (Lucile, female, 25).

> You can freak out for your buddies because you wonder what's happening to them, if they got hurt, if they're gonna be arrested so when you're at home games, you take your car and you go around to try and take three or four of them. (Sandrine, female, 28)

Gaëlle (female, 27) also talks about a trip to Kiev[13] during which the confrontations between Ukrainian fans and some fans from Saint-Etienne became very violent because Ukrainians fans used knives and pellet guns:

> I saw the Ukrainians coming to us so I crossed the street to stay aside. It didn't last long but when I crossed the street again, I saw a guy bleeding from everywhere so I gave him tissues, I tried to do what I could. Then I found Patrick [a member of her group] and he was also covered in blood so I tried to cure him a bit as I could.

Some of them can also be in charge of protecting the *matos* of the group:

> guys can entrust someone with the *matos* when she is an old hand and is in the core of the group. I've been in charge of the bans and the megaphone several times. In Bruges (Belgium), when the guys charged the opposing fans[14] I wasn't far from the central point of the fight even if it didn't last long, someone threw the *matos* in my arms and I ran away. In those moments, you run more to protect the *matos* than to protect yourself! (Elena, female, 30)

The stories of confrontations in Ukraine and in Belgium show how quickly those situations can change and that they require fast decision-making and action: stepping aside, running, taking shelter with the *matos*, standing up to the opponents, etc.

Finally, the most experienced female fans often assume the role of educator towards the beginners:

> I try to spot the little young girls in the group who, for most of them, can be very frightened because they are not used to it and I try to take them under my wing, so to speak, we try to protect each other and to step aside. I always have that reflex to say 'come on kids, let's step aside' because when you're young you can be petrified, paralyzed. I've seen some kids who were in the middle of a fight, not knowing what to do! (Elena, female, 30)

For Gaëlle (female, 27), they have to get the young women to understand that 'women can't participate to fights, it hinders the guys when there are girls in the middle. We had to tell Maureen who, instead of stepping aside, was stuck to her boyfriend!'

The followers

The followers are mainly composed of novices. Among them, some can have a good 'fight potential' and stay closed to experienced leaders, ready to follow them. They happen to participate in those situations: 'they [the leaders] never forced anyone to go for it. But when you went for it, you had to have balls and not to back up' (Liam, male, 27). Liam's remark shows that in every confrontational situation, particularly during fights, the reputation and the status of the group is at stake and everyone has to perform at one's best. Fabien (male,

25) underlines the importance of the practical and – mainly – the cognitive experience needed during those confrontational situations and he affirms, about some very young ultras: 'you don't take with you some people who are not totally prepared and who are not able to understand what's happening'. However, some youths get promoted by participating in those physical confrontations and by showing that they are skilful. When they are noticed by experienced members, they are quickly authorized to join the 'good guys'.

The 'good guys' and the 'first line'

The 'good guys' compose what the ultras call the 'first line' and are generally the most skilful. That is why they are considered as the leaders of the confrontations and initiate physical contact with the opponents: 'The same members always attack first. We know the good guys; I know who I have to follow. I know because I saw them act' (Liam, male, 27). They are known in the group because they are not afraid; they are able to give and to take punches and, for some of them, for their 'records' ie their several victories and trophies: *bâche* and *matos* stolen from the opposing fans but also helmets and batons stolen from policemen. Some guys have a reputation at the ultra world scale. Thus, their presence in the urban public space or at the stadium is interpreted in the same way by both opposing ultras and policemen: it is the sign that every violent issues of the situation will potentially be exploited.

> It's important to identify those who will punch. The worst is when you see ten *Magic* downtown with seven or eight *Green* and, would you believe! The *crème de la crème* of the elite. So we follow them, we track them. (Christian, male, spotter)

'Good guys' are particularly watched and tracked both by policemen and the opposing ultras. The analysis of the situation only differs in its finality: ultras are looking forward to fight with them when policemen surround them and keep sure that they do not provoke any misbehaviour. However, during confrontational situations, other members of the group can become leaders. They match the figure of the 'temporary leaders' (Collins 2008). The roles and the internal hierarchy of the group are redistributed, establishing other leaders for the duration of the confrontation. Those new roles correspond to 'actantial positions [that are] defined by the respective places of two people during the encounter' (Baszanger and Dodier 1997, 56). In fact, they are firstly defined by the interactional situation and the co-present actors. And this can lead policemen to rethink and re-examine the supervision dispositive during the situation. Beyond notorious fighters, policemen have to recognize fans who bear the behavioural and symbolic characteristics of a fighter: a casual clothing style; a typical stature (height, weight, muscular mass); an aggressive stare; the way they stay still, grounded, with arms at sides and clenched fists; the way they walk, straight and engaged; those are clues that help the most experienced policemen identify ultras. Clothes' brands, accessories (caps, badges, etc.) but also tattoos, haircuts or stature act as 'maps of meaning' (Hall and Jefferson 1975). 'People who are good at violence learnt to recognize situations of [confronting] interactions and know which methods work or not, according to situations' (Collins 2010, 243).

'When a group of three or four people walk nearby you and are into the stadium's spirit, you can see it to their style, their look, things happen very quickly and we identify them directly' (Quentin, male, 30). It is important when ultras look at each other. 'The aggressive eye contact' – writes Collins (2008, 276) using Elijah Anderson's expression – 'is part of behavioural signs that announce the beginning of a fight. Invectives, chants and throwing projectiles are also invitations to fight". All in all, the situations of confrontational tension will more easily become violent conflicts when there are actors with strong skills for emotional domination: these are the notorious and hardest fighters. But it only happens if opponents are willing to fight. Because situations of confrontational tension that become real physical and violent fights are rare: 'Humans have the capacity to be angry and to mobilize bodily energies to be forceful and aggressive' (Collins 2008, 27). However, most of the time, they hold this violence and keep it aside. It is even truer in the ultra world because those confrontational situations have rules.

Fight rules and strategies

No weapon and equality of fighters

> Theoretically, you fight with your bare hands. Sometimes, you use belts, PVC tubes and some cans may be thrown, as long as the guy doesn't take a can to hit you with it... In a way, you fight to hurt but not to put a guy's eyes out. (Guillaume, male, 26)

Ultras easily distort objects in their environment to use them as weapons or projectiles (belts, cans, flags' PVC tubes, pub's chairs, safety barriers, bins, stones, etc.): they fight with what they find within easy reach. Besides, some groups can prepare fights by making weapons, like groups from Marseille in the 1980s who used sharpened coins, or like groups from Nice who were 'equipped', ie came with batteries, nuts and bolts in their pockets. Others are considered 'real whores' because they do not respect the rules and do not hesitate to use knives, baseball bats or hammers. But in the ultra world, there is a tacit agreement to fight hand-to-hand.

> You've got the taste to punch but you won't go as far as stabbing someone. It's a bit the same competition as when you do *tifos* or chants; you want to sing louder than the others, to make a better *tifo* than the others... when you fight, it's the same, you want to be stronger than the others, make them move back. (Guillaume, male, 26)

The goal of those situations of physical confrontation is that one of the group gains the upper hand on the other. Punches are really given but also seem to be controlled because fights are not about seriously hurting the opponents, they are about submitting them to recognize that they are the weakest (Marsh 1978). 'Victorious armies [often] benefit from the confrontational tension experienced by the opponent' (Collins 2010, 243). It is about emotionally dominating opponents by imposing one's own rhythm (aggressivity, motivation, relying on the element of surprise). In many cases, the psychological and moral tension takes a bigger role in victory than the physical tension. All in all, 'violence is more about domination than conflict. To be violent, one firstly has to impose one's emotional domination in the situation' (Collins 2010, 254). Forcing the opponents to run is enough to win the confrontation.

Beside the use of weapons, the number of opponents is also taken into account: no prestige can arise from a victory against a group that would not have enough members. A situation of confrontational tension may not become a situation of fight if there are too few opponents. 'Theoretically, fifty guys don't fight with five guys, it's not right if it's not balanced! It's not fighting, it's lynching ...' (Bastien, male, 24). That is why sometimes those situations stay invitations to fight through aggressive stares, insults, provocative gestures or by throwing projectiles but they do not lead to a real situation of 'physical' contacts between fans: 'There's been no contact' say the ultras. In fact, real physical confrontations do not often occur. Situations of conflictual interaction are more likely to stay at a 'playful' and theatrical level that consists in a 'strength show' executed by both sides. 'Threat is a phenomenon that looks like a game because actions denote other actions while being different from them. Clenched fist is not yet a punch but it refers to the possibility of a future – but yet nonexistent – punch' (Bateson 1977, 251). Thus, the number of participants is important during confrontations. But to be in a balanced situation, they also have to take the 'equipment' into account. According to Arnaud (male, 20), it determines how they will take part in the confrontation: 'depending on how the others arrive, if they have weapons or not, if we fear for our lives. It really depends on the moment'. Ultras are kept on the alert in order to quickly read the situation: they are in a 'constant surveillance of the surroundings' (Goffman 1973, 227). Those situations require a quick evaluation, at a given moment, in order to adjust to any circumstance.

Discretion and avoidance strategies

To avoid being noticed by the police, ultras use tricks such as 'styling themselves' (*se looker*) with a neutral clothing style or choosing a discrete place to park like an underground parking lot and, mainly, walking in small groups that only gather at the last minute, ie just before meeting the opposing ultras. And in fact, what would be the interest if, as Vincent (male, 21) says it: 'you go downtown, you mess things up in the first pub you find, cops arrive, they escort you to the stadium and it's over, there won't be any occasion of contact with the other guys'? Discretion is appropriate during trips *en indépendant* – as casuals – until ultras find some opposing fans. Arriving at different times (some of them arriving at the beginning of the afternoon, others later on, etc.) and with different means of transport (car, train, J9[15]) can also be some necessary tricks. The idea is to get around security measures and to surprise policemen: 'It's tricky! Anything can happen, as soon as three companies of CRS[16] arrive in one go that's out' (Laurent, male, 28). Policemen have to face an 'unpredictable environment, constantly evolving, where constraints and obligations change tremendously, [their organization] is inevitably characterized by some tacit, ambivalent and flexible agreements' (Manning 2003, 357). They have to secure the space and to take quick decisions: 'We decide to arrest someone only if it's not likely to provoke more serious incidents. What's difficult is that the decision has to be taken quickly' says Paul (policeman). Those interactional situations can lead to several alternatives and can become overwhelming at any moment. Ultras appear to be fans who can quickly move from a peaceful behaviour to a violent behaviour, then disconcertingly come back to a peaceful behaviour. Facing such an undetermined situation, policemen are prepared to take urgent decisions and to make choices: intervene, arrest, let things quiet down, etc. Finally, for them the ultra world is 'an ambiguous environment with adaptive rules of conduct as well as blurred and uncertain success criteria that can only lead to uncertainty for actors who keep looking for concrete benefits' (Skolnick 1966, 180[17]). Both ultras and policemen face this uncertain environment by resorting to 'enlightened suppositions' (Manning 2003, 357), such as the strategies they use on the ground.

A search for adrenaline

The ultras' strategies to avoid security measures and meet opposing fans prove that 'it is not just about being tough; one should also have organizing and plot skills, skills that are also new, more subtle sources for excitement along with the need for secrecy and concealment, 'looking like innocents but being able to hit anywhere [...]' (Mignon 1998a, 134). The adrenaline coming with this 'cat-and-mouse game' with security forces is very appreciated by fans who travel *en indépendant* (as casuals) and who develop various practical skills such as locating foot patrols or unmarked patrol cars, locating security cameras, staying discreet while being recognizable by opposing fans whenever they want to, etc. Sometimes, the very shiver, the mix of fear and excitement given by walks in an enemy territory will satisfy fans who could not fight because they did not find their opponents or were restricted by police action. 'What I like is when you walk through town, you squat the town, you're searching, you don't know if you're gonna find, you don't know what's gonna happen' (Vincent, male, 21). Ultras from Saint-Etienne seem to appreciate the undetermined aspect of the situation and the adrenaline that comes with it, as opposed to the too organized nature of *fights* which are not worth of interest to them. In fact, they like the adrenaline shot given by the moment before fights and live this shot as a game: 'violence as fun and entertainment' (Collins 2008). Thus, it is not surprising that the movie *Fight Club* (Fincher1999), promoting hand-to-hand fights as a hobby is known to be the Paris fans' favourite movie, especially casuals from the *Kop of Boulogne*.[18] And as a fact, many ultras practise combat sports and use the techniques they have learnt during fights with other fans.

Conclusion

The ultra world would favour the acquisition of a confrontational culture that reinforces the acquisition of a deviant activity (watch skills, use of violence, throwing projectiles, dodging police controls, etc.) and emphasizes the use of physical force. Some ultras, especially those who like to travel as casuals prefer a practice based on confrontations and fights with other fans, revealing technics that are specific to fights (exerting an 'emotional domination'; hand-to-hand fights; taking, giving and avoiding punches) and developing new skills. In this way, this world is closed to a 'fighting school' that provides on-the-ground experience of confrontations and their organization. Women's involvement is not usually highly regarded nor taken seriously; and yet, they are also socialized to this confrontational culture. If most of them restrict themselves to distant confrontations (chants, insults, gestures), some of them have a taste for physical confrontations and real aptitudes for fights, at least because they are not afraid to fight. Thus, situations of confrontational interactions reveal other skills that some women may master better than some men:

> In Greece[19] I saw some guys who were known to be hard guys who hid in the stadium's toilets asking for their mother or their wife because they were scared, something that I never saw with a girl so it shocked me very much. (Karine, female, 29)

Those situations disrupt the roles established by the group, reveal aptitudes and allow other leaders to emerge; as well as they can give women some responsibilities (protecting the *matos*, locating adverse fans, etc.).

Notes

1. In compliance with the French legislation regarding associations. T.N.
2. In a stadium, terraces are the cheapest areas of the stands, located behind the goals. T.N.
3. Italian word that refers to displays using sheets of plastic or of cardboard, fabric, scarfs, balloons, confettis, flares, smoke bombs, etc.
4. It is a small magazine (mostly in an A5 format) that contains illustrated reviews of home and away games, as well as articles about the activities of the group, the club or the city.
5. This term mainly refers to objects bearing the group's name, logo or design that are sold during games or at the group's premises: scarfs, clothes (sweatshirts, tee-shirts, beanies, caps, polo shirts, etc), lighters, badges or stickers.
6. Main emblem of the group, it is made with plastic, measures several tens of metres and bears the name of the group. It is unfolded in front of the terrace during home games and away games.
7. Ph.D. thesis defended in public in October 2013, Université Jean Monnet in Saint-Etienne.
8. Created in July 1991, they occupy the northern terrace.
9. Created in February 1992, they are in the southern terrace, in front of the *Magic fans*.
10. For more anonymity, first names have been changed and quotations from ultras from Saint-Etienne will only refer to their sex and age and will not mention the name of their group.
11. When written in italic, *fights* will refer to scheduled fights which are also called *fights* by French ultras. When written in a regular font, 'fights' will refer to the French 'bagarre' (brawl). T.N.
12. That is what she writes about penitentiary world.
13. Season 2014–2015, Europa-League match in Kiev opposing Ukrainian club FC Dnipro Dnipropetrovsk and ASSE.
14. Season 2008–2009, Europa League match opposing Bruges to ASSE. A fight took place between Belgian fans and fans from Saint-Etienne on the way to the stadium, nearby the town centre.
15. A van of nine seats capacity. T.N.
16. Compagnie Républicaine de Sécurité (French riot squad). T.N.
17. In Manning 2003, 357.
18. This group has been dissolved by justice in 2010.
19. Olympiakos/ASSE, season 2008–2009.

Disclosure statement

No potential conflict of interest was reported by the authors.

References

Baszanger, I., and N. Dodier. 1997. "Ethnography: Relating the Part to the Whole." In *Qualitative Research: Theory, Method and Practice*, edited by D. Silverman, 8–23. London: Sage.

Bateson, G. 1977. *Vers une écologie de l'esprit* [Steps to an Ecology of mind]. Paris: Seuil.

Bouton, E. 2011. "Corps sublimés : le prix de la virilité et de la gestion du pouvoir pour des jeunes de la culture des rues." [Sublimated bodies: the price of the virility and the management of the power for young people of the culture of streets.] *International Review on Sport and Violence* 3: 95–108.

Bromberger, C. 1995. *Le match de football, Ethnologie d'une passion partisane à Marseille, Naples et Turin*. [The soccer game, Ethnology of a partisan passion in Marseille, Naples and Turin.] Paris: La maison des sciences de l'homme. doi:10.4000/books.editionsmsh.4077.

Bufford, B. 1999. *Parmi les hooligans* [Among the Thugs]. Paris: 10/18.

Bujon, T. 2009. *Boxing Club: Sociologie d'une salle de boxe thaïe en banlieue.* [Boxing Club: sociology of a Thai boxing gym in suburb] Saint-Etienne: PUSE

Collins, R. 2008. *Violence: A Micro-sociological Theory*. Princeton, NJ: Princeton University Press.

Collins, R. 2010. "La violence en situations. Entretien avec Randall Collins." [The violence in situations. Interview with Randall Collins"] *Tracés* 19: 239–255.

Dunning, E., P. Murphy, and J. Williams. 1988. *The Roots of Football Hooliganism: A Historical and Sociological Study*. Londres: Routledge & Kegan Paul.

Elias, N., and E. Dunning. 1986. *Quest for Excitement*. Oxford: Blackwell.

Fincher, D. 1999. *Fight Club*. Fox Pictures.

Ginhoux, B. 2013. "Les Ultras. Sociologie de l'affrontement sportif et urbain [The Ultras: Sociology of the Sportive And Urban Confrontation]." PhD diss., University Jean Monnet Saint-Etienne.

Ginhoux, B. 2015a. "Comment devient-on un « gars du groupe » quand on est une fille ? Carrière et combines des supportrices ultras." ["How to become a "guy of the band" when we are a girl? Career and tricks of the Female Ultras' football fans"] *Agora Débats / Jeunesses* 71: 7–21. doi: 10.3917/agora.071.0007.

Ginhoux, B. 2015b. "En dehors du stade: l'inscription des supporters « ultras » dans l'espace urbain." ["How to become a "guy of the band" when we are a girl? Career and tricks of the Female Ultras' football fans"] *Métropolitiques* Accessed http://www.metropolitiques.eu/En-dehors-du-stade-l-inscription.html.

Goffman, E. 1968. Asiles. Etudes sur la condition sociale des malades mentaux. [Asylums: Essays on the Social Situation of Mental Patients and Other Inmates] Paris: Éditions de minuit.

Goffman, E. 1973. *La mise en scène de la vie quotidienne. La présentation de soi* [The Presentation of Self in Everyday Life]. Paris: Éditions de minuit.

Goffman, E. 2003. *Les rites d'interaction*. [Interaction Ritual] Paris: Les éditions de Minuit.

Guilhaumou, J. 1999. "Renaud Dulong, le témoin oculaire. Les conditions sociales de l'attestation personnelle." [Renaud Dulong, the eyewitness. The social conditions of the personal certificate] *Mots* 59: 138–140.

Hall, S., and T. Jefferson. 1975. *Resistance through Rituals, Youth Subcultures in Post-war Britain*. London: Hutchinson.

Hourcade, N. 1998. "La France des Ultras." [Ultras of France] *Sociétés et représentations* 7: 241–261.

Hourcade, N. 2004. "Les groupes de supporters ultras." [The ultras football fans] *Agora - Sports et identités juvéniles* 37: 33–43.

Lepoutre, D. 1997. *Cœur de banlieue, codes, rites et langages*. [Districts Suburb Heart, codes, rites and languages.] Paris: Odile Jacob.

Louis, S. 2006. *Le phénomène ultra en Italie*. [The phenomenon ultra in Italy] Paris: Mare & Martin.

Manning, P. K. 2003. "Le jeu des « Stups », l'organisation policière comme miroir social." ["The game of "Drug squad", the police organization as social mirror"] *Les cahiers de la sécurité intérieure, Connaître la police, grands textes de la recherche anglo-saxonne*, Hors-série 2003: 351–360.

Marsh, P. 1978. *Aggro, The Illusion of Violence*. London: J. M. Dent & Sons.

Mignon, P. 1998a. *La passion du football* [The soccer passion.] Paris: Odile Jacob.

Mignon, P. 1998b. "Supporters ultras et hooligans dans les stades de football." [Ultras fans and hooligans in football stadium] *Communications* 67: 45–58. doi:10.3406/comm.1998.2015.

Rostaing, C. 2010. "On ne sort pas indemne de prison. Le malaise du chercheur en milieu carcéral." [We do not emerge unscathed from prison. The faintness of the researcher in prison] In *La relation d'enquête. La sociologie du défi des acteurs faibles*, 23–37. Rennes: Presses Universitaires de Rennes.

Spaaij, R. 2008. "Men like Us, Boys like Them: Violence, Masculinity, and Collective Identity in Football Hooliganism." *Journal of Sport & Social Issues* 32 (4): 369–392. doi:10.1177/0193723508324082.

Strauss, A. 1992. *Miroirs et masques*. [Mirrors and masks] Paris: Métailié.

Polish ultras in the post-socialist transformation

Radosław Kossakowski, Tomasz Szlendak and Dominik Antonowicz

ABSTRACT

The world of radical football fans across Europe is dominated by anti-system groups. While their sympathies in the west of the continent are mostly leftist, the ultras in the east tend to display right-wing attitudes. Poland makes a particularly interesting case in point, as the most intensive and emotional ideological criticism of the processes of 'transformation' and 'modernisation' is to be observed at the stadiums. As a result of historical developments, opposition against the system in the country can only be expressed using Catholic–patriotic symbolism, which in the case of collective actions of radical football supporters has produced sociocultural and aesthetic effects not to be found anywhere else in Europe.

Revolt of the ultras in the covert class society

In Poland, symbols of social revolt are rooted in religion and function within the frame of a class conflict which, however, is not openly defined in class terms. Indeed, the new (post-socialist) class system which emerged in Polish society after 1989 is still developing. In addition, the process is taking place in a cultural and historical environment which makes the notion of 'class' perceived as highly dangerous, a conviction stemming from 45 years of authoritarian rule of the nominally working-class state. Consequently, no one makes any explicit reference to class struggle, although the most committed fans, who support their clubs from the stands behind the goals, certainly feel subordinated, disadvantaged within the social structure and perceive themselves to be at the bottom of economic hierarchy and on the margins of Polish economic transformation. For them, the stadium has become the place where they demonstrate not only their love for the club but also their views, which they express in a particular socio-economic context, where the central process involves the emergence of new social inequalities (Karwacki and Szlendak 2010).

Dynamically emerging inequalities fuel the discontent or even frustration of those excluded, which is manifested to the world at the stadiums. However, unlike in a number of Western European countries, stadium performances of Polish football fans do not make use of leftist symbols or the rhetoric of 'class struggle'. Indeed, Che Guevara, the hammer and sickle, portraits of Stalin (used by, eg Livorno fans), anti-capitalist slogans (St. Pauli) are not to be seen in Polish stadiums. Consequently, we do not make use of critical theory along with the concepts and analytical tools originating in Marxist thought. While, naturally, they are used in research devoted to Western Europe (Taylor 1971; Kennedy and Kennedy 2010), we do not think they hold potential to explain the antagonism between the fans and the establishment in Poland.

Our analysis is based on the assumption that what we can observe in Poland involves a class dispute expressed by means of a set of symbols of protest stemming from national–Catholic ideology, including the heroic and tragic struggle of the Polish Underground State (*Polskie Państwo Podziemne*) (1939–1945) against the German and Soviet occupation. Although the majority of the most committed fans forming the ultras movement are not religious or practising believers, they hold a set of values, and display an inclination towards symbols, familiarized by the Polish popular class, which is deeply rooted in ritualized folk Catholicism. As a result, in their match-day choreographies they can only rely on the values and symbols they acquired in the process of socialization in the post-working-class and post-peasant communities: (1) patriotic cult of the nation understood as an ethnic community, (2) fear of the stranger, (3) Catholic symbolism, (4) symbols connected with the so-called Cursed Soldiers (*Żołnierze Wyklęci*),[1] (5) anti-leftist attitudes (in the sense of opposition to the leftist intellectuals and their liberal morality), (6) anti-feminism, (7) homophobia, (8) the macho cult.

In this way, Polish football stadiums came to function as enclaves of the sociocultural activity of the communities excluded from the processes of modernization, and places where they could manifest their social discontent. However, since the announcement of Poland and Ukraine as co-hosts of the UEFA Euro 2012 finals, modernization has invaded 'their' space. As a result, in the absence of any other public space 'familiarised' by the popular class which could serve to express sociopolitical conflicts, the stadiums have become a venue of the current conflict between social categories from the opposite ends of the social spectrum: those who are the beneficiaries of the great sociocultural transformation in Poland and those left on the margin.

Although the ultras movement in Poland is a community expressing opposition to the current 'system', it does not suggest any clear-cut alternative order which could follow its hypothetical overthrow. In the absence of such an idea, the situation is a case of 'unrealistic conflict', ie one where the conflict is only a form of release of frustration and accumulated aggression, with the antagonist making a 'suitable' target under the circumstances (Coser 1956). While this is particularly true about the younger generation, characterized by a strong rebel spirit, its representatives do not fully comprehend the reasons of their underprivileged situation (Szlendak 2015) and misdirect their revolt by targeting wrong social actors, or release their frustration in stadium activity which only relatively recently has acquired a political dimension.

An anti-government slogan exceedingly popular among the fans and shouted in the stadiums across the country a few years ago: 'Donald [Tusk] you moron, hooligans are going to overthrow your government' (*Donald matole, twój rząd obalą kibole*) can hardly be treated in terms of a manifesto proclaiming the contest for political power or a change of the system. Rather, Donald Tusk, the Polish Prime Minister at the time, became the symbolic enemy figure, even though he was not the only person responsible for the new legislation (including restrictions against fans), or for the processes of modernization which dealt a blow to the ultras movement. Tusk became a symbol of demonizing ultras movement in order to meet his political goals. And radical fans perfectly fit the picture of folk's devil and stir up moral panic (Cohen 1972). Although the fans had accumulated considerable social capital, and (considering the context of the day) displayed an exceptional cohesion and solidarity, they did not form a social movement posing an actual threat to the Polish political system. In fact, the fan movement in the country is largely fragmented, bound mainly by the revolt against commercial rules of today's world. While official fan associations in different cities pursue a broad range of activity outside the stadiums, they are mostly focused on pro-social actions (such as donating blood, helping children in foster care institutions) generally limited to the local community.

Stadium performances have become the principal means of communication of the fan community with club management, players, other fans and also, in broad terms, with the public opinion. Following the eradication of physical violence from the stadiums (a regular feature in the 1990s, typically involving fights between supporters of opposite teams and acts of vandalism (Zieliński 1997), match-day performances – including slogans, banners, flags and large-scale choreographies – frequently resort to the use of symbolic violence. In this way, spectacular fan performances, rich in aesthetic value and organized with great technical panache, have, to an extent, found their way to mainstream Polish culture: they are often featured in television coverage and on popular web portals, and are highly appreciated as an important contribution to creating a unique atmosphere at the matches.[2] Considering that no other anti-system group in Poland is engaged in the performative sphere to an extent observed among football fans, an analysis of stadium performances seems to be crucial in establishing the principal elements of the identity which shapes ultras culture, and in investigating the major lines of social conflict in Poland today.

Performance theory as a frame of analysis

The world of football fans has been the subject of many different academic interpretations: long dominated by the study of 'football hooliganism' (Frosdick and Marsh 2005; Spaaij 2006), research in the field has more recently focused on such issues as attitudes to the commercialization of football (Dubai 2010; Kennedy and Kennedy 2012), female fans (Pope 2011) or global networks (Millward 2011). Although, as can be seen, a variety of paradigms and research tools available in social sciences have been used to study the community of football fans, performance theory has rarely been applied in such research (Guschwan 2009; Doidge 2015). This is quite surprising, considering that in nearly every country fans make use of performance as a tool of manifesting their identity or their concern with social problems which affect them. Indeed, from match-day choreographies of ultras groups, through rhythmic clapping and jumping, to stadium chants, the world of football fans abounds in performative and dramatic activity. Performance theories are a relatively new phenomenon in social sciences. Based on anthropological analyses of rituals (Durkheim 2008) and concepts developed in the study of arts and drama (Schechner 1976), performance theories fostered the evolution of the analysis of rituals towards semiotics, cultural studies, dramaturgy; the concept of performance has also been used in the investigation of everyday life of individuals (Goffman 1959). The variety of the possible applications of the term stems from the variety of its meanings in different domains: 'In business, sports and sex, "to perform" is to do something up to a standard, to succeed, to excel. In the arts, "to perform" is to put on a show, a play, a dance, a concert. In everyday life, "to perform" is to show off, to go to extremes, to underline an action for those who are watching. In the twenty-first century, people as never before live by means of performance' (Schechner 2013, 28). Alexander (2006) identifies several elements of performance: systems of collective representation (background symbols and foreground scripts), means of symbolic production, actors, observers/audience, *mise-en-scéne*, and social power, with an effective performance depending on the authentic interrelatedness of all these elements.

Performances essentially involve the (direct or mediated) presence of the audience, are delimited (have a more or less specific beginning, middle and end) and are never the same, even if they repeat the same motifs in the same space. In our opinion, these features describe performances displayed by ultras, as they are shown before the audience (other fans), have a marked beginning and ending (eg unfolding, presentation and folding up the banner) and are never repeated (a strictly observed rule of match-day choreographies prepared by Polish fans). What is more, the tools/material means of aesthetic expression presented during the match are most often destroyed once the show is over.

For the purposes of the present analysis, we combined two different dimensions of the concept of performance, as outlined by Carlson (2004, 4): 'the display of skills' and display of 'a recognised and culturally coded pattern of behaviour'. Performance, then, manifests not only the experience of individual actors taking part, but also the culture whose values they intend to communicate. As Alexander observes, '[c]ultural performance is the social process by which actors, individually or in concert, display for others the meaning of their social situation' (2006, 32). Considering that football fans engaged in performance present their experience arising in a particular social and cultural context, it is thus worth analysing the sociocultural contents from which they derive. The form of ultras' 'display of skills' is rooted in a specific culture of fandom and, as such, should not be examined in isolation from 'the deep background of collective representations' (33).

In order to understand the phenomenon of Polish ultras one needs to consider a wider sociopolitical context in which their performances have been displayed. We shall see them (performances) through the prism of communication between social classes even so the latter have not have developed its identity. Notwithstanding that, there is little doubt that there is a widespread feeling of growing inequalities (or even polarization) in the Polish post-socialist society that are symbolically magnified and manifested in stadiums (Janicka and Słomczyński 2014). From the critical perspective, it could be observed that the stadiums built or refurbished for the Euro 2012 become a venue where the ultras and their performances function as a kind of commodity, with affluent users of skyboxes who represent the other end of the social spectrum as consumers. We can even talk about the class segregation of experience: with a view to turning a profit, the stadium is to provide different experience to different social classes and categories. In spite of the Polish fear of class, manifested in disguising the concept, class differences are clearly visible in Polish stadiums, where the popular class functions as entertainment and commodity for the middle class, professionals and the establishment.

Generally speaking, contemporary participants in culture (ie effectively all of us) are increasingly becoming a 'commodity' within the system of cognitive capitalism which feeds on millions of actions of Internet users (cost-free from the perspective of media corporations). Convinced that they lead a normal social life, they are in fact sold, as their experiences, emotions, discussions and comments are subject of trade. Every day, millions of posts on the social media, millions of virtual performances provide material which is turned into corporate income. Sometimes, if there are revenues involved, being such a performer means to engage in a ludic occupation (*zawód ludyczny*, the term borrowed from Zawadzka 2011, 230) providing an income in return for the display of one's ordinary or extraordinary experience in public space.

In the neoliberal reality, there are also people who perform their ludic occupation quite unwittingly: those whose performances do not stem from the culture-generated compulsion to manifest their own personality to the world, or from the desire to become the focus of public attention, but from the rules of their native local culture in which they were socialized. Polish ultras are among them. Today, they are 'fed' to other social categories which more and more frequently visit the stadiums. Polish football arenas have become the space of contact between at least two social worlds which are very distant in mental, economic and spatial terms outside the reality of the stadium. Stadium owners and club managers attract the middle class and urban elites (managers of business enterprises, successful doctors and lawyers, local and national politicians) with purpose-built skyboxes and VIP boxes. However, the Polish league still does not guarantee an attractive sports show in regards to quality of football. What is offered as an attraction instead is *Żyleta* ('the Razor', the terrace of Legia hardcore fans) in Warsaw, where a few thousand supporters keep jumping in an elaborate performance for the entire duration of the game. These fans, who mostly come from the popular class, become an attraction, a commodity, a part of the content of the sports show which can be 'consumed' by VIPs when there is not much going on the pitch itself. In this way, the fifth-generation stadiums are a space of meeting between distant social classes and distant cultures (Szlendak et al. 2014). Unfortunately, their stadium encounters are almost always a form of exploitation which remains hidden both to the exploiting and to the exploited.

A short but turbulent history of Polish ultras

Until mid-1990s, hooligan groups dominating in the Polish fan movement (Antonowicz and Grodecki 2016) generally used only small, unimpressive flags in club colours. The most committed fans had an inclination to violence and were closely connected with the skin-head movement. The run-down Polish stadiums were a scene of frequent fights and riots interrupting the matches. It was not until the second half of the 1990s that the supporters of the biggest clubs began to display large, hand-made flags and use pyrotechnic devices (white or orange smoke flares). Flares were very difficult to obtain and were used mostly by fans from the seaport cities (Szczecin, Gdańsk, Gdynia) who had access to fishermen's supplies. The 1995/1996 season saw the first large crowd flags (eg Legia Warsaw, Widzew Łódź, ŁKS Łódź, Pogoń Szczecin), featuring the club colours only, with no inscriptions. It is worth noting that the first attempts to introduce choreographies in the stadiums were made by supporters of the largest clubs with the largest turnout of committed fans. Fan performances included an increasing variety of elements (balloons, large flags on poles) and came to function as a plane of rivalry in terms of their content and form (scale).

The 2001/2002 season marked a turning point when choreographies became an integral element of football matches. Initially, the rivalry focused mainly on the scale of the shows, measured by the number of fans taking part. While larger and better organized groups tried to introduce more variety into their choreographies and make them more sophisticated, supporters of smaller clubs contented themselves with displays of the names and colours of their teams. The following seasons brought a radical change, as fan performances became not only spectacular shows, but also came to include a message to the outside world.

What proved a factor conducive to the development of fan performances was the institutionalization of fan movement, mainly in the form of officially registered associations. The change was important considering that support shows became increasingly more complex and complicated, which required close cooperation with club management in terms of logistics (installation, mounting, storage on club premises). Institutionalization of ultras groups also facilitated raising funds for choreographies, whose costs often exceeded tens of thousands Polish złotych (PLN). Indirectly, the ultras introduced formal structure to the community of football supporters. As a result, the fan movement went on to discover different areas of activity outside stadiums and became a part of organized civil society. Since the activity of the ultras required a certain level of organization, logistics and budgeting, they played a major role in the process. Naturally, fan associations included not only the ultras, but also those responsible for charity actions, contacts with the club, etc. At the same time, however, performances organized by the ultras were a means of communication of the most engaged fans with the outside world.

In the initial stage of the development of the ultras movement, the content of performances was generally limited to the world of sport and fans. The change came with the process of accelerated modernization of Polish football and the introduction of restrictive legal regulations concerning the fans.[3] Under the circumstances, supporters were confronted with structural factors which brought a radical change to the stadium reality. Fan performances became an element of a debate in mainstream Polish politics and a voice of the younger generation of people excluded by the transformation as well those sympathetic to their cause. The ultras movement led the struggle to defend the traditional order at the stadiums and the established patterns of fandom against the commodification of sport. It is worth noting that in the Polish context, the slogan 'modern sport' referred mainly to the world of fans, as Polish clubs (owing to their semi-peripheral location) were far less exposed to the process of commercialization than those in England, Germany, France or Italy. The pro-European, neoliberal government responsible for the new regulations automatically became the main target of messages presented by ultras groups.

Considering that (for reasons mentioned above) references to class conflict were out of the question, the conflict with the establishment (the government and the mainstream media supporting its line) became transposed onto the plane of worldview and ideology. This meant that the most engaged fans, who largely represent economically underprivileged groups, did not so much become their advocates, as such a position would naturally make them adopt the leftist stand and use class rhetoric (which they saw as utterly compromised), but found a different plane to express a de facto class conflict: that of worldview. In doing so, they relied on the historically consolidated national–Catholic symbols of disobedience and revolt. A considerable proportion of those excluded from the benefits of economic modernization of the country also rejected its liberal–leftist cultural bias. In this way, football supporters transposed the class conflict onto the political and, most importantly, ideological plane.

Support shows of Polish football fans

The community of ultras fans makes a very difficult subject of academic study not only because of its considerable diversity, but also as a result of problems with a definition of the category of membership. At the same time, in our view, it would be difficult to find a better measure of analysis than the effects of the activity of the movement. As we see it, it is a particularly rich and varied subject matter of their stadium performances that distinguishes Polish ultras groups. The present study provides an overview analysis of issues raised by the fans in their match-day choreographies displayed in the stadiums. In doing so, we approach their support shows as a form of alternative culture that, by means of stadium performances, demonstrates not only its attachment to the club and its tradition, but also manifests its attitude to the world and to the direction in which it is changing. Based on photographic documentation provided by clubs and supporters, our analysis of support shows offers a typology including seven major subjects featuring in stadium performances.

Performances expressing collective identity

The most popular type of choreography highlights the manifestation of the unity and collective identity of the group, and celebration of the idea of the sacred club. While the main objective of such performances remains essentially the same, what varies is their match-day context, thus making the actual content unique. Since the content frequently includes strong references to particular opponents on the day or to local animosities, it needs to be decoded with the symbolic context in mind. Collective identity is consolidated by means of performances in which fans glorify their own club and its supporters, and at the same time demonstrate superiority over others in general and the current opponent in particular. The latter involves symbolic violence whereby the rival club and its supporters are an object of depreciation, mockery and ridicule. This type of performance relies on a clear-cut division: 'We' and 'You'. For example, fans of Legia Warsaw strongly stress their distinctness and superiority by frequently displaying a banner reading 'We are your capital' (*Jesteśmy waszą stolicą*). Although the slogan emphasizes the fact which has nothing to do with sport, it sends a subtle message of supremacy.

Similar choreographies can also be observed in the local context. In northern Poland, two football clubs (Lechia and Arka) from two neighbouring cities (Gdańsk and Gdynia) are fierce rivals for domination and the title of 'The rulers of the North' (*Władcy północy*). A banner featuring the slogan was first displayed by Arka fans. Seized by their opponents supporting Lechia, it was burnt during a match between the two teams, an act of depreciation and profanation of the identity of the rivals. Moreover, during the following matches, Lechia fans presented their own flag in their club colours with the same inscription. The word 'rulers' points at a characteristic feature to be observed in a number of choreographies: collective identity of ultras groups tends to stress, at least in symbolic terms, their own hegemony. It is thus hardly surprising that performances repeatedly aim to convince the audience of the 'power' of a particular group. This identity strategy culminates in such slogans as 'Cracovia is Us', 'Lechia is Us', 'Lech is Us' (*Cracovia to My, Lechia to my, Lech to My*), which not only define the unity of the group, but also associate its members with the symbol of the club. Although Polish fans are not represented in the ownership structure of football clubs (apart from a few cases in lower leagues), the conviction of the power of their collective identity enables their self-perception in terms of 'moral' ownership, which does not have to be reflected in the actual organization.

Discussing collective identity of the groups in question, what needs to be stressed is the importance of performances displaying antagonism. Indeed, the ideology of the Polish ultras movement is based on a radical opposition against different actors, including the media, the police, politicians and supporters of rival teams. This category can be approached in terms of both duration (the 'perennial' hatred of law enforcement agencies) and change (situational and contextual oppositions). These oppositions are a symptom of an ideology of revolt and of efforts to delimit an own homogenous culture rather than of 'class' struggle. At times, the self-definition of fan culture by means of antagonism stimulates the expressive content whose radicalism reaches the verge of interpretative potential, leaving no room for any ambivalence. An example can be provided by a support show displayed by Górnik Wałbrzych ultras: 'We were not brought up to hate, we were brought up by hate itself' (*Nie wychowaliśmy się w nienawiści, to nienawiść wychowała nas*), stressing that their antagonism results from the tradition of, and socialization in, the fan environment. A similar spirit was demonstrated in a Legia Warsaw choreography: 'Ultras – We hate everyone' (*Ultras – Nienawidzimy wszystkich*). Such a radical definition of the attitude to the out-group appears to pinpoint and resolve the problem of collective identity (Antonowicz and Wrzesiński 2009). It would appear that in the fan community there is no border culture forming a space which cannot be enclosed, a space of post-identity. Thanks to this uncompromising 'differentiation', identity is more easily transformed into a positive value and self-glorification.

Patriotic and historical performances

The question of identity is also addressed in historical performances, which in fact refer to the contemporary history of the Polish nation understood in terms of an ethnic community. In a way, this involves an extension of group identity and is focused on the nation as an imagined community. Commemorating the heroes or events of twentieth-century history (references to earlier periods are not frequent), this type of support shows is dominated by a few historical themes, such as the Warsaw Uprising of 1944, featuring in choreographies devised by most ultras groups in Poland. Quite naturally, Legia Warsaw fans are the ones who most often prepare performances devoted to the event. In addition, if their team plays a match around the anniversary (1 August), the heroes of the Uprising are invited to the stadium and the Polish national anthem is played. Apart from other nationally celebrated historical events, such as the outbreak of the Second World War, there are also support shows devoted to commemorating events important in the local communities (eg the Greater Poland Uprising (1918–1919), celebrated by Lech Poznań fans in the capital of the province).

In recent years, an increasing number of historical choreographies have been devoted to restoring the memory of the so-called Cursed Soldiers (*Żołnierze Wyklęci*), military fighting against both Nazi Germany and, later, against the communist regime in Poland. Most of them were executed by the communist authorities or murdered by the secret police. Although in view of the Conference in Yalta (1945) that laid ground for post-war political settlement that contained Poland their struggle was irrational and doomed to defeat, they steadfastly pursued their heroic aim. Glorification of the Cursed Soldiers by fans is hardly surprising. Indeed, with their utmost devotion, radicalism and uncompromising attitude (including also a messianic vision of history with Poland playing a central role), they ideally fit the description of heroes. A particularly impressive choreography devoted to the Cursed Soldiers was prepared by Legia Warsaw ultras, who unveiled a giant banner (two levels of the stand) featuring a huge wolf with flares burning in its eyes. Dominated by red and white, the Polish national colours, it also included an inscription reading: 'In the shadows of the night, in the darkness of the trees, called by the homeland' (*Wśród cieniów nocy, mroku drzew, wezwani na ojczyzny zew*).

At this point, it is worth asking what role the community of Polish ultras can play in the shaping of historical policy at the national level. They are excluded from the public debate by both out-group and in-group factors: the mainstream media and their own contestation of the system as such. However, numerous choreographies devoted to the Cursed Soldiers have certainly had a considerable impact on collective memory and contributed to including them in the mainstream historical narrative. The Cursed Soldier were largely forgotten as their radical attitudes stood at odds with policy to soften the communist past as many of today's intellectual elite were somehow fascinated by the communist ideological project in the early 1950s.

Anti-communist performances

A foreign observer wondering why Polish ultras never display any leftist performances (which sometimes can be seen in Western Europe) should note that – apart from explanations presented above (concerning the Polish socio-historical context) – the group is characterized by radically anti-communist attitudes. Indeed, over a quarter of a century after the change of the political system, the movement surprisingly persistently displays anti-communist support shows which are uncompromising in terms of their style and symbolism. Anti-communism is understood as anti-system opposition against the world of political and business elites.

For example, in one of their anti-communist choreographies, Lechia Gdańsk ultras presented a giant crowd flag featuring a few top officials of the communist party hanged on trees. The flag was highly criticized in the media for using means of expression utterly unacceptable in democratic discourse and for inciting to violence. As we see it, Polish ultras consciously adopt the attitude of 'outsiders' and 'deviants' allowing them to break all limits: declaring to 'hate everyone', they release themselves of any obligation to consider the feelings and attitudes of their opponents. In this discourse, there is certainly no room for any dialogue and 'Other' can be presented in any way they see fit. This would seem to explain why Polish ultras meet with so much criticism from the left, which is deeply attached to dialogue and compromise between different identities. However, fans take no notice of the opinion of the out-group and go against the tide of political correctness, often beyond the limit of what is decent and acceptable in democratic culture.

The motif of punishment for traitors of the nation was also clear when Lechia fans presented a crowd flag with the image of General Wojciech Jaruzelski (responsible for the introduction of martial law in 1981) burning in the fires of hell (with the devil pointing a trident at him) and an inscription reading: 'You sold the nation and hell will take you' (*Za naród sprzedany, piekło cię pochłonie*). Owing to their involvement in the fight against the system in the 1980s, the fans from Gdańsk are leaders in anti-communist performances today. Looking back, it is worth mentioning the match between Lechia Gdańsk and Juventus Turin (the Cup Winners' Cup) in 1983. As the local supporters shouted 'Solidarity' and 'Lech Wałęsa' (who was present at the stadium), communist-controlled public television jammed the broadcast to prevent the anti-system message from reaching the audience. Hatred of communism leads to a rejection of leftist values. This can be seen in such slogans as 'Good night left side', and crossed-out images of Che Guevara (treated as a symbol of the left) or the hammer and sickle (a symbol of the Soviet Union). When it comes to more modern leftist–liberal values, Polish ultras radically oppose identity policies of ethnic or sexual minorities.

Performances as comment on current politics

Performances devoted to current political issues have become the voice of the streets and are the most interesting type in terms of form and content. Apart from hip hop culture, they provide the most important means of articulating the opinion of groups unfavoured not only due to their material status, but also radical political views. Referring Anthony Kings' work on football hooliganism (King 1997, 585) we tend to see that Polish ultras as ones that want to creates the boundaries only to breach them and being marked out as dangerous, radical and even outlawed. This is a form of self-creation that helps to build sense of imaginative community (Anderson 1991, 6, 7) which help to sustain masculinist and nationalist identity for themselves.

Performances of this kind are not always politically correct and their message concerning both home and foreign affairs can be treated as the voice a certain proportion of Polish society which will never be heard publicly in mainstream politics owing to the rules of political correctness. For ultras their uncompromising identity is manifested in sharp, often mocking, sometimes scathing or even primitive choreographies. It becomes an integral part of the ultras culture and – to quote Anthony King's work on hooliganism (King 1997, 585) – *it added to the excitement of a Saturday afternoon, that fans could indulge their often fanciful notion that they were somehow beyond the pale and, therefore, a threat to society*. Regardless of our judgement, they need to be approached as a form of criticism of the political class expressed by today's working class, the voice of the precariat and those who sympathize with their cause. It has been a number of ultras performances that raised political issues includes such examples as: uneasy diplomatic relations between Poland and Lithuania (Lech Poznań vs. Žalgiris Kaunas: 'Lithuanian peasant, kneel down before your Polish master' [*Litewski chamie, klęknij przed polskim panem*]); the engagement of Polish authorities in Ukrainian politics ('We remember Ukrainian genocide against Poles in Volhynia in 1943' [*Pamiętamy ukraińskie ludobójstwo na Polakach z Wołynia'43*]). It should be mentioned that these painful issues has been rarely raised in official discourse (the past atrocities becomes a political taboo) in order to secure good relations with both neighbouring countries; hasty naturalization of foreign players before the Euro 2008 championships ('Roger, you will never be Polish' [*Roger nigdy nie będziesz Polakiem*]), referring to Roger Guerreiro from Brazil who was offered Polish citizenship only to play for the Polish national team. As Marsh et al. (1978, 87) would argue all these radical, nationalist and even xenophobic performances serve as re-construction of the manhood and re-affirmation of masculinity that has been under criticism (more mocking) expressed by intellectual elite, numerous celebrities and also main stream media.

Uncompromising attitudes which go often beyond the limits of political correctness have also produced such performances as 'Jihad Legia' (in Arabic-style lettering; Legia Warsaw vs. Hapoel Tel Aviv) and 'Homosexuality forbidden!' (*Zakaz pedałowania*) that refer to the concept of 'normal' males that should be able to protect their nation from internal and external threats. The latter are conceived as threats to both to the notion of 'nation' (such as Islam and transnational organizations) and masculinity[4] (eg homosexuality). And also because they are perceived as compliant to hegemonic transnational political projects, the fans manifest their resistance manifested through rituals and performances. Displaying such attitudes seems to correspond well with the findings of Hall and Jefferson (1993) in their seminal work *Resistance through Rituals.*

In this context we can recall study of Klause Theweleit (1987) and George Mosse (1985) that make strong links between manhood and the idea of nation conceiving them as isomorphic concepts (King 1997, 581). Thus, it should be no surprise that Polish football fans immediately responded to a raising issue of Islam in Europe with popular the slogan 'Stop the Islamisation of Poland' (*Stop islamizacji Polski*). It appeared in a number of stadiums at the same time and was often displayed along the banners reading 'We want repatriants, not immigrants' (*Chcemy repatrianta, nie emigranta*, the word 'repatriants' referring to Poles who were forced to stay in the Soviet Union after the Second World War). It is important to observe that since anti-immigrant feelings are shared by a considerable proportion of Polish society, ultras performances do not seem to express an isolated opinion. However, such manifestation helps the ultras (or even much wider group of fans) to highlight their liminal status and re-assert the traditional notion of manhood in the light of external enemy.

There are numerous studies that link the fandom culture with resistance to political, economic and cultural transformation (Groves 2011; Millward 2011; Numerato 2015). The performance of Polish ultras seem not to be an exception, although they tend to make reference to contemporary politics. So far, comments from the ultras on current politics have been concerned with issues related to the world of football and involved the conflict with the government in the period preceding the Euro 2012. 'Moral panic' (Cohen 1972) stirred up public outcry and calls for undertaking radical measures against fandom culture with the particular focus on ultras who spectacularly marked their resistance to the concept of 'modern football'. It helped ultras to strength their 'deviant' identity but also build an self-image of 'male-soldiers' in love with their clubs and country. Their hermetic perception of collective identity naturally results in establishing the lines of division from 'Others' of different cultures and religious backgrounds.

Extremist performances

The above examples indicate political contexts dominating among Polish ultras. It also needs to be stressed that sometimes their political 'incorrectness' leads to extremist messages, which beg the question of legal limits for stadium expression. What remains certain is that racist incidents are far less frequent than they used to be in the 1990s, when skinheads made up a sizeable proportion of the fans. This is an effect of a civilizing change fostered not only by legal regulations, but also by the evolution of the supporters themselves. Although today there are no performances which would make direct references to racial hatred, flags with the Celtic cross can sometimes be seen, mainly in small stadiums in lower leagues. For example, in the context of the migration crisis, the fans of Piast Żmigród (the Fourth League) presented a choreography including the Celtic cross and the slogan 'Poland only for Poles' (*Polska tylko dla Polaków*).

The ultras sectors sometime also become a venue of number of anti-Semitic performances, indirectly but clearly referring to the Jewish origins of the opponents with an intention of discrediting their value. A radical example of such a choreography was one displayed by Resovia Rzeszów fans (level four in the league system) featuring the slogan

'Death to the humped noses' (*Śmierć garbatym nosom*) and an image of a Jew wearing a blue-and-white-striped kippah, the colours of the local rival club, Stal Rzeszów. However, an outside observer might have associated the colour theme with the outfits worn by the prisoners of German concentration camps. The Jew is used as an emblematic figure of the 'Stranger' which can be used as an insult in an act of symbolic degradation. This symbolic mechanism can be observed in Łódź, where supporters of the two rival local clubs (ŁKS and Widzew) call each other 'Jews', and in Cracow, where the fans of Wisła are notorious for their malicious comments on the Jewish roots of Cracovia club (co-founded in 1906 by members of the Jewish community). Although anti-Semitic flags and banners are a rare occurrence in the stadiums (probably because of the penalties involved), both cities have a large number of graffiti aiming to stigmatize the opponents by associating them with Jewishness.

Hooligan and prison-themed performances

Restrictive legal regulations and modern stadium infrastructure (including CCTV surveillance) have eliminated hooligan incidents from Polish stadiums. Today, hooligan 'firms' arrange fights in secluded locations, away from accidental witnesses and football arenas. They also protect the ultras (particularly during away matches) and thus – although they are relatively small groups – have a considerable influence in the stands (Kossakowski 2015). For this reason, support shows also include elements of hooligan wars, often in the form of a message to the opponent, usually the local rival. The world of football hooligans is hermetic and uses its own linguistic code, often deriving from prison slang. On the top of it, the reference to the underground culture draw a symbolic boundaries that helps ultras distance themselves from the rest of spectators, the elite from the rest (King 1997).[5]

Also, the most committed fans tend to adopt the rules of prison subculture. For example, Lech Poznań ultras prepared a two-part choreography including two banners saying 'Never give up' (*Nigdy się nie poddawaj*) featuring boxing gloves, and 'Never plead guilty' (*Nigdy się nie przyznawaj*), featuring an emoticon with a fastened zip instead of the mouth. The performance made a reference to both the 'militant spirit' and the principal rule of all football fans: they are not allowed to cooperate with the police under any circumstances. As a result, even those who become victims of violence refuse to make any statements in the course of an investigation.

Although there are no sufficient data on the scale of the problem, the principle of non-cooperation with the police is associated with the fact that the world of hardcore fans is penetrated by organized criminal groups (Chlebowicz 2009). This appears quite natural, considering that the community in question is highly masculine and controlled by strong, charismatic individuals, often involved in practising martial arts. Other factors at play include the hermetic nature and military structure of the group, governed by hierarchy, mechanical solidarity and controlled by means of violence (both symbolic and physical). As the principal rule is 'Never plead guilty', it is hardly surprising that criminal groups try to use this structure to pursue their own aims. Cooperation with the police is regarded as the greatest disgrace of all. Those who engage in it become ostracized and are subject to symbolic degradation, often expressed in vulgar terms. In one of such cases, a Legia Warsaw fan who decided to testify as a protected witness in a trial involving fans is not only still held in disgrace, but also regularly degraded on banners displayed in stadiums, denouncing him as a 'slut', 'bitch', or 'punk' (*szmata, kurwa, cwel*). On the other hand, those members of the fan community who find themselves in prison (a fact that would seem to confirm the presence of criminal element; however, there is no available data whether their activity was connected with organized crime) not only remain part of the 'family' but also receive both practical (assistance to their families) and symbolic support from other fans. The latter type involves flags and banners displayed in the stadiums reading 'Greetings to prison', most often abbreviated as 'PDW' (*Pozdrowienia do więzienia*), a standardized message used in this context across the country.

Anti-modernization performances

The above examples illustrate a preoccupation with particular concerns which arise from the local aspects of a certain strand of Polish culture. Considering that Polish football and fans have not yet become subject to global flows, Polish ultras performances rarely make references to the slogan 'Against Modern Football' in the sense used in Western Europe. Unlike fans in Germany or the Netherlands, their Polish counterparts do not protest against an increasing commercialization of football mainly because there are no private investors comparable in scale to Arab sheiks or Russian oligarchs. The conflict between Legia Warsaw fans and the owner of the club was an exception to the rule. Having bought the club, the ITI media group (the owner of a large television company, a web portal and a chain of cinemas) tried to use the policy of 'pricing out' in order to replace the ultras with 'new consumer fans (Antonowicz et al. 2016)'. Following a few months of a heated conflict, including a boycott of the matches by the ultras, the fans reached an agreement with the owner and returned to the stadium.

In 2008, at the time of the dispute, Legia supporters displayed a confrontational giant crowd flag featuring two figures of fans ripping apart the logo of the ITI company; as the flag was unveiled further apart sideways, the orange letter 'T' in the middle was actually split revealing a huge red heart with the logo of the club in it. The entire performance conveyed a message that the fans are able to 'rescue' the depth of symbolic value hidden under the surface of commercialism. Indeed, the message was also stressed by a banner reading 'Our passion knows no limits. The power of love destroys the power of money' (*Nasza pasja, która nie ma końca. Siła miłości niszczy siłę pieniądza*).

Although ultras groups occasionally manifest their contempt for the UEFA and its policy, they are driven mostly by the local context (as in a Legia choreography presenting a giant banner with the UEFA logo, featuring a pig wearing a euro-patterned suit in the centre, and accompanied by the words 'Because football doesn't matter. Money does'). For Polish fans, 'modern sport' is associated mainly with the increasing penalization of, and draconian fines for, spectator misconduct in the stadium. Hence, anti-modernization performances mostly concern the passion of the ultras which the authorities decided to ban. In reaction, ultras groups, responsible for devising performances, manifest their protest against the policy aiming to limit their activity in, or even to ban them from, the stadiums. Anti-modernization support shows also express nostalgia for the traditional, unrestrained atmosphere in the stands. The use of flares became a local Polish symbol of resistance against modernization, and the ultras regularly include them as a means of aesthetic expression. The significance of pyrotechnics could be seen in a choreography presented by Lechia Gdańsk ultras, displaying a giant crowd flag featuring a group of fans wearing club colours gathered at a table with a display of an array of pyrotechnic devices; the masked man in the centre opens up his arms in a gesture of invitation. While the composition was a reference to Leonardo's 'Last Supper', the accompanying slogan – 'Take this, all of you, and burn it' (*Bierzcie i odpalajcie z tego wszyscy*) alluded to the Words of Institution of the Roman Rite Mass ('Take this, all of you, and eat it').

Conclusion

The community of Polish ultras holds an important position in European fandom. They are fortunate in that Polish football has not been dramatically affected by the process of commercialization eliminating the supporters from the lowest social strata. Consequently, ultras culture can continue to develop and provide commentary on various issues in match-day choreographies. As we have attempted to demonstrate above, ultras performances often include historical, patriotic, anti-communist and, recently, also anti-immigrant content which is not related to sport. They reflect the collective opinion of the socially excluded, and the stadiums have become a space of presenting this opinion. Ultras culture, just like football in general, has always been a fundamental platform of identity policy. Stemming from the context of Polish history and culture, the identity policy of Polish ultras is drifting towards radical right-wing, ultra-conservative values. In doing so, it recreates traditional divisions between 'Us' (pious, nation-loving, admiring tradition, etc.) and 'Them' (lefties, feminists, communists, liberals). The example of Poland demonstrates that, in spite of its global character, football serves to form and express local and particular collective identities.

Notes

1. The Polish term Cursed Soldiers (*Żołnierze Wyklęci*) refers to the soldiers of the Polish underground independence movement, members of different partisan organizations, towards the end of the Second World War and in the first years of the post-war period. They became the victims of communist repressions and it is only today that their memory is being revived, including such initiatives as monuments and the National Day of Remembrance of the 'Cursed Soldiers' (Narodowy Dzień Pamięci 'Żołnierzy Wyklętych').
2. After the Polish Cup final between Legia Warsaw and Lech Poznań at the National Stadium in Warsaw (2015), the President of the Polish Football Association (PZPN), Zbigniew Boniek, issued a letter to thank Lech fans for their 'excellent show of support involving impressive choreographies' which created 'an atmosphere of football festival'. On the other hand, interestingly, the club was fined for the use of several dozen flares by the fans. http://www.poznan.sport.pl/sport-poznan/1,124479,17915959,Prezes_Zbigniew_Boniek_napisal_list_do_kibicow_Lecha.html (accessed 12.03.2017).
3. 2009 Act on Mass Events Security.
4. In Poland, fandom is almost entirely masculine activity. Only very few individual female supporters are on the stands and the best to our knowledge, there are neither ultras nor hooligans groups solely by populated by women. In this respect Polish fandom seems to stand out from many other Western countries (see Cere 2002; Dunn 2014).
5. In the old-school fans jargon the regular spectators used to be called 'picnic fans' which shows best the contempt and willingness to distinct themselves from the rest of the audience.

Acknowledgments

The Radosław Kossakowski's research was conducted thanks to a research grant from the Polish National Centre of Science (no. 2013 /09/D/HS/6/00238).

Disclosure statement

No potential conflict of interest was reported by the authors.

References

Alexander, J. C. 2006. "Cultural Pragmatics: Social Performance between Ritual and Strategy." In *Social Performance. Symbolic Action, Cultural Pragmatics, and Ritual*, edited by J. C. Alexander, B. Giesen, and J. L. Mast, 29–90. Cambridge: University Press.

Anderson, B. 1991. *Imagined Communities: Reflections on the Origin and Spread of Nationalism*. London: Verso.

Antonowicz, D., and M. Grodecki. 2016. *Missing the Goal: Policy Evolution towards Football-related Violence in Poland (1989–2012)*. International Review for the Sociology of Sport. Advance Online Publication. doi:10.1177/1012690216662011.

Antonowicz, D., R. Kossakowski, and T. Szlendak. 2015. *Aborygeni i konsumenci. O kibicowskiej wspólnocie, komercjalizacji futbolu i stadionowym apartheidzie*. Warszawa: IFiS PAN.

Antonowicz, D., R. Kossakowski, and T. Szlendak. 2016. "Flaming Flares, Football Fanatics and Political Rebellion: Resistant Youth Cultures in Late Capitalism." In *Eastern European Youth Cultures in a Global Context*, edited by M. Schwartz and H. Winkel, 131–144. Basingstoke: Palgrave Macmillan.

Antonowicz, D., and Ł. Wrzesiński. 2009. "Kibice jako wspólnota niewidzialnej religii [Sport Fans as a Community of the Invisible Religion]" *Studia Socjologiczne* 1 (192): 115–150.

Carlson, M. 2004. *Performance: A Critical Introduction*. Oxford: Routledge.

Cere, R. 2002. "'Witches of Our Age': Women Ultras, Football and the Media." *Sport in Society.Culture, Sport, Society* 5 (3): 166–188. doi:10.1080/911094210.

Chlebowicz, P. 2009. *Chuligaństwo Stadionowe. Studium Kryminologiczne*. Warszawa: Wolters Kluwer SA.

Cohen, S. 1972. *Folk Devils and Moral Panics*. London: MacGibbon and Kee.

Coser, L. W. 1956. *The Functions of Social Conflict*. New York: The Free Press.

Doidge, M. 2015. *Football Italia: Italian Football in an Age of Globalization*. London: Bloomsbury.

Dubai, S. 2010. "The Neoliberalization of Football: Rethinking Neoliberalism through the Commercialization of the Beautiful Game." *International Review for the Sociology of Sport* 45 (2): 123–146. doi:10.1177/1012690210362426.

Dunn, C. 2014. *Female Football Fans: Community, Identity and Sexism*. Basingstoke: Palgrave Macmillan.

Durkheim, E. 2008. *The Elementary Forms of Religious Life*. Oxford: University Press.

Frosdick, S., and P. Marsh. 2005. *Football Hooliganism*. Devon: Willan Publishing.

Goffman, E. 1959. *The Presentation of Self in Everyday Life*. New York: Doubleday.

Groves, M. 2011. "Resisting the Globalization, Standardization and Rationalization of Football: My Journey to Bilbao." *Soccer & Society* 12 (2): 265–278. doi:10.1080/14660970.2011.548362.

Guschwan, M. 2009. "Riot in the Curve: Soccer Fans in Twenty-first Century Italy." In *Football Fans around the World. from Supporters to Fanatics*, edited by S. Brown, 88–105, Abingdon: Routledge.

Hall, S., and T. Jefferson. 1993. *Resistance through Rituals Youth Subcultures in Post-war Britain*. London: Routledge.

Janicka, K., and K. Słomczyński. 2014. "Struktura społeczna w Polsce: klasowy wymiar nierówności." *Przegląd Socjologiczny* 63 (2): 55–72.

Karwacki, A., and T. Szlendak. 2010. "Trust and Social Activity versus Income Range. the Spirit Level Concept in the Light of European Social Survey." *Kultura i Edukacja* 84 (5): 81–106.

Kennedy, D., and P. Kennedy. 2010. "Towards a Marxist Political Economy of Football Supporters." *Capital & Class* 34 (2): 181–198. doi:10.1177/0309816810365520.

Kennedy, P., and D. Kennedy. 2012. "Football Supporters and the Commercialization of Football: Comparative Responses across Europe." *Soccer & Society* 13 (3): 327–340. doi:10.1080/1466097 0.2012.655503.

King, A. 1997. "The Postmodernity of Football Hooliganism." *The British Journal of Sociology* 48 (4): 576–593. doi:10.2307/591597.

Kossakowski, Radosław. 2015. *Where Are the Hooligans? Dimensions of Football Fandom in Poland*. International Review for the Sociology of Sport. Advance Online Publication. doi:10.1177/1012690215612458.

Marsh, Peter, Elizabeth Rosser, and Rom Harre. 1978. *The Rules of Disorder*. London: Routledge.

Millward, P. 2011. *The Global League. Transnational Networks, Social Movements and Sport in the New Media Age*. Basingstoke: Palgrave Macmillan.

Mosse, G. 1985. *Nationalism and Sexuality*. Wisconsin: University of Wisconsin.

Numerato, D. 2015. "Who Says 'No to Modern Football?' Italian Supporters, Reflexivity, and Neo-liberalism." *Journal of Sport and Social Issues* 39 (2): 120–138. doi:10.1177/0193723514530566.

Pope, S. 2011. "Like Pulling down Durham Cathedral and Building a Brothel." *International Review for the Sociology of Sport* 46 (4): 471–487. doi:10.1177/1012690210384652.

Schechner, R. 1976. *Essays on Performance Theory*. New York: Drama Publishers.

Schechner, R. 2013. *Performance Studies: An Introduction*. Abingdon: Routledge.

Spaaij, R. 2006. *Understanding Football Hooliganism: A Comparison of Six Western European Football Clubs*. Amsterdam: Amsterdam University Press.

Szlendak, T. 2015. "Die jungen Polen und die Politik." *Polen-Analysen* 166: 2–7.

Szlendak, T., R. Kossakowski, D. Antonowicz, and M. Sipińska-Małaszyńska. 2014. "Stadiony piątej generacji jako 'maszyny do życia." *Prakselologia* 155: 231–259.

Taylor, I. 1971. "'Football Mad' – A Speculative Sociology of Soccer Hooliganism." In *The Sociology of Sport: A Selection of Readings*, edited by E. Dunning, 357–377. London: Cass.

Theweleit, K. 1987. *Male Fantasies, Vol. I: Women, Floods, Bodies, History*. Cambridge: Polity.

Zawadzka, A. 2011. "Przymus kreatywności." In *Wieczna radość. Ekonomia polityczna społecznej kreatywności*, edited by J. Sowa, 227–237, Warszawa: Fundacja Bęc Zmiana.

Zieliński, R. 1997. *Liga chuliganów*. Wrocław: Croma.

Ultras in Turkey: othering, agency, and culture as a political domain

Yağmur Nuhrat

ABSTRACT

Football administrators and non-fans or non-ultra fans in Turkey tend to posit ultras as either the 'fire of the show' or write them off as instruments of violence guided by irrationality. These two stances are the two sides of the same coin which points to a fascination/fear discourse that serves to produce ultras as the perfect other. The financially powerful actors of football tolerate and accommodate ultras so long as they don't challenge dominating commercial or political interests. This relegates ultras to the supposedly innocuous realm of culture divorced from politics, especially in the aftermath of the Gezi Uprising of 2013. However, through organizations like the Fans' Rights Association and in their everyday practices of fandom, ultras reject subjectivities assigned to them by the fascination/fear discourse, they agentively engage with their own spectacularization and othering as well as the legal or administrative efforts to contain and confine them.

Introduction: ultras in Turkey

Scholars working on ultras have both discerned defining criteria and conceded that substantial heterogeneity exists within ultras especially as the movement continues to spread globally (Kennedy 2013). Similarly, there is not a consensus within the football community in Turkey regarding whether or not ultras actually exist in the country. On the one hand, there are fan groups that self-label as 'ultras' (such as Galatasaray's UltrAslan) and those that reference ultras on their paraphernalia like Bursaspor's Teksas inscribing scarves with 'Ultras Green Boys' or 'Curva Sud'.[1] Especially after fan groups' political presence in the Gezi protests of 2013, more and more political commentary referred to Turkish fan groups as 'ultras' comparing their role to the role of ultras in Egypt (Bergfeld 2014; Dorsey 2013; Taştekin 2013). However, those who adhere to more rigid definition of ultras have opposed calling fan groups in Turkey ultras. Indeed, on-the-ground observation shows that more fans in Turkey refer to themselves as fans (*taraftar*), fanatics (*fanatik*), hooligans (*holigan*), children of the tribunes (*tribün çocuğu*) or as tribuners (*tribüncü*).[2]

Battini (2012) identifies the 1990s as the time when 'ultras model of fan support became common' in Turkey (703). He ties this development to the liberalization of economy under the leadership of Turgut Özal, a project that also included football and resulted in the intensification of Turkey's interaction with football in Europe (Irak 2010). According to Battini, fans in Turkey were thus influenced by Italian ultras, a historical process exemplified by the emergence of UltrAslan in 2001 and the modification of other fan groups to embrace practices and performances associated with ultras. My research shows that even fan groups that don't necessarily refer to themselves as ultras exhibit qualities of ultras such as designing elaborate choreographies involving pyrotechnics, drumming and vocal leaders (amigos), claiming certain sections of the stadium, selling their own merchandise, organizing transport to away games, protesting restrictions imposed by the federation, the police and the law, and socializing together as fans even on matchless days.[3]

On the other hand, some sports columns and online fan commentaries purposefully refrain from using the term 'ultras'. For example, Topal (2010), argues that fan groups of Istanbul's big three can hardly be considered ultras since they have negligible influence on club decision-making and are in fact regularly deployed or bought off by clubs towards intensifying club control over stadium stands. He adds that fan groups in Turkey lack coordination and cooperation with fellow ultras groups and that the foremost goal of any supporter group is simply to outshine fans of other teams. Positing Adana Demirspor's Mavi Şimşekler as an exception, Topal concludes that even though an intense fanaticism characterizes many fans in Turkey, they don't satisfy the criteria to qualify as ultras. Others who agree present reasons such as fan groups in Turkey expecting or receiving monetary help from their clubs, being unable to stand up to the dictate of broadcasting companies in relation to match times amongst other impositions by clubs, media and the federation, having hierarchical relationships within the group, and at times siding with the police (*Ekşi Sözlük* 2012).[4]

Highlighting differences among ultras around the world and drawing attention to the fact that some ultras groups may be engaged in activities (such as receiving monetary help from clubs) that ostensibly stand opposed to the philosophy of being ultras, Kennedy (2013) has concluded that 'it would be inappropriate to attempt any kind of analysis which fails to recognize the heterogeneity of ultra groups (133)'. As such, literature on ultras acknowledges this as a complex movement, sometimes even as a 'complex puzzle' (Spaaij and Viñas 2005). In this article, I consider this heterogeneity and concede that some of the fans I write about do not necessarily refer to themselves as ultras, even though their experiences are comparable to those of ultras in other parts of the world.

Club and federation administrators as well as non-fans or non-ultra fans in Turkey tend to posit ultras as either the 'fire of the show' or write them off as simple instruments of violence guided by irrationality and animal instinct. I show that these two stances are the two sides of the same coin which points to a fascination/fear discourse that ultimately serves to produce ultras as the perfect other in Turkey. I demonstrate that those benefitting from the interests of capital and power tolerate ultras so long as they don't challenge dominating commercial or political interests where a technique of this tolerance is by relegating ultras to the allegedly innocuous site of 'culture' divorced from politics or power relations, especially in the aftermath of the Gezi Uprising of 2013. However, through organizations like the Fans' Rights Association and in their everyday practices of fandom, ultras reject subjectivities assigned to them by the fascination/fear discourse, agentively engage with their own spectacularization and the efforts to contain and confine them.

Literature on postcolonialism as well as studies that engage theoretically with race and racism explain that fear and fascination go together in the construction of various social categories as 'others'. Sometimes the other is the Orient (Said 1978) other times it is a black man's body (Butler 1993; Hall 1997) but it is always a locus of mystery, danger and fascination at once. In this paper, I argue that for football authorities in Turkey, ultras compose such a group of other. For this reason, administrators and the media desire to repackage ultras' practices to be included in the site of football – consumable as a spectacle. Related to this, I contend that the othering of ultras is class-based since the various commercial and legal moves to contain them serve to achieve distinction for more advantaged groups (see Bourdieu [1979] 1984). In addition, class-based othering works towards containing ultras in the supposedly more innocuous realm of culture thereby both removing ultras from the political site and also realizing a specific political goal, which discursively disconnects the sites of culture and that of politics.

In what follows, I first describe how football administrators conjure ultras and how their description of 'good fandom' serves their financial interests. Then, I outline how ultras' subjectivity differs from the subject positions attributed to them through the discourse of fascination/fear by accounting for their agentive engagement. Finally, I challenge the desired depoliticization of ultras in Turkey by demonstrating the very political nature of this attempt. This article is based on fieldwork I conducted in 2010 and 2011, mostly in Istanbul but also in other cities around Turkey, exploring dynamics of watching, playing, mediating, administrating and refereeing football, with a specific focus on the concept of fairness. During this time, I attended 34 football matches; I travelled to away games outside of Istanbul and spent time in various locations where fans congregate. I held in-depth interviews with fans, former footballers, coaches, referees, journalists, football federation and club administrators. I also analysed online and printed media discourse circulated by administrators, players and fans of football in Turkey. Since 2011, I have continued to hold follow-up interviews with key interlocutors in Istanbul.

Fear and fascination: two sides of the same coin

It is common to find football authorities praise ultras' choreography, which in Turkey is most often referred to as 'fan shows' or 'tribune shows'. In June 2011, I spoke with two high-ranking administrators at Beşiktaş Football Investments Incorporated – the corporation of Beşiktaş's (BJK) football branch.[5] They readily accepted to be interviewed and welcomed me in their office. Among other things, I was interested in finding out how these administrators conceived of ultras and their presence in the stadium. One of my interlocutors, Mehmet Uygur explained to me that he goes to matches seeking 'the show and the adrenalin' and finds himself 'wanting to be a part of that show' albeit away from the centre of the eastern stands where 'the fighting' is.

çArşı, Beşiktaş's most prominent fan group, is one of the most significant ultras groups in the country.[6] Unlike ultras in general, çArşı is located in the centre of the upper eastern section of the stadium.[7] The eastern section is called the 'kapalı', literally meaning 'closed', referring to the roof over the top. Beşiktaş fans in general and çArşı in particular take pride in having won this section after violently battling fans of Galatasaray and Fenerbahçe for years back when the three teams used to play home games in the same stadium. Sleeping in the kapalı night after night, fending it like a fort and claiming it as theirs after years of fighting in the 1980s, çArşı has objected to all efforts geared towards their relocation in the stadium. In fact, when BJK's Serdar Bilgili administration decided to relocate çArşı to the southern stands in order to build box seats in the kapalı, there were massive protests in the stadium. Uygur's narrative shows that he is impressed by the intensity of fandom at kapalı.

At the same time, Both Uygur and his colleague, Sinan Ulu, were vehement in communicating their desire to rebuild and reorganize the stadium so that the eastern stands could be allocated to more affluent fans – a process that was completed through the reconstruction of Beşiktaş İnönü Stadium as Vodafone Arena. Calling this 'displacement', I asked from Ulu to comment on the process. He replied:

> We don't want them to lose that fervour or passion. We don't want silent people who only go there to applaud. That would kill the love for football … This is not displacement. All ultras groups around the world are situated behind the goal. They like being there. When they want to scream and shout they can go there. When they wish to show their girlfriends what Beşiktaş is all about, then they can buy two VIP tickets and go to the eastern or western section. We must make sure that ultras here can identify with the southern stands … just like in Germany and their terraces behind the goals. (Sinan Ulu, in-depth interview, June 2011)

As much as the southern positioning of ultras around the world can be taken for granted today, I hold that Turkey is currently experiencing this as a phenomenon of displacement, especially in the case of çArşı whose group and fan identity is partly composed by having won the eastern stands in the 1980s. As administrators see it, tribune shows are magnificent but they need to be contained and controlled. Uygur explained to me that in a 'world of those who manage and those who are managed, groups like çArşı or UltrAslan are the managed – a position they in fact desire'. As such, according to Uygur, good management can easily relocate them since 'they don't even need seats'. Wishing to be in total control of football as a spectacle, administrators praise or rather tolerate fervour and passion so long as they have the final say in relation to how they can be packaged – in a way that can generate profit for the club.

Uygur's words mark a fundamental misconception in regards to ultras' identity. As I discuss in the next section, ultras imagine their subjectivity as 24-h fans who congregate whether or not there is a match. This communitarian life reinforces their identity and allows them to keep organizing towards performing support for the team. On the contrary, administrators such as Uygur see ultras' identity as almost a piece of clothing that one may decide to put on or take off depending on the context. For them, ultras can easily shift between the position of entertainer and that of entertained depending on whether they feel like screaming or rather like purchasing VIP tickets so that their girlfriends (who are supposedly not familiar at all with the setting) may enjoy the show in peace.

Ultras relocation in the stadium, their repackaging as a passionate yet managed element within the spectacle of football is a manoeuvre towards employing ultras as money-making agents. This became clear to me when Mehmer Uygur described his version of the ideal fan as someone who not only cheers the team on but also spends money on licensed products and rejects pirated paraphernalia. He complained about how some fans who think they support the team in fact cause the club to pay fines because they swear too much when they chant. Uygur stressed that fans should consider the club's finances first and everything else second when they set out to demonstrate their fandom.

By containing ultras, club administrators can use them as a brand to attract more consumers. A relocated çArşı can provide entertainment for those who wish not only to watch football but also to breathe in the atmosphere of fandom at the stadium – albeit at a safe distance, from their more expensive seats in the eastern stands. The class-based motive came across also when I interviewed assistant referee Tolga Engin, who told me that whilst 'no one would want to lose the ultras since they have real heart and soul and are the fire of the show', clubs must relocate them if they wish for stadiums to be 'more refined' and generate 'financial success'.

This point of view is in line with the discourse and promotion of the Law to Prevent Violence and Disorder in Sport (aka Violence Law) (Resmi 2011) fashioned after many European examples, including the Taylor Report (Taylor 1990) with the mission to 'civilize', and 'Europeanize' football in Turkey eliminating violence in and around the site of football. As such, I argue that the desire to contain ultras are also related to the larger mission of clubs and TFF to legally reorganize and transform football in Turkey by criminalizing those components of ultras culture that do not avail themselves to generating profit. I became keenly aware of this when speaking to a TFF administrator, Hasan Yılmaz:

> We want fans to be informed and aware … who know that this is just a game and who are not inclined to violence. We make such a big deal out of football in this country … I think that some people use football to hang onto life. I'm sure there is nothing else in their lives, no lovers, no women, no hobbies … They think that they acquire clout when they join fan groups … We try to cleanse stadiums of these people – the amigos and the hooligans … As stadiums modernize, as they get more luxurious and as ticket systems change, the looters (*çapulcu*) won't be able to afford going to matches … (Hasan Yılmaz, in-depth interview, May 2011)

Yılmaz's words mark the transition from viewing fans as the 'fire of the show' to interpreting them as asocial good-for-nothings, incapable of treating football as 'only a game'. 'Amigos' or 'hooligans' are imagined here as looters or lowlifes with no social attachments to prevent them from acting violently.

This incriminating language is not too removed from the discourse put forth by the BJK administrators I quoted. If ultras act in ways that fall short from promoting the club, the federation or the 'beautiful game', if, for example, their actions accrue fines or they clash with the police, they are seen as unjustly invading the stadium and the site of football. Depicting ultras as naturally violent or as asocial creatures naturalizes this invasion. It is telling that Yılmaz is using the word 'looters' (çapulcu) to describe the group of people from whom he believes football must be cleansed. The term *çapulcu* took on a new meaning during the 2013 Gezi Uprising when then PM Erdoğan used this word to refer to the protestors demonstrating against the government. Those involved in the resistance immediately appropriated the term and began self-labelling as çapulcu – some of which were the very ultras Yılmaz describes as utterly purposeless.

Said (1978) described Orientalism as the construction of the Orient by the West as its other, a mysterious and exotic object to be feared, desired and possessed at the same time. Accounts of othering in relation to racism have described similar seemingly paradoxical dynamics where the racialized other would be attributed ostensibly opposing qualities. Stuart Hall (1997) wrote,

> … people who are in any way significantly different from the majority – 'them' rather than 'us' are frequently exposed to this *binary* form of representation. They seem to be represented through sharply opposed, polarized, binary extremes – good/bad, civilized/primitive, ugly/ excessively attractive, repelling-because-different/compelling-because-strange-and-exotic. And they are often required to be *both things at the same time*! (229)

As such, scholars of postcolonialism and race have discussed racialized others as super-masculine or feminine objects of sexual fantasy and fear at the same or as super-human wonders fascinating and endangering simultaneously (Butler 1993; Fanon 2008). I find that it is precisely a reincarnation of this age-old fascination/fear discourse that characterizes the ways in which administrators view ultras in Turkey.

This discourse feeds off of and into conventional characterizations of football fans as irrational and crazy people with perverse priorities or concerns. Over the years, telling people I was researching football in Turkey, the common reaction from non-fans was that I was working with crazy people to figure out the causes of fanaticisms. Non-ultra fans on the other hand, made a distinction between 'normal' fans (themselves) and 'fanatics'. The conventional othering of ultras, referred in Turkey as 'fanatics' or 'tribuners' feeds on the ways in which football's administrators circulate this discourse. But whilst non-fans and non-ultra fans may have similar points of views to the administrators I quote in this section, the bosses of football in fact have monetary gains from the reproduction of this discourse and the subjectivities it makes available (Foucault 1982).

Ultras' self-perception and agency

As I began to discuss in the previous section, a significant characteristic that marks ultras is the fact that they don't come together only for matches. Pilz and Wölki-Schumacher (2010) wrote: 'Unlike other fan club activities, a person is an ultra not only at a weekend game but also during the entire week. Everything is subordinated to football and/or the fan movement' (6). Speaking with two BJK fans who associate themselves with çArşı, live in Beşiktaş and frequent the kapalı, I heard similar descriptions. Their words also clarified for me how geographically grounded çArşı and Beşiktaş can be despite the popularity of the team across the country or the global reach of çArşı.

Emre was 26 years old when we met in January 2011. He is a web designer who was born and raised in Beşiktaş. Emre has been going to games with the same group of friends since childhood – a group that spends most of their time together in Beşiktaş writing songs, designing banners, discussing recruits and organizing trips to away locations. Emre told me, 'Beşiktaş is like a refuge for us. Here, we experience Beşiktaş even on matchless days as if there was a match. We talk about old games. We sing and cheer'. He was very keen on explaining to me that their concern went above and beyond particular games and that they were more interested in coming together as Beşiktaş fans, uniting over this 'common denominator'. He recounts that when Beşiktaş loses, it's easy to find his group of fanmates in Beşiktaş drinking to commemorate defeat after which the group eventually begins to sing cheers again as if they were celebrating a win. 'What's important is to always maintain the fervour' he says, 'the fervour keeps you attached. Otherwise, seasons come and go. Matches come and go'.

After I met Emre, I spent some time with his fanmates, going to games with them and following their discussions in their email group. I realized that a considerable amount of performing fandom 24/7 happens online where more than 50 messages may be exchanged on any day, with the conversation covering anything from a single refereeing call through random denigration of rival teams, to the problems of losing sleep over defeat. Through Emre, I met and interviewed Veysel, 32 when we met in 2011 and the editor of an online Beşiktaş news portal. He said he chose this job over an administrative position at Siemens and explained that he gave up on a secure job and a fixed income for his passion, Beşiktaş. We met at one of the popular fan hangout places in Beşiktaş, Külüstür pub which allowed him to describe how he and his fanmates, 'the whole tribune' in his words, gather at this precise location over the course of the week 'to prepare banners, chant and compose new cheers'. Referring to Beşiktaş as a 'common language', he also told me that fans gather to discuss whether or not any given player should be recruited, how much they approve of someone's salary and the problems they associate with the commercialization of football – in Turkey referred to as 'industrialized football'. Therefore, unlike the quotes I provide from BJK administrators, ultras don't see themselves as part-time devotees whose only significance for the club relates to generating profit. Furthermore, they are certainly not societal rejects with no attachments other than football. Expecting them to switch sections of the stadium, predicting that they are 'easily manageable', or claiming that they have no purpose in life other than to cause trouble in the stadium are, if nothing else, misconstrued.

When I spoke with administrators at BJK, they told me that they desire 'full' fans, using the word 'full' in Turkish (tam) as an acronym that stands for 'fan', 'member', and 'customer'. Indeed, the issue of how fandom relates to the commercialization of football is a substantial topic of discussion in Turkey. Whilst some ultras groups have integrated into this system for instance, by producing merchandise to be sold at the official club store like UltrAslan (Battini 2012), and some fans may indeed consider good fandom to be performed through good consumerism, there are ultras and other fan organizations, like the Fans' Rights Association in Turkey, that reject the label of customer. Against the point of view which posits fans' consumption of pirated paraphernalia as betrayal, my interviews showed that for some fans, purchasing pirated products is more desirable than buying licensed merchandise since the money spent generates income for people who are not so well off rather than the big corporation that is the club. çArşı leaders often say that one only needs to scream at the top of their lungs and feel the spirit of çArşı in order to belong. Whilst this requirement may be different in comparison to the recruitment process of other ultras groups, like the more formally organized UltrAslan, it shows that fans' perceptions of good fandom may differ considerably from that of club administrators'.

As I have alluded to before, the standpoint described in the previous section which portrays fans as potential criminals unless they are managed in the ways administrators desire, echoes the discourse of the Violence Law. Through this law, the government, the football federation and club administrators run a crusade to 'civilize' football in the country. This is a class-based mission geared towards eliminating those sectors who don't contribute to the industry of football as a bourgeois pastime – much like the process of the embourgeoisement of football in England that Armstrong and Young (1997) critique. In other words, the fascination/fear discourse does not only portray fans as objects of fascination or danger, it indeed creates endangering fan subjectivities. However, discursively constructing fans and fan subjectivities and spectacularizing the site of football are not processes that do not involve fan agency.

On the one hand, rising commercialization and legal restructuring increasingly produce football as a marketable spectacle in Turkey. On the other hand, some football fans, as active participants in that packaged spectacle, engage in practices that disrupt ideal spectacularization. They light flares and sing against the government in their pirated jerseys. The combined interests of state and capital desire an end product that is clean and tidily packaged as a spectacle, ready for the smooth consumption of those who can afford it. As such, the multiple economic, legal and spatial ways in which this spectacularization unfolds in Turkey may be said to attest to Debord's (2008) notion of the spectacle as containing cultural manifestation. However, a careful study of fan agency as different from a Debordian spectator may allow us to complicate the concept of spectacle.

Describing the media spectacles of football in Hong Kong, Francis Lee (2005) critiques Debord by stating that football fans are distinct from 'spectators' because they are active and not merely passive consumers of spectacle. Football fans in Turkey may be legally banned from executing their desired chants in the stadium; displaying their banners or visiting their teams' away games. But they theoretically challenge and practically protest these decisions through organizations like the Fans' Rights Association founded in 2012. Therefore, it is in fans' necessary insertion into spectacle that we might trace subversions in the idea and practice of spectacle. If football fans are subjected to bodily and conceptual reconfiguration because their propriety is critical for the presentation of the spectacle, they also work from within the spectacle to disrupt and/or transform it as agents – amounting to a phenomenon that is far more complex than simply 'managing problematic fans' by relocating them in southern stands.

Politics vs. culture: a political dichotomy

Above I argued that there are particular financial goals behind administrators' desire to contain fans in specific ways. In this section, I show that those financial goals are tied to political motives. Various ultras groups around the world have explicit political affiliations (Doidge 2013; Spaaij and Viñas 2005; Testa 2009). In Turkey, whilst many ultras demonstrate nationalistic tendencies, some also align with specific political stances. For example, Beşiktaş's çArşı self-describes as anarchists, Fenerbahçe's Vamos Bien and Galatasaray's Tek Yumruk are leftist groups. A momentous development in relation to ultras identifying with political viewpoints took place during and in the aftermath of the Gezi Uprising. It was also at this time that football and government authorities vehemently discouraged 'mixing politics with football'. In this section, first I describe the political football atmosphere of Gezi. Then, I analyse the discourse, which separates football from politics as a specifically political discourse aimed at silencing political opposition. As such, I argue that the perception of ultras as a socially problematic group is tied not only to the interest of capital but also to the interrelated interest of governing power.

In late May 2013, what started out as a peaceful sit-in to protest the demolishment of Gezi Park in Istanbul quickly turned into a full-fledged uprising against the government. Demonstrators all over the country organized park or square occupations and marches to protest what they felt like were governmental infringements on basic social rights. The uprising saw a remarkable cooperation between different sectors of society as Kurds, nationalist Turks, secularists, Sunnis, Alevis, 'anti-capitalist Muslims', LGBTI activists, university students, environmentalists and animal rights groups marched and camped together. They were all met with very intense police violence, mostly in the form of tear gas, water cannons and plastic bullets – indeed fatal across the country.[8] Another group that left their mark with Gezi were ultras.

In Istanbul, the first week of June saw çArşı's involvement in Gezi as group members organized to defend both the Gezi Park and the neighbourhood of Beşiktaş to where battling between protestors and police had spread (Gürmen 2013). Soon after çArşı came out in solidarity with other protestors, the fans of their archrivals Galatasaray and Fenerbahçe joined (McManus 2013b; Nuhrat 2013). Referring to themselves as 'Istanbul United' the age-old rivals fought shoulder to shoulder for the rest of the summer, namely until the season started. However, some ultras purposefully chose not to join the uprising. A few days after fan groups became conspicuous in protest, UltrAslan made the declaration that they were 'saddened' by the politics of Gezi, highlighting their lack of affiliation or alignment with any political stance (*Hürriyet* 2013). UltrAslan's decision was protested at Gezi, drawing antagonism also from fellow Galatasaray ultras Tek Yumruk whose presence at Gezi was conspicuous.

As soon as the season started, fans against the government began to recite Gezi slogans in various stadiums around the country. In fact, some of my older interlocutors pointed out that they recognized this pattern since stadiums were the only legitimate gathering sites for politically motivated masses in the aftermath of the 1980 coup in Turkey. Gezi chants were overwhelmingly met with stadium authorities randomly blasting songs from the loudspeakers to drown out fan voices. There were increasing discussions among sports commentators as well as politicians debating whether or not football and politics should mix. The reigning point of view desired football to remain as 'the game that it is' uninvolved in politics and confined to the supposedly apolitical realm of culture. Finally, then Minister for Youth and Culture, Suat Kılıç stated, 'Taking Gezi inside stadiums would be the end of football' (*Radikal* 2013).

Kasapoğlu (2013) has noted the inconsistencies one may find studying football, media and government authorities' discourse against the mixing of football and politics, especially drawing attention to how manifestations of political conformism go without discouragement or reprimand. Indeed, many overtly political practices go either unnoticed or unchallenged in football in Turkey. Some examples include footballer Emre Belözoğlu signalling the *rabia* after scoring a goal, football commentator Rıdvan Dilmen siding with then PM Erdoğan against Fenerbahçe fans who accused the PM of corruption and numerous manifestations of Turkish nationalism that range from official club banners condemning the Kurdish cause to the routine recital of the Turkish national anthem before every domestic game in the country.[9] As such, the separation of football from politics is prescribed only when the said politics stray from the interests of power. The discourse pushing for an unmixing of football and politics are thus already a political discourse.

In addition, underlying the wish to remove politics from football is the desire to confine both football and ultras to the realm of entertainment or the supposedly innocuous site of culture safely removed from the 'adulterating' influences of politics. Anthropology has long ago dismantled the assumption that culture and politics occupy different spheres, demonstrating various ways in which what people understand and experience as culture is laden with power relations (Abu-Lughod 1991; Bourdieu [1979] 1984; Gupta and Ferguson 1992; Merry 2003). However, conventional wisdom still relegates culture to a realm of entertainment aggressively trying to 'protect' it from what is supposed to be the corrupting effect of politics. This separation discursively blinds the eye to politics that continue to play out in and through culture. By denying the political nature of culture, this discourse serves to disadvantage further those that are already less powerful within any given cultural sphere.

In September 2013, following a Beşiktaş vs. Galatasaray derby marked with Gezi slogans as well as supposedly a pro-government BJK ultras group invading the pitch, a total of 62 ultras leaders woke up to home raids and detentions. Mostly charged with exchanging tickets on the black market, 36 were released within a month. Their fanmates meeting them at the courthouse sang, 'We are fans, not terrorists'. Soon after, nearly 100 members of çArşı were taken into custody for being involved in Gezi, the last 35 of whom were on trial without arrest for reasons of forming a terrorist organization and plotting against the state until December 2015 when they were acquitted. During the course of the trial, the Fans' Rights Association engaged in mobilizing fellow ultras to come together in solidarity with çArşı, arguing that the çArşı case represented a larger problem threatening not only çArşı but all other groups that wished to contradict desired fan behaviour.

The powerful authorities in and around football issue a definitive distinction between culture and politics where this distinction is informed both by a wrongful, depoliticized conceptualization of culture and also contentious criteria in relation to the identification of the political, based on conformism vs. dissent. Labelling dissent as terrorism, they further posit ultras as always and already endangering just by virtue of being ultras (see Butler 1993). Thus, the discourse of fascination/fear not only serves the interests of power – the neoliberal football economy in Turkey that needs and can tolerate ultras in one very specific and limited way.

Conclusion

Scalia (2009) has written against the marginalization of ultras in Italy as a 'violent mob'. Rather than contradicting the fact that ultras engage in violence, he asserts that 'violent acts can be the consequence of the multiple, contradictory and complex emotional meanings that supporters give to a football match and also express through it', thereby offering social background and rationale for violent events rather than positing them as natural occurrences caused by an essentially violent group. Not only does Scalia push for the social and political grounding of footballing violence, he also asserts that 'football supporting [is] a phenomenon that is only distantly related to the rules of fair play …' thereby, challenging the official representation of fairness through the ideal of fair play (42, 43). Armstrong and Young (1997) have similarly put forth that footballing brawls have a certain ethical code the comprehension of which is necessary to evaluate these instances in order to analyse them within the context they unfold. Scholars on Turkey have also shown that in order to account for violence in football it is crucial to consider both the related non-footballing factors that inform it and to study dynamics of fandom that feed it (Akın 2004). These studies, including the present paper, write against the line of thought that foresees criminal justice as the only way to curtail violence in football as well as the standpoint that naturalizes violence in football by demonizing fans.

The attempts to 'manage' ultras in Turkey through the effects of the fascination/fear discourse and legal instruments such as the Violence Law are not measures that stand out given the social and political constellation in the country during the 2010s. The ultras roundup discussed above is yet another manoeuvre by the government in Turkey to control and regulate every facet of society including imposed urban regeneration projects, top-down changes to the education system, intrusive efforts to organize gender, family and sexual relations, and the use of new demographic and surveillance techniques in multiple social sites (Nuhrat and Akkoyunlu 2013). Indeed, the last few years in Turkey have witnessed aggressive governmental intrusion in multiple social sites with the purpose of introducing a desired order and social morality. A discourse of anti-violence and security is deployed to fend off the system's 'others' – those factors that stand in the way of reconfiguring social sites to satisfy the interests of capital and a conservative neoliberal politics. This serves to continually radicalize and marginalize dissent in Turkey, creating subject positions for the 'disorderly' and the 'violent', thereby creating moral panic and effectively othering sectors of society that refuse to identify with discursive constructions that serve the government. Furthermore, by defining good fandom through consumption and propriety, those who have higher class positioning achieve distinction from fans who allow their passions to overtake them, forgetting that football is 'only a game' (Bourdieu [1979] 1984).

In this paper, I have focused on one such group of people, ultras, or the 'fanatics' of football in Turkey – a group that is consistently produced as the perfect societal 'other' which is the object of fascination and fear at once. I have demonstrated how it befits both the interests of capital and of power to deploy this discourse in relation to ultras that ultimately only allocates ultras a role in the neat spectacularization of football as a product. At the same time, I have added that through fan mobilization movements as well as political participation, ultras in Turkey refuse to be passive subjects of 'management' as club administrators desire. I have outlined the tense dynamics between how ultras are overwhelmingly represented by the rest of society, the interests that are served by this representation and the agentive presence of ultras that work to subvert this representation. Acknowledging the differences among ultras in Turkey especially in regards to how they relate to power on the spectrum of conformity and dissent, I show that the fascination/fear discourse others ultras in the interest of neoliberal politics, a process not uncommon in Turkey and that ultras who experience this daily through the reconfiguration of the site of football agentively engage with their own othering.

Notes

1. Beşiktaş, Galatasaray and Fenerbahçe are the three most popular football teams in Turkey. They are all based in Istanbul and are commonly referred to as the 'big three'. Bursaspor is the football team from Bursa, one of the two other teams to have ever won the league title in the country.
2. Stadium stands are referred to as 'tribunes' (*tribün*) in Turkey.
3. The term 'amigo' is used to refer to stadium and/or fan group leaders in Turkey after the self-labeling of the first group of such leaders.
4. Ekşi Sözlük is a collaborative online wiki with approximately 400,000 registered users. On the wiki, there is a topical thread for nearly every football game, among other issues, where members discuss issues pertaining to that game in their entries.
5. I don't specify rank and I use pseudonyms for all of my interlocutors for privacy reasons.
6. *Çarşı* means 'marketplace'. çArşı is the most prominent Beşiktaş fan group, named after the Beşiktaş marketplace. They consider themselves to be leftist and anarchic even though some members admit that it is difficult to substantiate those claims today. Regardless, they spell the word *çarşı* with a capital 'A,' mimicking the symbol of anarchy. I follow that spelling in this paper. For more on çArşı, see: Kytö (2011), and McManus (2013a).
7. Here, I refer to the Beşiktaş İnönü Stadium, the reconstruction of which lasted for three years until its reinauguration in 2016.
8. For more on the Gezi Uprising see Yıldırım and Navaro-Yashin (2013).
9. Kurds in Turkey have been engaged in peaceful political movements and armed struggle since the 1980s towards social and legal recognition and the establishment of an autonomous government. The routine recital of the national anthem before every domestic match is a practice that started in the 1990s in response to the activities of PKK (Kurdistan Workers' Party) – classified as a terrorist organization by the Turkish State.

Disclosure statement

No potential conflict of interest was reported by the author.

Funding

This research for this article was partly supported by The Middle East Research Competition.

References

Abu-Lughod, Lila. 1991. "Writing Against Culture." In *Recapturing Anthropology: Working in the Present*, edited by Richard G. Fox, 137–162. Santa Fe: School of American Research Press.

Akın, Yiğit. 2004. "Not Just a Game: The Kayseri vs. Sivas Football Disaster." *Soccer & Society* 5 (2): 219–232. doi:10.1080/1466097042000235227.

Armstrong, Gary, and Malcolm Young. 1997. "Legislator and Interpreters: The Law and 'Football Hooligans'." In *Entering the Field*, edited by Gary Armstrong and Richard Giulianotti, 175–191. Oxford: Berg.

Battini, Adrien. 2012. "Reshaping the National Bounds through Fandom: The UltrAslan of Galatasaray." *Soccer & Society* 13 (5–6): 701–719. doi:10.1080/14660970.2012.730771.

Bergfeld, Mark. 2014. "Turkey's Ultras at the Forefront of Resistance." *Al Jazeera*, December 16. Accessed March 19, 2017. http://www.aljazeera.com/indepth/opinion/2014/09/turkey-ultras-at-forefront-resi-201492310517225921.html

Bourdieu, Pierre. [1979] 1984. *Distinction: A Social Critique of the Judgment of Taste*. Translated by Richard Nice. Cambridge: Harvard University Press.

Butler, Judith. 1993. "Endangered/Endangering: Schematic Racism and White Paranoia." In *Reading Rodney King, Reading Urban Uprising*, edited by Robert Gooding-Williams, 15–22. New York: Routledge.

Debord, Guy. 2008. *The Society of the Spectacle*. New York: Zone Books.

Doidge, Mark. 2013. "'The Birthplace of Italian Communism': Political Identity and Action Amongst Livorno Fans." *Soccer & Society* 14 (2): 246–261. doi:10.1080/14660970.2013.776471.

Dorsey, James. 2013. "Turkish and Egyptian Ultras Fight for their Existence." *The Turbulent World of Middle East Soccer*, September 30. Accessed March 19, 2017. http://mideastsoccer.blogspot.com.tr/2013/09/turkish-and-egyptian-ultras-fight-for.html

Ekşi Sözlük. 2012. "Ultras." December 13. Accessed March 19, 2017. https://eksisozluk.com/ultras–205807?p=3

Fanon, Frantz. 2008. *Black Skin White Masks*. New York: Grove Press.

Foucault, Michel. 1982. "The Subject and Power." In *Michel Foucault: Beyond Structuralism and Hermeneutics*, edited by Hubert L. Dreyfus and Paul Rabinow, 208–226. Chicago, IL: University of Chicago Press.

Gupta, Akhil, and James Ferguson. 1992. "Beyond 'Culture': Space, Identity, and the Politics of Difference." *Cultural Anthropology* 7 (1): 6–23. doi:10.1525/can.1992.7.1.02a00020.

Gürmen, Esra. 2013. "Talking to Besiktas' Bulldozer Joyriding Fans about their Role in the Turkish Uprising." *Vice*, June 17. Accessed March 19, 2017. http://www.vice.com/en_uk/read/patrolling-democracy-in-the-streets-of-beikta

Hall, Stuart. 1997. "The Spectacle of the Other." In *Representation: Cultural Representation and Signifying Practices*, edited by Stuart Hall, 225–279. London: Sage.

Hürriyet. 2013. "Gezi Park Demonstration Declaration from UltrAslan." [UltrAslan'dan Gezi Parkı Eylemi Açıklaması.] June 9. Accessed March 19, 2017. http://www.hurriyet.com.tr/gezihaberleri/23467345.asp

Irak, Dağhan. 2010. "The Transformation of Football Fandom since the 1970s." MA thesis, Boğaziçi University.

Kasapoğlu, Çağıl. 2013. "Can Politics Stay out of Football?" [Siyaset Futbolun Dışında Kalabilir mi?.] *BBC Türkçe*, December 31. Accessed March 19, 2017. http://www.bbc.com/turkce/spor/2013/12/131230_futbol_siyaset

Kennedy, David. 2013. "A Contextual Analysis of Europe's Ultra Football Supporters Movement." *Soccer & Society* 14 (2): 132–153. doi:10.1080/14660970.2013.776464.

Kytö, Meri. 2011. "'We are the Rebellious Voice of the Terraces, we are Çarşı': Constructing a Football Supporter Group Through Sound." *Soccer & Society* 12 (1): 77–93. doi:10.1080/14660970.2011.530474.

Lee, Francis L. F. 2005. "Spectacle and Fandom: Media Discourse in Two Soccer Events in Hong Kong." *Sociology of Sport Journal* 22 (2): 194–213. doi:10.1123/ssj.22.2.194.

McManus, John. 2013a. "Been There, Done that, Bought The T-Shirt: Beşiktaş Fans and the Commodification of Football in Turkey." *International Journal of Middle East Studies* 45 (01): 3–24. doi:10.1017/S0020743812001237.

McManus, John. 2013b. "Turkish Protests: Look at Football Match Policing for an Explanation." *Guardian*, June 4. Accessed March 19, 2017. http://www.theguardian.com/commentisfree/2013/jun/04/turkish-protests-football-match-policing

Merry, Sally Engle. 2003. "Human Rights Law and the Demonization of Culture (and Anthropology Along the Way)." *Political and Legal Anthropology Review* 26 (1): 55–76. doi:10.1525/pol.2003.26.issue-1.

Nuhrat, Yağmur. 2013. "Fans at the Forefront of Occupy Gezi." *Ballesterer*, July 20. Accessed March 19, 2017. http://ballesterer.at/aktuell/football-fans-at-the-forefront-of-occupy-gezi.html

Nuhrat, Yağmur, and Karabekir Akkoyunlu. 2013. "Turkey at a Suffocating Intersection." *Open Democracy*, October 16. Accessed March 19, 2017. https://www.opendemocracy.net/ya%C4%9Fmur-nuhrat-karabekir-akkoyunlu/turkey-at-suffocating-intersection

Pilz, Gunter. A., and Franciska Wölki-Schumacher. 2010. "Overview of the Ultra Culture Phenomenon in the Council of Europe Member States in 2009." Paper presented at the International Conference on Ultras, Vienna, February 16–17. Accessed March 19, 2017. http://www.coe.int/t/dg4/sport/Source/T-RV/T-RV_2010_03_EN_background_doc_Prof_PILZ.pdf

Radikal. 2013. "Taking Gezi Inside Stadiums would be the End of Football." [Gezi'yi Statlara Taşımak Futbolu Bitirir.] August 11. Accessed March 19, 2017. http://www.radikal.com.tr/politika/suat_kilic_geziyi_statlara_tasimak_futbolu_bitirir-1145650

Resmi Gazete. 2011. "Law to Prevent Violence and Disorder in Sport." [Sporda Şiddet ve Düzensizliğin Önlenmesine Dair Kanun.] April 14. Accessed April 24, 2016. http://www.resmigazete.gov.tr/eskiler/2011/04/20110414-6.htm

Said, Edward. 1978. *Orientalism*. New York: Random House.

Scalia, Vincenzo. 2009. "Just a Few Rogues? Football *Ultras*, Clubs and Politics in Contemporary Italy." *International Review for the Sociology of Sport* 44 (1): 41–53. doi:10.1177/1012690208101682.

Spaaij, Ramón, and Carles Viñas. 2005. "Passion, Politics and Violence: A Socio-historical Analysis of Spanish Ultras." *Soccer & Society* 6 (1): 79–96. doi:10.1080/1466097052000337034.

Taştekin, Fehim. 2013. "Ultras: The Surprise Kids of Turkey's Uprising." *Al Monitor*, June 4. Accessed March 19, 2017. http://www.al-monitor.com/pulse/originals/2013/06/instanbul-football-clubs-help-protesters.html#

Taylor, Peter. 1990. *The Hillsborough Stadium Disaster Final Report*. London: The Home Office.

Testa, Alberto. 2009. "The UltraS: An Emerging Social Movement?" *Review of European Studies* 1 (2): 54–63. doi:10.5539/res.v1n2p54.

Topal, Fırat. 2010. "Ultra Culture and Turkey." [Ultra Kültürü ve Türkiye.] *Birgün*, August 19. Accessed March 19, 2017. http://www.birgun.net/haber-detay/ultra-kulturu-ve-turkiye-10142.html

Yıldırım, Umut, and Yael Navaro-Yashin. 2013. "An Impromptu Uprising: Ethnographic Reflections on the Gezi Park Protests in Turkey." *Fieldsights – Hot Spots, Cultural Anthropology Online*, October 31. Accessed March 19, 2017. http://www.culanth.org/fieldsights/391-an-impromptu-uprising-ethnographic-reflections-on-the-gezi-park-protests-in-turkey

'The East' strikes back. *Ultras Dynamo*, hyper-stylization, and regimes of truth

Daniel Ziesche

ABSTRACT

This case study deals with *Ultras Dynamo*, the leading group in the active fan scene of Eastern German (the term Eastern Germany is used within this paper to refer to the territory on which the GDR existed from 1949 to 1990; it entails the federal states Brandenburg, Mecklenburg-Vorpommern, Sachsen, Sachsen-Anhalt, Thuringia and the eastern part of Berlin) side SG Dynamo Dresden (throughout the paper, the club's full name 'Sportgemeinschaft Dynamo Dresden' will be shortened using either Dynamo Dresden or simply Dynamo. Among the fans, the club is mostly called SGD (abbreviation of Sport[G]emeinschaft Dynamo) which is also used on flags, banners and in fan chants). The paper analyses styles of self-representation of the active fan scene at Dynamo and critically analyses the claim made by the group to being apolitical. The process of collective identity construction is linked to media images of the group and a 'regime of truth' is identified: a self-sustaining and interdependent cycle which overarches the process of image- and identity-construction at Dynamo Dresden and which can be traced back to processes of labelling, stigmatization and secondary deviance.

Setting the scene: the ugly face of football

When Dynamo Dresden is playing a match in North-Rhine Westphalia we have to assume that around 500 to 600 potentially violent offenders will come. And I deliberately do not speak of fans but of offenders.

Arnold Plickert[1]

The effect that a visit of Dynamo Dresden to almost any part of Germany has among the local community, police authorities and media can usually be described by two words: Unrest and panic. Dynamo is treated like an uninvited guest; Dynamo Dresden is German football's '*persona*' *non grata*. The club received the hardest punishment ever imposed by the German football authorities when it was excluded from the German Cup competition after repeated misconduct of its fans in the 2011/2012 and 2012/2013 season. Still, after fan violence occuring before and after an away match in Bielefeld in the 2013/2014 season,

Arminia Bielefeld's CEO Marcus Uhlig discussed even further-reaching measures: 'After these incidences, it needs to be contemplated if Dresden should be excluded from the league competition, as well' (qtd. in *Neue Westfälische*, 07 December 2013).[2] Dynamo Dresden's active fan scene polarizes: For some, the fanatic fans count among the best supporting groups in German football. For others (and the larger part) it is an 'uncontrollable horde' which deems itself to be standing above the law and which should be excluded from German football. Thus, media depictions usually alternate between rather positive depictions of the fans' fierce support for the club and the much more negative stylization as a violent posse and 'a disgrace for German football' (qtd. in WAZ 12 December 2013) – very much in line with Cohen's ([1972] 2002) conception of 'folk devils'.[3] On the following pages, the endeavour to grasp the complex dynamics and the reciprocity between internal and external identity construction which encompasses this group.

The research questions for this paper are how collective identity is constructed and represented within the active fan scene of Dynamo Dresden, which values and stances can be singled out, and how these can be traced back to historical and societal processes. Two hypotheses accompany my research. The first one relates to the self-perception of *Ultras Dynamo* (UD) and their play and interplay with (political) icons, symbols and codes: (T1) While considering themselves an 'apolitical group' (Dynamofan TV 2012) with no room for extremism from either side of the ideological political spectrum, UD regularly furnish themselves with a particular political identity and take a very distinct political stance. The second hypothesis is related to the media image of the club and characteristic patterns in media coverage of UD: (T2) Patterns in media coverage and externally constructed images on stereotypes of Dynamo's fan scene flow back into the scene and sustainably shape the group's self-perception.

I will start by elaborating on the theoretical framework of this study and will then move on to introducing the specifics of the club's history within the turmoil after German reunification until today and link it to the emergence of UD in the early 2000s as it is impossible to understand UD without acknowledging the historical context of their emergence. I will then move to analyse different aspects of UDs self-understanding and self-representation, focussing on aspects of masculinity, nostalgia, victimization and deviance. I will then link UDs stylization to its self-conception as an apolitical group – and the perception that the terraces should be apolitical. This claim is critically analysed and problematized as I will argue that UD show a very ambivalent but still distinctive political stance, mainly fuelled by defiance. This interplay of deviant self-imagery and defiant political attitude have, as I will argue in the fourth part of this paper, formed a self-sustaining 'regime of truth' which overarches the process of collective identity- and value-construction at Dynamo. In the last section of the paper, I will conclude the analysis with a summary of the specifics that make Dynamo Dresden's active fan scene 'different' and discuss which insights can be gained from this case study.

Without being decidedly deductive in character, the paper has a wider social constructivist theoretical outlet which frames the hermeneutical, mixed-method approach. I have based the study on qualitative, hermeneutical methods of content-analysis and participant observation. The method of participant observation has a long tradition of (rightful) critique. As most of the analysis of UD in this paper follows an interpretational approach – which always bears the flaw of being potentially subjective – it is supplemented by content and data analysis in an effort to place the arguments made within this paper as far on an 'objective' side as possible. Material used for the analysis reaches from video addresses, the groups own fanzine (*Zentralorgan*) and pictures published by the group to banderols, banners, chants and other visual and vocal demonstrations. This mixed method approach is still of a qualitative, cultural-analytical nature, without exactly being what Clifford Geertz famously termed 'thick description' (1972, 3). Rather, it employs multiple theories and concepts which do not necessarily complement each other but instead serve the purpose of analysing one particular 'reality of everyday life' (Berger and Luckmann 1967, 19).

Labelling theory, outsiders and secondary deviance

Deviant behaviour among supporter groups within football culture is neither a new nor particularly under-researched phenomenon. Analysing the use of violence and hooliganism as well as masculinity within sport and football (exemplarily Taylor 1971; Elias [1986] 2008; Giulianotti, Bonney, and Hepworth 1994), researchers engaged with the topic from the first days of the emergence of the field of football studies. During the 1990s, with the transformation of English (and later on also European) football to a consumer-friendly, commodified spectacle, research interest increasingly shifted towards consumption-critical behaviour among football supporters and the evolvement of new subgroups within football culture (exemplarily Portelli 1993; King 1997, 1998; Giulianotti 1999; Williams 1999, 2006; Wagg and Crabbe 2004) and then moved on to supporter-owned clubs as political manifestations as well as to protest against neoliberalism and politics of excess within football from the mid-2000s onwards (exemplarily Crabbe and Brown 2004; Brown 2008; Ziesche 2011; Numerato 2015).

The Ultrà-movement as it originated on the *curves* of Italian stadia has always been at the forefront of this consumption-critical mentality, and, especially in Italy, it is also strongly connected to ideological-political positioning (cf. Testa 2009). Ultras are in their self-conception bound to be deviant in one way or the other. This is attested by goals like the self-regulation of the *curve* along with the anti-police stance in many groups, the sometimes rule-breaking rituals of football folklore, and the simple fact that Ultrà groups are first and foremost a youth-cultural movement. 'Deviance' describes behaviour as apart from formal or informal norms, as contradictory to the modus vivendi of what could be called 'the mainstream' or, at least, the more powerful group. Deviant behaviour leads to labelling and stigmatization (cf. Goffman, [1959] 1980, [1963] 1986) of an individual as an 'outsider' (cf. Becker 1973). Edwin M. Lemert argued that engaging in deviant behaviour ('primary deviance') can become essential to the individual identity formation of a person. The stage when a person incorporates this deviant identity in their self-conception is what Lemert termed 'secondary deviance' (cf. [1963] 1972, 62).

These processes can also be transferred to groups of individuals, i.e. repeated deviant behaviour by individual members of a group can lead to the whole group becoming labelled as outsiders and stigmatized. Instead of evicting the rule-breaking members, the group solidarizes with them and repeats acts of primary deviance. In consequence of repeated labelling as 'deviant' in some form, the group builds up a collective deviant identity and by incorporation of this identity into its self-conception reaches the stage of secondary deviance. Of course, the labelling process works in both directions, on the labelled as well as the labellers. Groups repeatedly labelled as deviant are thus conceived as abnormal or antisocial by other groups or wider society. If such a reciprocal relationship repeats itself over and over again, we can speak of the establishment of a 'regime of truth' which then prefigures the discourse on the deviant phenomena (cf. Foucault 1980).

From Liverpool FC to VfB Zittau: the unlikely fall of a football star

When Dynamo Dresden – Eastern Germany's biggest football club until today – last appeared in the European football theatre, they played against FK Red Star Belgrade in the quarter final of the 1990/1991 European Cup. After a 3–0 loss in Belgrade, during which the visiting Dynamo fans had been attacked by Belgrade supporters and the police force, the second leg at home was suspended at 1:2 because of massive spectator violence.[4] Consequently, Dynamo was banned for two years from European Cup qualifying rounds. However, the punishment never had to be put into practice since, after the incidences against Belgrade, Europe became nothing more than a nostalgic and distant memory to the club's fans. Having been drained of its player potential in the weeks and months after the fall of the wall[5], the constantly mismanaged club was unable to compete both on the sporting as well as on the financial level in the newly formed all-German 1st *Bundesliga*[6] and finished last in the 1994/1995 season. However, Dynamo relegated straight to the third level because the German football authority DFB refused to grant the playing licence for the 2nd *Bundesliga* due to a debt of around 10 Million DM.[7] This marked the beginning of general discontent with and critique of the football authorities among the supporters of Dynamo Dresden. In the following years, the perception of being treated unfairly and being the scapegoat of all that is wrong with (Eastern) German football nurtured this stance and the credo 'us against the rest' became *doxa* and an elementary part of the (active) fan scene's identity.[8]

Ultras Dynamo appeared on the stage around five years later, when the Italian *ultrà*-movement reached numerous clubs in Germany and elsewhere and when the scene started to grow into the dominant form of football fan culture on the terraces in most of Europe's stadiums. When UD was founded in December 2000, the fan scene in Dresden had radically changed. With about 40,000 visitors at international matches during the most successful years in the 1980s, numbers had dropped to 5000 after the relegation to the *Regionalliga* and further dwindled in the fourth level *Oberliga* years from 2000 till 2002. The club still was renowned for their comparably strong supporter numbers. In 2002 Dynamo returned to the third level and in 2004 even promoted to the 2nd *Bundesliga* but was relegated again after just one season. The club fulfilled the qualification for the newly introduced *3. Liga* in 2008. After three seasons in the newly founded league, Dynamo promoted to the 2nd *Bundesliga* at the end of the 2010/2011 season where it stayed for three consecutive seasons until relegation at the end of the 2013/2014 season.

With the top level of German football continuously out of reach along with financial troubles and club-internal personnel issues, the fan scene moved more closely together, especially when the club played in the *Oberliga*. Until today, these two years are memorized and mythologized in a popular chant:

> *Oberliga, Oberliga, Oberliga* was so beautiful – rampage and riots, *Oberliga* was so beautiful.[9]

Unlike any other club in Germany, Dynamo Dresden has achieved the image of a 'chaos club' – both in club-internal matters (but then more regionally noted) and in the club-external effects of its fan scene, which – according to media reports – seems to be 'uncontrollable' and 'unreachable' by the club. While, with over 15.000 members, it is the most popular club from Eastern Germany until today, Dynamo Dresden is the epitome of a bad club: the public image mainly circulates around right-wing extremism, hooliganism and the assertion of having been the *Stasi*-club during the times of the GDR.[10]

Authenticity, self-representation and hyper-stylization

Those useless actions like 'we whack a crapper into pieces' or 'we kick some adverts apart' – seriously lads, we have to keep that within bounds a little. It's not like in the old days anymore.

Lehmi[11]

Those Dynamo fans are not from this world – they are monsters.

Marcus Uhlig[12]

To find out about the elementary parts of UD's self-understanding, how it is stylized and enacted, which symbols and codes carry which messages, and which specific sub-cultural identity is constructed, reconstructed and represented, I mainly refer to the scene's own audible and visual output. First, I use three video addresses by the capo of UD, 'Lehmi', for the seasons 2012/2013, 2013/2014 and 2014/2015. These addresses were intended to sum up the past season and prepare the active scene for the upcoming season, especially problematizing issues within the scene. Second, I cite the UD's own fanzine *Zentralorgan*, introduced in the 2003/2004 season and published for almost every home game and cup matches since. This serves as a source for analysing UD's self-representation and public appearance. Furthermore, I analyse the style and content of banners and banderols as well as chants and vocal demonstrations.

Like other ultra-groups, UD generally stylize themselves in an 'in your face'-manner: The group's symbol, the *Böse Ball* (transl. evil ball) is a comic-style, black-white football with a grimace, its red eyes looking angrily from above at the onlooker while it bares its teeth. However, the group's name is quite plain and does not follow other ultras groups' preference for a distinctive group name with military- or worker's movement-related references.[13] This is especially unusual as the number of clubs bearing 'Dynamo' in their name is quite high, especially, but not exclusively, in eastern Europe.

Ultras Dynamo and Eastern German identity

The main visual element in home games is the group's banner, spelling '*Ultras* Dynamo', with the 'evil ball' in the middle of the two words. Usually, this banner is connected to others which are much smaller and mounted on top. One of these is the 'Official SGD Hooligans' banner, another one is the 'Red Kaos' banner from the ultras of FSV Zwickau, a befriended fan group.[14] Left and right of the main banner are the ones from other fan groups, the further up in hierarchy the closer they are positioned towards the banner of UD. While I am completely aware of the fact that hooligans and ultras are crucially different phenomena of fan culture, in the case of Dynamo these borders seem to blur more than within other fan scenes. Still, even though it might be intriguing, I refrain from using term 'Hooltra' with regards to the ultra-related parts of the Dynamo's fan scene. While this term comes up in the debate about fan behaviour every now and then especially in Germany (cf. DeuPol

2005; Hess 2009), I do so for two reasons: First, because of its grand elusiveness and second because UD has never referred to themselves as 'Hooltras', as other groups have done. While surely nothing like *the* ultra or *the* hooligan (or *the* fan) exists, but instead many shades of 'in-between' and orientations towards the one or other conception of fandom, I consider it useful to keep these two phenomena of fan groups separated. It is the nature of sociology that the ideal type of a group does usually not exist in 'reality'. More often than not, we as sociologists are confronted with exceptions from the rule and try to outline characteristics and specifics which differentiate one group from another. It is hard to single out specifics which separate ultras from hooligans. In the German case (which is the case I am referring to), political orientations vary from one ultras group to another or one hooligan group to another. Often, these orientations also vary from one member to the next within the same group, as in most scenes, political orientation is not the first identifying factor for the members but allegiance to the club they support. The crucial difference I would single out between hooligan and ultras groups lies in their stance towards violence. Hooligan groups 'actively seek' violence, whereas ultras groups usually do not refrain from using violence when confronted with violence or see it as a probate means to an end (e.g. avoiding body controls at the stadium entrance). Also, ultras put the support of the club first (and actively seeking violence would often contradict this aspiration), whereas support is only secondary (if at all) to hooligan groups (cf. Pilz and Wölki-Schumacher 2010, 16). This might be debated, as the borders between 'actively seeking' and 'not refrain from using' do often blur in real-life events. I would still argue that most ultras groups try to avoid violent encounters – especially with hooligan groups whose members are usually older, physically superior and much more experienced. Surely, in most fan scenes, ultras and hooligan groups mingle, and members can be part of both groups. However, in many cases and in Dresden as well, these groups still exist separately with their own agendas. Thus, the combination which the term 'Hooltra' also implies – a group with both an ultras and a hooligan agenda – cannot be found at Dresden.

In further banners of the active fan scene which read 'Facefisters', 'Fighters', 'Brutal Fans Dynamo Dresden', the mythologized brutality of Dynamo Dresden fans is addressed as well. Apart from this myth, another anchoring point for the construction of a collective identity among UD is the Eastern German background, the reunification and the stylization as losers of this historic event. In a subliminal narrative, the reunification-myth and its (alleged) effect on inequality and social deprivation in Eastern Germany is told by the direct selling of scarfs by UD which read 'children of the reunification'. The slogan refers to two dimensions of UD's identity: The age of its members and the historic cause for 'why they are what they are'. Eastern German symbolism is further presented by flags which bear the counterfeit of *Pittiplatsch*, a famous fantasy figure from Eastern German television. The figure is displayed in various adaptations, ranging from cute to brutal.

Dressing for the carnival

The (unofficial) dress code of the scene is losely oriented towards a casual-sportive style. As far as jackets are concerned, the colour black dominates and the brands are typically The North Face or Jack Wolfskin; shirt colours are usually yellow, black, white or claret – colours that resemble the club emblem or parts of it. For some matches, UD sell hats or other accessories prior to the matches to guarantee a uniform appearance. On special occasions, theme trips are announced. These might be on a small scale, e.g. 'everybody wears a white shirt', or the active scene might hyper-stylize themselves as cliché post-reunification Eastern Germans. The away match in Bielefeld in the 2013/2014 season, was announced to be one of these theme trips, seeing members of the active scene dressed with fake mullets and wigs, (real) moustaches, bomber jackets, sun glasses, and the oldest jerseys, jumpers and high-waist trousers they could find in the wardrobe. Even accessories like a comb in the back pocket, golden necklaces or a walk-man were part of the costume. This self-depiction as cliché Easterners, as antisocial 'hillbillies' from the 'Valley of the Clueless'[15], as reunification losers or other stereotypes about post-1990s East Germans, is clearly ironic and represents a quite recent trend within the fan scene of Dresden: a trend which I would like to call 'de-seriousization' – a decrease in seriousness or graveness in the scene's self-representation. This tongue-in-cheek-attitude is quite popular at other fan and ultras scenes but had never been at Dynamo Dresden. Occurrences of ironic self-depiction could thus be interpreted as a sign to a relaxed self-understanding of a collective's identity. However, quite ambivalently, these costumes also resemble and imitate the looks of people in the 1990s, arguably the most violent years in Dynamo's history. Thus, the appearance could also be used to restrengthen the fan scene's violent image – especially when the scene generates media images as it did in Bielefeld before and after the game. Even more ambivalently, the whole active fan scene was dressed in yellow rain capes on the way to the stadium – a sight quite surreal and intimidatory at the same time.

Self-representation in the media

For quite some time, the Youtube channel of UD was called 'Elbkaida TV' – a portmanteau merging the Elbe River at which Dresden is situated and the terroristic group 'Al Qaida' – until it got renamed as 'DynamofanTV' in 2013. The quite direct reference to a terrorist group was controversially discussed and eventually led to the change of the name. The channel is the platform for the presentation of videos which show montages of spectacular choreographies and apperances of UD. It also provides the seasonal speeches by UD's *capo* Stefan Lehmann, three of which exist so far and address the active fan scene: The first for 2012/2013, the second for 2013/2014, and the third for the 2014/2015 season. The first two videos are around 20 minutes long, while the duration of the last one is only 12 minutes. They all show the *capo* in different settings. The first stages 'Lehmi' sitting on the *capo* tower in the K-Block, the standing area of Dynamo Dresden's stadium and 'home' of UD. The second video is filmed at the banks of the Elbe River – with Dresden's picturesque *Elbterassen* in the background, the reason for the city's nickname *Elbflorenz*.[16] The third and last one is filmed in the rooms of UD, with the 'evil ball' sprayed on a wall in the background. All three videos address the active fan scene, discuss the past season and communicate rules of appearance and behaviour for the upcoming season at home and away games. Also, issues with the media and the police are addressed as well as 'highlight matches'. The speeches are exemplary for the ways in which UD try to act out influence on the active scene, to bind 'uncontrollable' forces and to communicate, i.e. foster the group's self-understanding. They also address and represent a consumer-critical, anti-neoliberal stance identified by Dino Numerato (2015) by criticizing consumption-friendly fans, processes of marketing and commodification, and processes of efficiency enhancement and optimization within football culture.

Interestingly, all three videos address at some point the misuse of alcohol, especially during away games. According to the videos, the 'useless rampage' (Dynamofan TV 2012) caused by this misuse as well as the unnecessary stadium evictions needed to be reduced; also, support would suffer under the influence of too much alcohol (cf. Dynamofan TV 2014). Further topics in the videos include the 'highlight matches' which will not be dictated by the media but which will be chosen by the scene on its own terms. Therefore, more discipline (i.e. non-violent behaviour) was required during non-highlight games. Further, fans are asked to trust the scene more than club officials or players who are mostly 'legionaries from the west' and will be gone in some months or years. In addition, the proclamation is made that all away matches will be attended, no matter what. The subtext here is that UD will be present at all matches, even if visiting fans are not allowed (to whatever circumstances). Further points include discipline during choreographies, the outer appearance of fans ('you only need one scarf'), police actions in the past season and the principle of non-communication with the police, and the general attitude towards football culture which should be more intense and unlike that at many of the other clubs. This includes pyrotechnics being part of UDs understanding of a living and authentic football culture (cf. Dynamofan TV 2012, 2013, 2014).

In summary, UD embrace a (hyper-)stylization of themselves as the 'Other'(cf. Hall 1997). They orchestrate themselves as societal misfits; as villain-like, defiant 'savages' from the 'wild East'. Mantra-like, media narratives on fan-misconduct during matches of Dynamo Dresden repeat and augment this story. While police and club officials usually get their say in TV reports, UD or members of the active fan scene remain unheard. UD has long taken up a 'no-comment' stance towards the media, and most parts of the active scene follow their lead. Thus, the public image of the active fan scene is externally constructed by omission of its core part. The pillars of these strongly biased narratives are usually the same: While the club has made great efforts to change things for the better, the uncontrollable parts in Dynamo's fan scene do not just entail a few misguided individuals (subtext: as it is the case with other clubs), but there is assumed to be a general over-aggressiveness and uncontrollable mind-set, an abnormality present in the fan scene of Dynamo Dresden which cannot be reasoned with. In the following, I will focus on the claim made by UD to be an 'apolitical group' and problematize this claim in different dimensions of politics.

Problematizing the apolitical

> All political chants can be left out of the stadium. We are an apolitical terrace, we always will be and there is just no room for anything which is left or right.
>
> Lehmi[17]

While the fellowship of Dynamo was renowned for its strong hooligan scene especially in the years after reunification, the club had the most trouble fighting right-wing extremism among its supporters. With the early 2000s, the scene became more diverse. The presence of members from the right-wing scene and especially their presence on the terraces clearly decreased significantly although never completely disappeared. However, in light of this past, claims like the one made above by UD's capo seem highly problematic. The recurrence to an 'apolitical' stance carries with it several issues: In how far can an ultras group be truly apolitical if every action is discursive and every discourse considered to be a political action?

Can a subcultural scene as publicly visible (and audible) as the ultras scene, primarily active in the political landscape of a football stadium (cf. Guschwan 2014), claim an apolitical stance? And furthermore, do UD live up to this claim? The claim I make here is that they cannot. On the contrary, I will argue that UD take a very distinctive political stance – even if it cannot be clearly assigned to either left or right of the spectrum of ideological politics.

As is the case with many other ultras groups, anti-discriminatory positions which form the basis for the formulation of European standards of human rights – which are, in fact, societal minimum standards – are considered to be left or extreme left political positions (cf. Wark and Diekert 2012). Being an apolitical group is an illusion many ultras – and UD – have succumbed to.[18] In leaving these societally relevant areas and debates untouched or, as I will show on the following pages, even in confronting them by an anti-stance, leaves the scene open to reactionary, discriminatory, right-wing positions.

Football and fan activism

In Germany, the ultras, originally a highly politicized (and ideologized) fan movement from Italy, have established themselves since the end of the 1990s and gained astonishing momentum with regards to their widespread dissemination in German (and European) football culture during the early 2000s. While still upholding most of the fan-political components from the Italian tradition (anti-commercialization, autonomous organization of fan curves, anti-police dogma, etc.; i.e. an anti-modern football stance), the German ultras predominantly followed a rather 'celebrative' interpretation of the term *ultrà* in comparison to their Italian counterfeits and role models (cf. Doidge 2015). This is not to say that ultras lifestyle would be interpreted less seriously in Germany, but the focus is not as much on ideology-driven, 'hard' political topics as it is in Italy. Thus, while still the 'wild boys' (and meanwhile to some extent also the 'wild girls') on German terraces, the focus of German ultras lay predominantly in the creation of choreographies, ongoing, intense support of the club on match days, and the prioritization of the club above everything else in life (cf. Pilz and Wölki-Schumacher 2010). Fan-political engagement and inter-group networking have increased from 2010 onwards, especially during fan campaigns against a strategy paper for increased stadium safety and security in 2012 (cf. Spiller 2012; Ziesche, forthcoming). With regards to ideological positioning, though, apart from a few clubs where the active fan scene takes a clear position in the left/right scheme (although usually left) as at St. Pauli, Babelsberg 03, and – to some extent but less open – at Carl-Zeiss Jena, Union Berlin or Fortuna Köln, most ultras groups in Germany consider their stance as 'neutral'.[19] UD do not constitute an exception from that rule. However, there are issues shared and addressed by most – if not all – ultras groups (including UD) which are of social political, sport political and security political character. When protesting against a rise in ticket prices, increased security measures or league authority's legislation, different dimensions of the aforementioned areas of politics are involved.

With regards to club- and football-related political stances, UD are highly active. The renaming of the club to SG Dynamo Dresden in 2007 and the changing of the emblem colours back to the traditional style in 2002 were surely two of the biggest successes of the group's political agenda setting.[20] Furthermore, the group was able to convince the club to maintain a comparably large area for the attachment of banners in the stadium instead of selling them to sponsors. UD also played a huge part in the agreement of a fan charter which is exclusive in German football and which contains agreements between club and fans on detailed policies with regards to fan cultural issues. Moreover, this charter also contains an explicit positioning against any discrimination on the basis of ethnicity, religious beliefs, sexual orientation or physical or mental disabilities[21] – a fact which makes the occurrences described in the course of this paper even more ambivalent. UD have also founded the *Schwarz-Gelbe Hilfe*[22], an initiative in the vein of the *Schwarz-Rote Hilfe*[23] at 1. FC Nuremberg and similar initiatives at other clubs, which offers help and advice for fans who are in trouble with the police or face a stadium ban. The *Zentralorgan* also holds room for football and fan activist statements and analyses past matches with regards to police work and fan behaviour, regularly assessing which developments the scene considers relevant in these areas.

Anti-media and anti-authority stances

As previously mentioned, an anti-authority stance is one of the main parts of UD's self-understanding. As with most ultras groups, the police are the number one enemy. ACAB[24]-postulations in chants and banners are thus visible and audible in the stadium. Almost equally high in the enemy positioning of the scene is the German football association, the DFB. While football and league authorities are certainly criticized by all ultras groups at some point, the hatred expressed in Dynamo's fan scene against the footballing authority is arguably more intense due to the self-perception of having been punished unrightfully too often in the past(cf. *Zeit Online*, 07/03/2013).

Another banner that is quite often visible during home games bears the word *Lügenpresse*[25] and has been present for some years now, also as a chant among the fans (typically extended by 'Auf die Fresse', a call to violence against the press). Within the context of Dynamo, the banner criticizes the perceived undifferentiated media reports on the club and its fan scene. Although even journalists have meanwhile assessed a biased 'West'-German press with regards to reporting on Dynamo Dresden and other Eastern German football clubs especially with regards to reports on fan troubles (cf. Ruf 2012), the perception of the 'bogeyman press' within the active fan scene persists, as shown in the previous section. However, the term *Lügenpresse* is highly political: it originated in the mid-eighteenth century and later became popular among the national socialists – and directed against the so-called 'system press'. Nowadays, it is one of the main audible and visual slogans of the *Pegida*[26]-movement.

Ideological political activities

Despite their proclaimed 'neutral' stance, UD have attracted attention with regards to 'real', ideological political positioning in the past, as well. Even though the active scene rarely displayed any bigger scale statement (visual or audible) against racism, sexism or homophobia as other German ultra-groups have done[27], there are still political quarrels being fought out within the scene. In 2012, the right-wing fan group *Faust des Ostens*[28] was pushed out of the terrace with their banner disappearing from the K-Block, (cf. Vorderwülbecke 2012; LVZ 2012). The matter was solved internally and in a manner of self-regulation with the details about the 'how' and 'why' being kept under wraps. Interestingly, in 2011, the cover of the *Zentralorgan* contained a collage of fan banners including a picture of the *Faust des Ostens*-banner and the motto 'Young or old doesn't matter – as long as we stand together' (UD 2011).[29] The leading article speaks of struggles within the scene which should be laid aside for the games ahead to focus on 'what truly matters' (UD 2011, 6). Still, at the end of these struggles, *Faust des Ostens* was forced off the terrace.

Other positioning against right-wing extremism includes a banner against anti-Semitism by the anti-racist fan group *1953 International* during a home game against TUS Koblenz in the 2010/2011 season, and the general rule put out by UD that racist and anti-Semitic chants are off the charts – a rule meanwhile mostly respected and abided by. However, given the history of Dynamo's fan scene and the dominant role right-wing extremism had during the 1990s until the early 2000s, clear postulations against such political positions by the active scene still remain a rarity. Rather, the scene coquettes with political incorrect and antisocial behaviour – especially during matches against leftist clubs – as I will show in the following part of the paper.

Discriminatory and exclusionary political activities

With racist and anti-Semitist[30] chants almost entirely banished from the stands, recourse to homophobia and sexism still seems to remain acceptable in the active scene. The discriminatory and exclusionary banners and chants fall in line with a maintaining of hegemonic masculinity and the subordination of what is not deemed 'truly manly' (Bourdieu 2005, 90 pp.). As Michael Meuser (2008) has shown, football matches are one of the last arenas for the contesting and re-enactment of a dominant masculinity which also includes the de-masculinization of the opponent.

While banderols like 'Sexism is a fan chant – you cunts'[31] or 'Ultrà Sankt Pauli women out of the away end – so the kitchen may live'[32] cannot necessarily be considered representations of a solidified, general political stance of the individual members but are intended to hit the opponent at their respective political attitudes – i.e. their core identities – they are still manifest of which measures are accepted and tolerated within the scene and within its fan-folklore.[33] How drastic this acceptance can be acted out became apparent in 2015 during an away match against Preussen Münster when Dynamo fans displayed a banner which can almost be interpreted to be a hyper-signifier of the non-conformist self-conception. It responded to an anti-*Pegida* picture by *Femen* activist and former politician of the *Piraten* party Mercedes Reichstein who had written the words 'Bomber Harris – do it again! #noPegida'[34] on her naked torso while raising a middle-finger as part of an (alleged) *Femen*[35] campaign.[36] In response to this action, Dynamo fans lifted a distasteful banderol which contained pure sexism and a clear rape reference: 'Do it again: Bombing the assholes of *Femen*-cunts with cum.'[37] Needless to say, provocations are an elemental part of fan folklore and, especially within the footballing context, content which might otherwise be ostracized (for whatever reasons) deemed fit. However, this banner understandably alienated parts of Dynamo's own fan scene and onlookers from other scenes alike (cf. Heiser 2014; Reinbold 2014) and bluntly shows how far into the discriminatory and antisocial side UD is willing to venture.[38]

While the previous example can partly be seen as an archaic, sexualized, hyper-stylization of masculinity and in terms of its extreme message must be seen as an exception, it also contains something quite typical for the assertion of maleness within the active fan scene of Dynamo Dresden: a reference to violence, physicality, and fighting. Values such as 'honour', 'virility' and 'fidelity', as well as terms like 'blood', 'scars' and 'death' are present in many of the group's chants, banderols and choreographies. Of course, these proclamations can also be read within the context of football folklore; still, UD and the active fan scene deliberately play with their image and label present in the wider football (and non-football) public.

Interestingly, neither the club nor UD have taken position against this movement, while media images and reports have proven that fans of Dynamo (although not necessarily parts of the active scene) take part in the demonstrations and two major hooligan groups affiliated with Dynamo serving as a 'security service' during the demonstrations (cf. Sundermeyer 2015a).[39] Apart from the passivity with regards to the *Pegida* movement, the club has launched some actions against racism in the past. Exemplarily, the slogan 'racism is not a fan chant' is displayed on the stadium screen during matches. For special occasions, the team kit does not have a sponsor but the slogan 'Love Dynamo – Hate Racism' printed on its chest – an action in cooperation with *1953International*. Also, refugees have recently been invited in larger numbers to the stadium on match days and scouting and training events for refugees have been held (cf. *Sächsische Zeitung*, 23/04/2015). However, these actions remain mostly in the hands of the club; the active scene (apart from *1953International*) has never been part of or addressed these actions in a bigger scale.

Binding it together: Identity construction and political attitude

While the banners and postulations mentioned in this section might be considered singular and case-related occurrences, they are at the same time also representative for what could be identified as a 'policy' among UD: to hold anti-positions, to be '*anti*-anti'. The mediated violent stigma of the fan scene in general thereby serves as a main repository for other anti-social trespassing and verbal and visual breaks with conformity and political correctness. The hyper-stylization as '*Assis*', the German short word for asocials, is present in chants as well: 'Black throat, yellow fingers we are the *Assis* from Dresden Zwinger.'[40] In contrast to other fan groups with an '*Assi*-stance' (e.g. as in *Ultrà St. Pauli* in terms of a punk attitude), UD's is defined by an anti-stance towards a perceived political correct mainstream football culture. Thus, UD differentiate themselves further from groups which also consider themselves to be different from the mainstream football culture – by a hyper-stylization as a villainous, trashing mob without a social conscience. Thereby, the use of the 'virtual' fear the group and its appearance causes is a key element. Thus, without having a clear political stance, the group leaves the interpretative framework consciously open and coquettes more often with right-wing or conservative than with 'left' or liberal positions – which is arguably inevitable if a group considers itself to be revolting against the cleansing of football culture which goes along with an alleged, overly present mainstream-leftism within society. At Dynamo Dresden, the anti-stance towards what came to be called 'modern football', such as consumerism and a consumer-friendly football environment, has led to a discriminatory and deviant stance which, by the forms of its protest, is open to right-wing, conservative political attitudes and content. Thus, the football political stance of UD, combined with the claim of being 'apolitical' has direct ideological political effects. While anti-consumerist and anti-modern fan activist stances foster, if any, rather a left-leaning ideological political agenda of football groups (see exemplarily A.S. Livorno, FC St. Pauli, SV Babelsberg 03, Athletico Bilbao, FC United of Manchester), UD tried to express this stance via an over-aggressive, anti-leftist, and antisocial stance which is by its nature neither apolitical nor non-ideological.

Still, both the reputation of the scene as its collective identity have to be continuously legitimized. These legitimization processes happen on three levels: Self-assuring of the collective about its identity by 'highlight matches', self-assertion within the football public, i.e. gaining the 'respect' of other ultra-groups, and legitimization of the media image by the images produced during these games. This cause-and-effect cycle is a closed one and highly efficacious within both the scene and public perception: Even though misconduct of Dynamo's fans has decreased significantly in the past decade and other (same league) clubs have received higher financial punishments by the football authorities than Dynamo in the seasons 2013/2014 and 2014/2015, the reputation of Dynamo Dresden remains unchanged. The club is perceived synonymously with violence and misbehaviour around football matches – a reputation definitely caused by the fans but hardened into public collective memory by media narratives. While within the 'football public' other clubs have a difficult reputation as well, Dynamo's is even known outside of the footballing world and present in the wider public's memory. The 'regime of truth' which has developed about Dynamo's fan scene is self-sustaining and self-fulfilling. The fetishization of violence and antisocial behaviour by the scene has evoked cultish practices of repetition and public display. It could be argued, that Dresden's active fan scene and UD at its forefront have incorporated their deviant identity and are thus acting out a secondary deviance: The repetition of victimization, stigmatization and punishment has led to the adopting of the rowdy-image as an integral part of the collective's identity and thus making it unable to think of itself outside of this 'regime of truth'.[41]

'Dresden is different' – but how exactly?

> The club has a distinctive myth around it. The people in Dresden are positively nuts.
>
> Rainer Calmund[42]

> The communal sharing of culture never starts from a tabula rasa. The process of sharing value draws on prior sharing of history, communal identity, experiences, and rituals.
>
> Amitai Etzioni[43]

'Dresden is different' is another mantra repeated by club officials, onlookers and UD themselves all the same. Within the course of this paper I have intended to de-construct the self-conception of *Ultras Dynamo*, connecting it to the historical and (sport-)political developments in Eastern Germany and identifying both the self-perception and the media image of the group as an established 'regime of truth' in the Foucauldian sense. I have identified this regime and its mechanisms as self-preserving and, furthermore, as a stable and a core part of internal and external identity and image construction, despite all of the dynamics which have shaped this process.

As with any other case of fan identity construction, UD's case is a highly complex and dynamic one, as I have shown. In fact, many of the specifics which make out the phenomenon Dynamo Dresden can be found elsewhere, in other clubs in Germany and abroad. Fanatic fans who consider themselves to be unique, a club which has a glorious past, a rather mediocre present and big goals for the future, and which is permanently in financial trouble and under 'special treatment' by the football authorities and the media. Still, it is argued here that the amalgamation of all these parts formed a specific Dynamo culture within the fan scene that has crystallized within *Ultras Dynamo*.

After the fall of the club in the mid-1990s, a young generation of football supporters had to re-define their identity. In the early 2000s, this generation faced the sportive wasteland of the reality of fourth league football while still being told about a legendary past of cup-victories and European matches by the older generation. On an off-the-field level, the years after the reunification and the downfall of Dynamo were marked by spectator violence and almost a decade of hooliganism. Today's self-understanding draws on all of these elements: the glorious past, the years in the no-mans-land of German football, the violent and turbulent late 1990s, the repeated punishments by the authorities, the stigmatization of the club's fan scene in the media, etc. All these parts taken together have created an 'us against the rest' mentality which condenses into an anti-everything, an antisocial stance. Following Glynis M. Breakwell, identities which are perceived to be under threat are enforced even harder by its bearers (cf. 1986, 1993). The self-stylization along an Eastern-German loser mentality and the (antagonistic) self-understanding as better, more authentic, more true than the rest is employed and fetishized by the scene – and being legitimized, this self-understanding thereby 'demands' to 'strike back' from time to time.

With regards to the leading questions of this paper, the findings only allow for a tentative conclusion. Both assumptions have proven to hold true. What has become astonishly clear is that UD's claim to be an apolitical group has to be refuted. Also, I have laid out the interrelations and interdependencies between the group's self-stylization and the mediated image of the active fan scene. However, especially the complex and manifold dynamics within the scene make it hard to pinpoint a distinctive political stance UD employ. It is an ambivalent construction, in wide parts antagonistic and anachronistic.

Considering the presented research and results, the effectiveness of UD in the active fan scene at Dynamo Dresden remains questionable. UD show tendencies of self-regulation and value definition from inside and in some ways the group might even serve as a corrective for the actions of the active scene, though so far much more on a football political, fan activist level than on a general level within the fan scene. However, these tendencies are counteracted by the repeated self-assurance of the scene's core identity. To break these cycles is a long-term process in which the values and aspects of UD's identity and the active fan scene's identity have to be re-negotiated. In how far this can be achieved by UD as the leading group of Dynamo's fan base has to remain the subject of further investigation.

Notes

1. President of the union of the police force of the federal state of North-Rhine Westphalia, qtd. in WDR (2014).
2. A survey linked in the same article asked the readers whether Dynamo should indeed be excluded from the league. The result was that 73% of the readers opted with 'yes' (cf. ibid.). However, it has to be pointed out that the news paper is a very regional or even local one.
3. Exemplarily see: Lohse (2012), MDR (2015), Spiegel TV (2012) and WDR (2012, 2014).
4. As media reports indicate, this massive violent outbreak was also caused by hooligans who came from all over Germany, most notably Hamburg (cf. Sport Journal 1991). The match in Dresden was declared to be revenge for what had happened in Belgrade (cf. Sport Journal 1991).
5. The sell-out of the most successful GDR teams to West German teams, most notably Bayer 04 Leverkusen, changed the balance of power among the former GDR football teams dramatically,

even making then chancellor Helmut Kohl intervene. It is one of the reasons formerly less known and less successful clubs have become the representatives of Eastern German football teams in the 1st and 2nd *Bundesliga* for some years, e.g. Energie Cottbus, Hansa Rostock or Erzgebirge Aue. Since the 2009/2010 season, no team from Eastern Germany has competed in the 1st *Bundesliga*; in the 2005/2006 season this was the case as well.

6. The club never reached a top ten position from 1991 to 1992 till the relegation in 1994/1995.

7. 1995 this equalized about £4,4 million.

8. The term 'active scene' is used by UD and entails the group itself and those fans and fan groups who partake in chanting and the visual display of the club during matches (with banners and flags) but are not necessarily members of UD. There is no membership number of UD available, core members of the group are estimated to count about 30–50 people.

9. *Oberliga* was also the term for the highest level of the league pyramid in the football system of the GDR. Thus, the chant refers both to the club's successful GDR past as well as to the absolute low point interms of sportive success from 2000 to 2002.

10. While right-wing extremism and hooliganism are associations made with almost all clubs from Estern Germany, it was in fact BFC Dynamo Berlin which was the club of GDR's secret service – the *Staatssicherheit* (*Stasi*). Dynamo Dresden was affiliated to the GDR's police force (*Volkspolizei*). For a historical overview on the concept of Dynamo-sport centres and networks during the times of the Soviet Union, see Edelmann, Hilbrenner, and Brownell (2014, 603 pp.) and Collins (2013, 100 pp.). For an analysis of the GDR sport system and its football clubs: Anderson (2011).

11. Stefan Lehmann, *Capo* of UD, qtd. in: Dynamofan TV (2012). The *Capo* is the main figure and in most cases also the 'conductor' of an ultras group. In the case of UD, Stefan Lehmann is known by his nickname 'Lehmi'.

12. CEO of Arminia Bielefeld, quoted in: *Neue Westfälische*, 07 December 2013.

13. Group names which contain 'Commando', 'Brigade', '*Bande*', or 'Inferno' are especially popular in German and international ultras groups.

14. This is complemented by a banner from FK Sarajevo, to which's *Horde Zla* (transl. hordes of evil) UD have built up a friendship since 2012. Members of both groups regularly pay visit to matches of the other team. The same accounts for the friendship with *Red Kaos*.

15. The German expression *Tal der Ahnungslosen* was applied to GDR citizens living in the north-east and – primarily – in the south-east, especially in the area of Dresden. The term refers to the detachedness of these areas from the general information stream as it was impossible to receive terrestrial Western television or radio.

16. transl. Fiorentina of the Elbe.

17. Stefan Lehmann, *Capo* of UD qtd. in: Dynamofan TV (2012).

18. For the wider issue of an apoliticization of sport stadiums see Guschwan, 'Stadium as public sphere'.

19. Still, the diversity of *Ultrà*-groups is enormous and does thus not allow for generalization. As mentioned earlier, the political affiliations differ vastly from group to group and ask for a differentiated, case-to-case analysis. The scenes in Aachen, Braunschweig and Düssledorf in particular have found themselves in severe struggles about political cleavages.

20. The club played as 1. FC Dynamo Dresden from 1990 to 2007 and sported a green/white emblem instead of thetraditional claret/white emblem from 1990 to 2002. In 2011 the whole emblem was redesigned in the style of theclub's emblem from 1968 to 1990.

21. Orig. 'Der Verein SG Dynamo Dresden und die Fans stehen aktiv gegen Rassismus, Fremdenfeindlichkeit und Diskriminierung (aufgrund ethnischer Zugehörigkeit, religiöser und sexueller Orientierungen sowie körperlicher und geistiger Beeinträchtigung) innerhalb und außerhalb des Stadions ein.' (Dynamo Dresden 2015, Section 1.2).

22. transl. black-yellow help.

23. transl. black-red help.

24. Acronym for the slogan 'all cops are bastards'. Referring to the position of the letters in the alphabet, this slogan is also codified as '1312'.

25. transl. lying press.

26. Acronym for what transl. Patriotic Europeans Against the Islamisation of the Occident – a movement comparable to the English Defence League which has its starting point and highest mobilizing potential in Dresden.
27. E.g. the anti-homophobic choreography by queer fan club 'Meenzelmänner', which was supported by the *Ultras* of FSV Mainz 05. With regards to right-wing extremism see numerous banderol displays by the *Ultrà* groups 'The Unity', 'Schickeria' or 'Ultrà Sankt Pauli' at Borussia Dortmund, FC Bayern München and FC St Pauli, respectively.
28. transl. Fist of the East.
29. German orig.: 'Egal ob jung oder alt, was zählt ist der Zusammenhalt'.
30. Antiziganism remains to be a problem until today.
31. Displayed during the away game in Babelsberg in the 2010/2011 season.
32. Displayed during the home game against St. Pauli in the 2011/2012 season. The banderol was later stolen and presented by women from USP on the website in typical *Ultrà*-style: The women held burning flares and – ironically – kitchen utensils.
33. Folkloristic elements draw on the variety of shared cultural experiences present within the collective memory of a society or community (cf. Cohen, [1972] 2002 55–56, 66).
34. The slogan 'Bomber Harris – Do it Again' is popular among the left-extremist scene in Dresden who.
    criticises the annual 'victimization' of the casuals of the bombing raids in February 1945.
35. *Femen* are a feminist group who appear in public places usually with their torso stripped naked and political messages written on them. Usually, sites for appearance are chosen due to their potential to cause civil unrest.
36. A similar action had already taken place a year ago: cf. Reinbold,'Hickhack um Protestaktion'.
37. Orig.: 'Do it again: Femen-Fotzen das Arschloch mit Wichse zubomben!!'.
38. Although the banner was not signed with 'UD' but with the signature of a smaller fan group it still represented the active fan scene in the moment it was lifted and is featured on the website of UD.
39. Similar observations were made in Leipzig and other cities where *Pegida*-equivalent demonstrations have been held. Hooligan groups from the local football club act as demonstration security and keep opposing demonstrators and members of the press at a distance (cf. Sundermeyer 2015b; Völker 2015). Although club policies forbid the use of the club emblem and memorabilia in political contexts, the club has not criticised the appearance of Dynamo fan merchandise in the crowds of *Pegida* demonstrations – much in contrast to other clubs confronted with the same issue (e.g. FC Lokomotive Leipzig). In addition, the club has encouraged a dialogue with the *Pegida* movement – arguably to not alienate any of the opposing factions, knowing well about the 'mind-set' of some of the stadium visitors (cf. Ruf 2015). Interestingly, UD positively recall the organised flood help by the active fan scene in 2013 in their video for the 2013/2014 season (cf. Dynamofan TV 2013). The 'flood help' allegedly built networks and tied knots between cadres of the right-wing movement and served as a starting point for the *Pegida*-movement (cf. Sundermeyer 2015b).
40. Transl. 'Schwarzer Hals, gelbe Finger wir sind die Assis vom Dresdner Zwinger'. The *Dresdner Zwinger* is a sight-seeing monument in Dresden.
41. Cf. Foucault (1980).
42. Former CEO of Bayer Leverkusen and voluntary advisor to Dynamo Dresden in 2010, quoted in: *Neues Deutschland,* 18 October 2010.
43. Etzioni (2001, 93).

Disclosure statement

No potential conflict of interest was reported by the author.

References

Anderson, S. 2011. "Soccer and the Failure of East German Sports Policy." *Soccer and Society* 12 (5): 652–663. doi:10.1080/14660970.2011.599584.

Becker, H. S. 1973. *Outsiders: Studies in the Sociology of Deviance*. New York: The Free Press.

Berger, P. L., and T. Luckmann. 1967. *The Social Construction of Reality: A Treatise in the Sociology of Knowledge*. New York: Random House.

Bourdieu, P. 2005. *Die männliche Herrschaft* [Masculine Domination]. Frankfurt am Main: Suhrkamp.

Breakwell, G. M. 1986. *Coping with Threatened Identities*. York: Methuen.

Breakwell, G. M. 1993. "Social Representations and Social Identity." *Papers on Social Representations* 2 (3): 198–217. http://www.psych.lse.ac.uk/psr/PSR1993/2_1993Brea1.pdf.

Brown, A. 2008. "'Our Club, Our Rules': Fan Communities at FC United of Manchester." *Soccer & Society* 9 (3): 346–358. doi:10.1080/14660970802008967.

Cohen, S. [1972] 2002. *Folk Devils and Moral Panics*. 3rd ed. Abingdon: Routledge.

Collins, T. 2013. *Sport in Capitalist Society: A Short History*. Abingdon: Routledge.

Crabbe, T., and A. Brown. 2004. "'You're Not Welcome Anymore': The Football Crowd, Class, and Social Exclusion." In *British Football and Social Exclusion*, edited by S. Wagg, 26–46. Oxon: Routledge.

DeuPol. 2005. "Vom Kuttenfan und Hooligan zum *Ultrà* und Hooltra – Wandel des Zuschauerverhaltens im Profifußball." [From Kuttenfan to hooligan to Ultrà to Hooltra - Changes in spectator behaviour in professioanl football] *Deutsche Polizei 11/2005*. 6–12. Accessed August 25, 2015. https://www.gdp.de/gdp/gdp.nsf/id/wmsafe/$file/DeuPol0511_Titel.pdf

Doidge, M. 2015. *Football Italia. Italian Football in an Age of Globalization*. London: Bloomsbury Academic.

Dynamo Dresden. 2015. *Fan Charta*. January 2015. Online. Accessed August 25, 2015. http://www.dynamo-dresden.de/fans/fancharta.html

Dynamofan TV. 2012. "Es Geht Wieder Los! K-BLOCK Saison 2012/13." YouTube Video. Online. Accessed August 25, 2015. https://www.youtube.com/watch?v=PHdEqWcFcc0

Dynamofan TV. 2013. "Es Geht Wieder Los! K-BLOCK Saison 2013/14." YouTube Video. Online. Accessed August 25, 2015. https://www.youtube.com/watch?v=tNQRiOSvlTM

Dynamofan TV. 2014. "Es Geht Wieder Los! K-BLOCK Saison 2014/15." YouTube Video. Online. Accessed August 25, 2015. https://www.youtube.com/watch?v=GD6fAZZfNn0

Edelmann, R., A. Hilbrenner, and S. Brownell. 2014. "Sport Under Communism." In *The Oxford Handbook on the History of Communism*, edited by S. A. Smith, 602–614. Oxford: Oxford University Press.

Elias, N. [1986] 2008. "An Essay on Sport and Violence." In *Quest for Excitement. Sport and Leisure in the Civilizing Process*. Rev. Ed., edited by N. Elias and N. Dunning, 150–174. Dublin: University College of Dublin Press.

Etzioni, A. 2001. *The Monochrome Society*. Princeton, NJ: Princeton University Press.

Foucault, M. 1980. *Power/Knowledge*. Brighton: Harvester.

Geertz, C. 1972. *The Interpretation of Cultures: Selected Essays*. New York: Basic Books.

Giulianotti, R. 1999. *Football: A Sociology of the Global Game*. Cambridge, UK: Polity Press.

Giulianotti, R., N. Bonney, and M. Hepworth, eds. 1994. *Football, Violence and Social Identity*. London: Routledge.

Goffman, E. [1959] 1980. *The Representation of Self in Everyday Life*. New York: Anchor Books.

Goffman, E. [1963] 1986. *Stigma: Notes on the Management of Spoiled Identity*. New York: Simon & Schuster.

Guschwan, M. 2014. "Stadium as Public Sphere." *Sport in Society: Cultures, Commerce, Media, Politics* 17 (7): 884–900. doi:10.1080/17430437.2013.806036.

Hall, S. 1997. "The Spectacle of the 'Other'." In *Representation: Cultural Representations and Signifying Practices*, edited by S. Hall, 223–290. London: Sage Publications.

Heiser, S. 2014. "Piratinnen Feiern Bomber Harris." [Female members of the *Piraten*-party celebrate Bomber Harris] *taz*. February 21. Accessed August 25, 2015. http://www.taz.de/!5048076

Hess, P. 2009. "Fußball als Gewalt-Event: 'Hooltras' als die neue Problemgruppe." [Football as an event for violence: 'Hooltras' as the new problematic group]*Frankfurter Allgemeine Zeitung*. March 13. Accessed August 25, 2015. http://www.faz.net/-gtm-15cd4

King, A. 1997. "The Lads: Masculinity and the New Consumption of Football." *Sociology* 31 (2): 329–346. doi:10.1177/0038038597031002008.

King, A. 1998. *The End of the Terraces: The Transformation of English Football in the 1990s*. London: Leicester University Press.

Lemert, E. M. [1963] 1972. *Human Deviance, Social Problems, and Social Control*. 2nd ed. New Jersey: Prentice Hall.

Lohse, S. 2012. "Die zwei Gesichter der Dynamo-Dresden-Fans: Schwarz-Gelbe zwischen Gewalt und Kampagne." [The two faces of the fans of Dynamo Dresden: Black-yellows between violence and campaigning] *Dresdner Neueste Nachrichten*. September 9. Accessed August 25, 2015. http://www.dnn-online.de/dresden/web/dresden-nachrichten/detail/-/specific/Die-zwei-Gesichter-der-Dynamo-Dresden-Fans-Schwarz-Gelbe-zwischen-Gewalt-und-Kampagne-649819349

LVZ (Leipziger Volkszeitung). 2012. "Großrazzia in Sachsen gegen Dynamo-Dresden-Fangruppierung 'Faust des Ostens.'"[Larg-scale raid in Saxony against fan group of Dynamo Dresden '*Faust des Ostens*'] *Leipziger Volskzeitung*. June 5. Accessed August 25, 2015. http://www.lvz.de/Leipzig/Polizeiticker/Polizeiticker-Mitteldeutschland/Grossrazzia-in-Sachsen-gegen-Dynamo-Dresden-Fangruppierung-Faust-des-Ostens

MDR (Mitteldeutscher Rundfunk). 2015. "Schwere Krawalle Durch Dynamo Dresden Hooligans." *Documentary Piece*. Accessed August 25, 2015. https://www.youtube.com/watch?v=LY8gIGRj_zE

Meuser, M. 2008. "It's a Men's World. Ernste Spiele männlicher Vergemeinschaftung." In *Ernste Spiele. Zur politischen Soziologie des Fußballs*, edited by G. Klein and M. Meuser, 113-134. Bielefeld: Transcript.

Neue Westfälische. 2013. "Marcus Uhlig: 'Der Liga-Ausschluss von Dresden sollte überlegt werden.'" [Marcus Uhlig: 'The expulsion of Dynamo Dresden from the league should be considered'] *Neue Westfälische*. December 7. Accessed August 25, 2015. http://www.nw.de/sport/dsc_arminia_bielefeld/9839980_Marcus-Uhlig-Der-Liga-Ausschluss-von-Dresden-sollte-ueberlegt-werden.html

Numerato, D. 2015. "Who Says 'No to Modern Football?' Italian Supporters, Reflexivity, and Neo-Liberalism." *Journal of Sport and Social Issues* 39 (2): 120–138. doi:10.1177/0193723514530566.

Pilz, G. A., and F. Wölki-Schumacher. 2010. "Overview of the Ultra culture phenomenon in the Council of Europe member states in 2009." Expertise for the European Council. Accessed August 25, 2015. https://www.sportwiss.uni-hannover.de/fileadmin/sport/pdf/onlinepublikationen/pilz/T-RV_2010_03_EN_background_doc_Prof_PILZ.pdf.

Portelli, A. 1993. "The Rich and the Poor in the Culture of Football." In *The Passion and the Fashion: Football Fandom in the New Europe*, edited by S. Redhead, 77–88. Aldershot: Ashgate.

Reinbold, F. 2014. "Hickhack um Protestaktion: Femen und der Weltkriegsbomber." [Squabbling around protest action: Femen and the World War bomber] *Spiegel Online*. February 19. Accessed August 25, 2015. http://www.spiegel.de/politik/deutschland/Femen-aktion-in-dresden-zu-bomber-harris-sorgt-fuer-streit-a-954246.html

Ruf, C. 2012. "Die Macht der Medien-Wessis." [The power of the West German media] *taz*. November 11. Accessed August 25, 2015. http://www.taz.de/!5079688

Ruf, C. 2015. "Gespaltene Stadt, gespalterner Verein." [Divided city, divided club]*Spiegel Online*. January 12. Accessed August 25, 2015. http://www.spiegel.de/sport/fussball/dynamo-dresden-ist-gespalten-im-umgang-mit-pegida-a-1012508.html

Spiegel TV. 2012. "Fankrawalle in Hannover." [Fan riots in Hanover] *News Magazine Piece*. Accessed August 25, 2015. https://www.youtube.com/watch?v=mFm-uMyGkmc

Spiller, C. 2012. "Die Fans sind keine unkritische Masse mehr." [Fans are not an uncritical mass anymore] *Zeit Online*. Accessed August 25, 2015. http://www.zeit.de/sport/2012-12/fussball-fans-sicherheitskonzept-dfl

Sport Journal. 1991. "Dynamo Dresden – FK Roter Stern Belgrad Europapokal der Landesmeister." [Dynamo Dresden - FK Red Star Belgrade European Champuon Clubs' Cup] *News Magazine Piece*, Orig. Aired. March 20. Accessed August 25, 2015. https://www.youtube.com/watch?v=7FVOm7autos

Sundermeyer, O. 2015a. "Die Pegida-Miliz aus dem Stadion." [The Pegida militia out of the stadium] *Zeit Online*. January 12. Accessed August 25, 2015. http://www.zeit.de/sport/2015-01/pegida-dynamo-dresden

Sundermeyer, O. 2015b. "Hooligans als Schutztruppe." *Frankfurter Allgemeine Zeitung*. Online. Accessed August 25, 2015. http://www.faz.net/-gu9-7za31

Taylor, I. 1971. "Football Mad: A Speculative Sociology of Football Hooliganism." In *The Sociology of Sport: A Selection of Readings*, edited by E. Dunning, 352–377. London: Frank Cass.

Testa, A. 2009. "The UltraS: An Emerging Social Movement?" *Review of European Studies* 1 (2): 54–63. doi: 10.5539/res.v1n2p54.

Ultras Dynamo. 2011. *Zentralorgan*. Accessed August 25, 2015. http://*Ultras*-dynamo.de/ud2010/files/11-04-06-zentralorgan-erfurt.pdf

Völker, M. 2015. "Die Unterwanderungbewegung." [The infiltration movement] *taz*. January 20. Accessed August 25, 2015. http://www.taz.de/!153116

Vorderwülbecke, P. 2012. "Aus der Kurve: In Dresden versuchen die Fans selber, ihr Image durch Taten zu verbessern." [From the terrace: In Dresden the fans try to better their image by deeds] *Deutschlandfunk Online*. March 6. Accessed August 25, 2015. http://www.deutschlandfunk.de/aus-der-kurve.1346.de.html?dram:article_id=197030

Wagg, S., and T. Crabbe. 2004. *New Perspectives on Sport and 'Deviance'*. Abingdon: Routledge.

Wark, T., and H. Diekert, dirs. 2012. "Die Braunen im Blick." [Keeping an eye on right-wingers] *Documentary Piece. ZDF SPORTreportage*. Accessed August 25, 2015. https://www.youtube.com/watch?v=kOKIIXYQcYg

WAZ (Westdeutsche Allgemeine Zeitung). 2013. "'Das sind Kriminelle' – Dynamo Dresden distanziert sich von Randalierern in Bielefeld." ['These are criminals' - Dresden dissociates itself from hooligans in Bielefeld] *Westdeutsche Allgemeine Zeitung*. December 12. Accessed August 25, 2015. http://www.derwesten.de/region/anhaenger-von-dynamo-dresden-randalieren-in-bielfeld-id8746143.html#plx99495637

WDR (Westdeutscher Rundfunk). 2012. "Skandalclub Dynamo Dresden." [Scandal club Dynamo Dresden] Documentary piece. WDR Sport Inside. Accessed August 25, 2015. https://www.youtube.com/watch?v=eUwXY2kTXG8

WDR (Westdeutscher Rundfunk). 2014. "Ein Pulverfass." *Documentary Piece. WDR Sport inside*. Accessed August 25, 2015. http://www.ardmediathek.de/tv/Sport-inside/Ein-Pulverfass/WDR-Fernsehen/Video?documentId=23789610&bcastId=1493328&mpage=page.moreclips

Williams, J. 1999. *Is It All over? Can Football Survive the Premier League?* Reading: Garnet.

Williams, J. 2006. "'Protect Me from What I Want': Football Fandom, Celebrity Cultures and 'New' Football in England." *Soccer & Society* 7 (1): 99–114. doi:10.1080/14660970500355637.

Ziesche, D. 2011. *Reclaiming the Game? Soziale Differenzierung, Exklusion und transformative Prozesse in der Fußballkultur Englands*. [Reclaiming the Game? Social Differentiation, Exclusion and Transformational Processes in England's Football Culture] Berlin: Wissenschaftlicher Verlag.

Ziesche, D. Forthcoming. "Well Governed? Stakeholder Representation in German Professional Football Clubs." In *Football and Supporter Activism in Europe: Whose Game is It?* edited by B. García and J. Zheng. Basingstoke: Palgrave Macmillan.

The (Re)Constitution of football fandom: Hapoel Katamon Jerusalem and its supporters

Netta Ha-Ilan

ABSTRACT

Hapoel Katamon Jerusalem, a fan owned club in Israel, was established in 2007 by fans of Hapoel Jerusalem, in protest against the management of the original club. The fans have adopted anti-racism, opposition to violence and inclusiveness as markers of their identity, while stressing their links with the surrounding community. The paper emphasizes the role of reflexivity and agency, as the fans built the new club to embody their aspirations. The emphasis on reflexivity is required to integrate in the analysis, both macro-social elements, and processes linked with 'everyday life'. The paper stresses the unintended consequences of the fans' success, in creating a football club owned by them. The performance of HKJ fandom forged, over a short time, an inclusive 'protected space', wherein norms of solidarity and trust were developed. Such a space attracted several thousand persons – many of them coming to football for the first time – and cultivated a sense of 'community' that has become of growing importance in the fans' collective identity.

Introduction

This paper examines the constitution of fandom of a supporter-owned football club, and the social processes behind it. To a certain extent, fans' ownership of their club is the mirror image of most 'ultras' groups. Both are forms of committed fandom, resisting commercialization, with a high degree of emotional attachment to a team (Kennedy 2013). However, they usually represent opposite positions on issues of identity, social inclusion and involvement with club management.

By concentrating on the case of the fans of one football team, Hapoel Katamon Jerusalem (HKJ), the essay argues that there are various structured patterns of fandom culture that stem from the reflexive acts of social agents (Giddens 2013). It tries to describe the 'origins' (Dixon 2013) of a fan-owned club fandom, and how interacting fans produced and reproduced a particular pattern of support.

The aim of the paper is twofold: firstly, to illustrate the implications of fan ownership for the constitution of fandom and the formation of the fan identity, and secondly, to analyse fandom as form of reflexive social agency in modern society. After a brief description of

HKJ fandom and its development, the first part of the paper examines the formation of its collective identity, the design of its traditions, and the challenge of 'authenticity' in an inclusive environment. The second part reviews issues of inclusion and exclusion, and examines fandom as a 'space' produced and updated through interactions between fans from varied backgrounds. The third part deals with fan ownership as an institution, and describes how the supporters managed the tension between their cultural capital and the financial needs of their club. It also surveys the ways they confronted issues of authority and legitimacy in the club that they own.

Introducing HKJ

HKJ is an Israeli supporter-owned football club founded in 2007 by fans of Hapoel Jerusalem (HJ) in protest against its mismanagement. The original team was established in 1926 by the local branch of the Histadrut (Trade Unions General Federation). Financial troubles during the 1980s led to its sale to local real estate businessmen at the end of the decade as part of the privatization of Israeli football (Ben Porat 2012). The club's financial decline continued, however, and the number of supporters was down to a few hundred by 2006, while the local rival team, Beitar Jerusalem, linked to the nationalist right wing, thrived. Fearing that their team was heading towards its disappearance, the supporters organized several protests against the club owners.

The supporters who eventually founded HKJ had originally planned to buy their old club, and set up a nonprofit association for that purpose. However, after HJ owners refused to sell the club, the fans bought the managing rights, but not the ownership, of a club playing in Israel's third division, and changed its name to Hapoel Katamon. In 2009, the association members decided to set up a new club, owned by them. The new team, HKJ, started playing in Israel's fifth division that year, reaching the second tier in 2015 after a series of promotions. As of the end of August 2015, the association had 700 dues-paying members and several thousand home supporters, with the number rising to 4000–6000 for important matches. Fans come from diverse backgrounds in terms of politics, attitudes towards religion and economic ideology. The association members annually elect the club's board on a one-man, one-vote basis.

The club opposes racism and homophobia, rejects violence, and dedicates time and efforts to communal projects. About a fifth of its budget is used to finance community activities, the highest proportion in Israeli football. HKJ organizes five groups of boys and three groups of girls playing in the leagues of the football federation. Its community activity includes two leagues for boys and girls from Jewish and Arab schools in Jerusalem, a setting that enables Jewish and Arab children to become acquainted with each other. It runs a system of mentors in Jerusalem schools and two sport projects for at-risk youth, one Jewish and one Arab. It also runs a football school attended by children from all parts of the city, and sponsors a football team for adults with mental health problems.

The initiative to form a new club came from a group of young people, most of them in their 30s. They became HJ supporters during its decline in the 1990s, and were very active in the protests against its owners. Joining them were older supporters from the 1970s and 1980s – former activists in political extra-parliamentary groups opposed to Israel's occupation of the West Bank and Gaza. The third group involved in the establishment of HKJ consisted of traditional HJ fans in their 40s and 50s for whom the club was part of their childhood in the city's southern neighbourhoods.

People outside these three groups joined HKJ after it was established, attracted by its opposition to racism and violence and the idea of fan ownership. Their number and importance have increased steadily and, as stressed below, their arrival set in motion the process of creating HKJ fandom. In practice, it is a new fandom, combining all the groups, with a distinctive collective identity. HKJ fandom includes 'traditional fans' and persons who originally were not HJ followers, some of them not even football fans at all, who joined the club in search of a social framework that would express their aspirations. Thus, HKJ supporters created a committed fandom, best described as a form of both social activism through football and resistance to racism and discrimination.

This case therefore makes it possible to follow the social processes behind HKJ fandom constitution, and to examine the dynamics of its development as a form of collective behaviour. The analysis below is based primarily on fans' posts in the club's online forums in 2010–2015. As explained below, the main debates among the fans were conducted in these forums.

Additional sources include:

- The association's constitution, collectively drafted by rank-and-file members and approved in 2011.
- Recordings of the fans' biweekly podcast containing interviews with individual supporters and groups.
- The minutes of three round table discussions between 80 association members, during the May 2015 'HKJ Association Day'.
- Minutes of a meeting of the association's board with association members on January 2014 to discuss means of increasing the club's revenue.
- Interviews with three founding members of the association for the purpose of putting some of the issues reviewed here into context.

HKJ fandom and its symbolic definitions

Studies on football fandom find that for committed fans, supporting a team is a significant, continuous and stable part of their identity (Ben Ben Porat 2012). Football fandom is seen by the fans themselves as a lifetime practice rooted in family traditions or local context. This feature of fandom is usually stressed to highlight its contrast to the commercialization and globalization of football (Giulianotti and Robertson 2004). Furthermore, fandom stability stands out against the background of fluid or liquid modernity (Best 2013).

However, fandom is rooted not only in tradition, but also, and primarily, in the everyday and institutionalized social life of the fans (Stone 2007). Fandom is a dynamic process shaped by fans monitoring of, and reflection on, their lives, the social symbols and boundaries that regulate their interaction with others, their chances in the market, and their links with public and state institutions (Numerato 2015). Therefore, fandom practices and meanings, including 'traditions', are updated by the fans' reflexive efforts to handle the conflicts and problems woven into their daily lives (Dixon 2011). Expressions of football support are not limited to the pursuit of stability or connectedness in a diffuse reality.

The case of Hapoel Katamon highlights the importance of reflexivity in generating collective symbolic definitions, and the eventual formation of a collective identity. The monitoring and self-awareness of those fans played a key role in forging their collective identity. HKJ fans aimed to form a football club that would fulfill their aspirations, and to become its fans, in ways that would express their perceptions and values. Their aspirations are best described as particular attempts to transcend the divisions created by the particular and primordial definitions of identity in Israel.

Social trends display a high level of income inequality, weak solidarity among groups, erosion of the welfare state, and decreasing levels of trust in social and government institutions. In the urban space of Jerusalem, those trends are marked, owing to the unequal status of social and national groups in the city and its high levels of poverty (National Insurance Institute 2015). Everyday life in the city is constituted and negotiated along the overlapping cleavage lines of nationality (Jews – Arabs), ethnicity (Oriental Jews – Ashkenazi Jews), and religion (religious – secular).

Those social boundaries constitute the everyday horizon that HKJ fans aspired to transcend and transform. The association's most active members in its first days were young people who became HJ supporters during the decade of the 90s, coinciding with rising tensions between Jews and Arabs in Jerusalem. Furthermore, for some of them, membership in the HKJ association was an extension of their involvement with other grassroots organizations seeking social change. Moreover, as wage earners and members of young families, they had suffered the consequences of privatization, outsourcing of social services and deterioration of labour conditions. Therefore, in their eyes, football's privatization was part of a wider trend. Establishing a fan owned club, and turning it into a focal point of communal initiatives constituted an act of resistance that expressed their outlook.

The new club soon attracted people who had similar experiences, or were active in community activities, education, environment protection, urban planning, trade unions or fighting racism. HKJ was set up at a period of rising public attention to the effects of economic policy and privatization on welfare and income distribution. Thus, the founding of a fan-owned club by HJ fans manifested a wish to save their team, while echoing a set of ideas and projects emerging in the public sphere. Those ideas eventually led to the outburst of the social protest in July and August 2011, when hundreds of thousands took to the streets to protest economic policy.

In February 2011, close to four years after the establishment of the association, the members approved its constitution. Eight months earlier, in June 2010, a group of founding members had proposed to draft a constitution, in view of the large number of newcomers joining the association. They argued that it was no longer possible to assume that there was a common set of implicit principles for its management, and these therefore had to be stated explicitly and included in a formal document.

However, the same interactions led the new arrivals to accept the declared principle of 'reuniting Hapoel Jerusalem'. Placing it at the opening of the new constitution was not an insincere acceptance of the 'till-death-us-do-part' approach of HJ fans; rather, it constituted a merging of the perspectives of both 'old' and 'new' fans. These mutual perspectives became the cornerstone of HKJ's inclusive character and the basis of a fandom composed of supporters from various backgrounds.

The analysis of the emergence of common symbols is related to the fans' uses of online communication. Online forums, set up by the fans in 2007, played a central role in the protest against the owners and the proposal to buy the team. The initiative to set up a new club owned by the fans developed in the online and offline social networks connecting members of the group of young supporters. The online forum also connected the young supporters to older fans who had distanced themselves from HJ after its privatization and decline.

After the establishment of HKJ, its open forum became a place where non-association members could also place posts. Moreover, its importance rose steadily as new fans joined the club and took part in the debates. It displays the same features found in any forum of football fans and, helped develop the fans' bond with the new club (Gibbons and Dixon 2010). In addition, there were lively discussions of the club's goals, the relationship between fandom and politics, issues of authenticity, and the role that HKJ should play in advancing the fans' ideals. Therefore, the online interactions turned the forum into a permanent assembly that generated key markers of a collective identity, and where the diverse fans' perspectives merged.

One of those debates took place in March 2012, after hundreds of Beitar Jerusalem fans, leaving the city stadium after a match, attacked Arab employees at a nearby mall. HKJ fans discussed the incident during a discussion lasting two days, with a general condemnation of racism and criticism of police impotence. The debate turned on the event's significance as part of the growing phenomenon of violence against Arabs in Jerusalem and a harbinger of future events. It also covered the best ways of responding to the attacks. The proposals included aiding attacked employees to file a complaint with the police and sending HKJ volunteers to the mall after Beitar Jerusalem matches to protect Arab employees.

This example is one of several instances where fans defined themselves through collective condemnation of racism and violence, while creating a symbolic space of resistance to an urban environment that became threatening. The same definitions appeared in the discussion held in May 2015, when association members held several round table discussions to debate its goals, failures and achievements. One member summarized the day's debates as follows, 'As a social worker, I witness racism every day. HKJ is my choice to partner with people who see the danger and feel threatened'.

The performance of HKJ fandom

Football support traditionally expresses itself in social settings; it is an experience full with emotions and shared with others. During matches, there is a collective expression of support for a team, often described as 'passion' (The Social Issues Research Center 2008), involving singing, jumping, banner waving and wearing of scarves, hats or shirts with the team colours (Clark 2006). Although it is possible to support a team privately, 'true' fans knowingly display their loyalty not only on match days, but when interacting with others in their everyday life.

Football fans assert their identity by their collective performance, inside and outside the stadium, based on the mutual symbols, traditions, norms and values composing their social knowledge (Stone 2007). Moreover, by performing their support, they cultivate their links with other supporters in face-to-face encounters or through online social networks. At the same time, they update their shared knowledge, thus becoming active participants in the construction of the meanings of fandom (Dixon 2011).

The expression of support for HKJ during match days developed as a process that reflected the changes in its fandom – from a narrow range of support forms, commanded by the founding group of young fans, to a variety of expressions that suited the diversity of fans. The process took place alongside the debates about the nature of 'genuine' support. In its early stages, the discussion involved the young supporters, and was restrained to a narrow definition of support. They agreed that 'true' support involved standing together, choreographically coordinated movements while singing, and chanting accompanied by drums. Any behaviour that did not correspond to this pattern, which is suitable for young males, was not considered 'support'.

The debate was whether to organize 'genuine supporters' and set apart a section of the stands for them. Those proposing such a move also used the term 'ultras' to describe the desired form of support. Opponents of that approach identified ultras with violence, and stressed their opposition to creating a hierarchy of support among fans attending matches. Establishing a hierarchy of fans is a part of creating 'authenticity (Fiske 1992)'. Thus, the opposition to setting apart a group of 'dedicated' fans undermined the idea of 'genuine' support that the young supporters were trying to advance.

This paradox is explained by the agreement of the fans debating 'genuine support' to open the club's doors to anyone accepting its principles. Moreover, they deliberately excluded from the association's constitution any distinctions between old and new fans. The decision to adopt such an inclusive strategy was based on both principle and practical motives. A fan-owned club needs a broad base of supporters from which dues-paying association members are recruited. Inclusiveness also means that a many fans attending matches are women and families with children. Diversity itself became one of the markers of HKJ identity, and constrained the possibilities of developing a male support culture. Thus, it changed the perception and definition of 'authentic support'.

In November 2011 several women supporters appeared on the club's podcast and spoke at length about female fandom. They expressed their satisfaction with the ability to express support in a way that suited them, without imitating male patterns. 'I do not have to join the "supporting block" of males. I can find my way of supporting the team without joining them'.

Some newcomers were attracted to HKJ because of its rejection of violence and its communal work, while others came because it was a 'family-friendly environment'. Once diversified forms of support became legitimate, they could join and internalize the social knowledge associated with fandom: knowing the players, attending away matches, singing the songs, and wearing the team shirt on match days.

However, from the perspective of HKJ young founding supporters, their acts had brought about an ambivalent outcome. The diversification of fandom they had introduced eventually challenged their notion of 'authenticity'. The question of what constitutes 'genuine support' is behind recurring online debates about fans' behaviour during matches and, in particular, the place of cursing and verbal aggressiveness. Although cursing in football might appear devoid of importance, for HKJ followers, it was a question about the form and content of identity creation and the acquisition of norms associated with its fandom.

One example of this debate took place in July 2012 on the online forum, after fans attending the stadium with their families demanded, at the association's annual assembly, the banning of 'verbal violence' in the stands. In response, some young fans described curses and verbal attacks as 'part of football culture'. They called football 'an emotional sport' with 'no room for softness', and proposed setting up a designated 'sterile' zone for families, thus enabling 'other fans to express themselves'. One post summarized the case for 'authenticity' by saying that at the original club, no one had ever thought of banning cursing. He also criticized applauding the players after they lost a match, a practice introduced by newcomers, which he called 'defeatism'.

This dispute has never been formally settled; nevertheless, each time the diversity versus authenticity question emerged, it was the former that prevailed. Groups of supporters habitually fill specific sections of the stands, but there is a constant movement of people during the match. The 'supporting block' usually occupies the middle stands, singing, jumping, and waving flags during the match. It includes supporters from 'Brigada Malcha', the organized fans of HJ basketball team, who have no special status during football matches. Other groups express support by applauding, sporadic shouts and sometimes joining the singing. Several times during the matches, all of the fans perform a joint chant, preceded by silence, thus affirming their collective identity.

Identity is also affirmed and commemorated through ceremonies sometimes held before home matches. Banners with legends against racism and violence are displayed, or children attending the community projects are invited to the pitch before the match. During 2015, the rainbow flag was displayed several times to mark the club's rejection of homophobia.

Fans' practices of support outside the stadium are similar to those of other supporters around the world. They organize meetings and parties and five-a-side tournaments, there is a club fanzine and a biweekly podcast, the club organizes an annual event for families before the season opening, and children are enrolled in its football school. These activities generate committed fans with a strong attachment to the club and to other supporters.

However, the performance of support for the club also includes practices directly linked to its rejection of racism and its affirmation of social solidarity. Like the ceremonies preceding matches, these practices load HKJ support with emotions, and help forge a collective identity. They also portray HKJ support as a social agency driven by the reflexive acts of supporters.

In December 2014, a classroom in Jerusalem's bilingual (Hebrew–Arabic) school was set on fire by members of a racist Jewish organization. The school is attended by Jewish and Arab children, whom are often invited by the club to attend its home matches. The club enlisted supporters and team players to help the school and play with the students. The attack and the club's response were widely commented on the supporters' online networks. Like the social worker quoted above, they also saw the action in support of HKJ as creating a 'safe space' free from racism.

Community projects are a more standardized form of expressing support for the club outside the stadium. HKJ operates a network of volunteers that involved in those projects who are enlisted through the online forums. During the period under review, from January 2010 to May 2015, there was a constant flow of messages on the fans' forums celebrating those projects and calling them 'the club's essence'.

Agency and reflexivity played a key role in defining supporters' practices and identity formation, as they did in shaping their opposition to racism. During the round table discussions held at the 2015 association day, one of the members described the club's partnership with an institution for at-risk adolescents. She ended her description as follows: 'They now have a football team that includes Arab kids from a neighbouring village. It shows that HKJ makes it possible to turn abstract ideas about justice and coexistence into a reality'.

Oral traditions, memories and fandom

Fandom as collective identity is always connected to the team's history as narrated by the supporters to each other. Knowing what to remember, what to forget and how to narrate the past is a basic feature of a collective identity and its updating (Assmann and Czaplicka 1995). Memories are oral traditions that develop in supporters' social networks and express, in their view, the spirit of their team, 'Genuine' supporters are loyal to their team in the present and to its past, as they perceive it. Moreover, the supporters' collective identity attaches itself to geographical sites with special significance in the team's history, usually a stadium, a neighbourhood, or a city (Fitzpatrick 2013). Thus, the traditions and the memories are part of the intangible assets, the cultural capital, held by the fans (Richardson and Drachan 2006).

The establishment of a new club, like HKJ, owned by its supporters, poses a special challenge to issues of continuity and tradition. HKJ was named to honour Katamon stadium, where the original team played for more than 25 years before it was sold to real estate developers in 1978. The reference to the old stadium in the new club's name was a way of connecting it to the traditions of the original team. In addition, the 'memories' adopted by the fans were translated into practices that in turn reaffirmed 'traditions'. The schools league, the fans' annual five-a-side tournament, and the activities of the club's 'football school' for children are all referred to by both the club and its fans as expressions of values passed to the next generation.

Another element they adopted from what they called 'HJ history' was the rejection of racism. In 1968, Hapoel Jerusalem became the first club to include an Arab player in its team, and he became one of its legends. Thus, an event from the past, the presence of one Arab player at HJ, was transformed into a constitutive element of the 'traditions' adopted by HKJ fans. The emphasis on tradition reinforced their argument that they were the heirs to the spirit of their original team. But it was not merely a matter of symbolically recovering the team of their past; it was about connecting their present situation, in modern Israel to what they regarded as an earlier tradition. The stories they told about the team's past were a reflexive choice of social agents resisting racism.

In contrast, Beitar Jerusalem, HJ's local rival for many years, never hired Arab players. Furthermore, BJ fans are usually identified by their racism and hatred of Arabs and Muslims. Through their rejection of racism, HKJ supporters asserted their communal identity, while defining a distance from BJ fans who were consequently perceived as 'others'. The process was similar to the creation of identity through supporters' rivalries in other parts of the world (Benkwitz and Molnar 2012).

In November 2013, the HKJ team captain publicly criticized Beitar Jerusalem players for not condemning racism among their fans. His statements were heavily criticized in the news media for 'mixing football with politics', triggering an angry response from HKJ fans over online platforms. These fans used the occasion to affirm their anti-racist identity and praised the player, calling him 'our captain' and 'a source of pride for the club'.

The contents of the fans' commentaries reflected the daily reality in Israel and their awareness of the rising tide of racism. Furthermore, rejection of racism became one of the features linking founding members and newcomers, because the latter could identify with the club's stance. Therefore, new fans of a club established a few years before could see themselves as part of a 'tradition', and merge their perspectives with those of the founding supporters. Thus, 'memories', always an elusive subject, became the unquestioned content of a narrative uniting 'new' and 'old' fans.

Reconstructing authenticity

Merging diverse perspectives and creating a common identity was not a trivial process; rather, it involved negotiating meanings and updating symbolic definitions of identity. It involved a long and sometimes acrimonious debate about what constitutes a genuine supporter. Research on football fandom has analysed the 'authentic' fan from several points of view: social knowledge and cultural capital, the unconditional and emotionally loaded connection with the team, and the social and family bonds involved in lifetime fandom (Davis 2014). Here, authenticity is related to the fans' own experience and their ability to categorize and assess their behaviour and of other supporters, according to their social knowledge (Dixon 2014).

This notion is important, because it played a central role in defining a collective identity by negotiating meanings and adopting common definitions. As described above, the debate on authenticity among HKJ supporters involved the definition of 'genuine' support on match days, but such a discussion centred on the forms of support during matches. A more profound and far more important debate took place in the summer of 2013 and between January and April 2014 concerning two proposals to merge HJ and HKJ.

Since 2009, there have been several initiatives, most of them from third parties, to reunite HJ and HKJ. In 2013, HKJ gained promotion to Israel's second division, meaning the team would face HJ in the next season. Immediately after promotion was secured, the mayor of Jerusalem made an unsuccessful attempt to reunite the teams. Then, in January 2014, a private businessman offered to buy HJ and let HKJ's association manage it as a united and privately held club, with all of its community projects becoming part of the merger.

The two proposals, especially the second, triggered a vigorous debate on the fans' online forums and in several association general assemblies. The possibility of 'returning home' constituted a challenge for the ways the founding members defined and portrayed themselves as 'authentic'. What was at stake was a question of the primary goal of the new club. For some founding members HKJ is a temporary arrangement designed to eventually save HJ from bad management. Thus, genuine fans were exclusively those who supported the original club and aspired to 'return home'. New supporters claimed that HKJ was a club on its own right. It symbolizes a beginning for fans from various backgrounds, who reject racism and advocate supporters' ownership of their club.

On the online forum, some founding members complained that for the newcomers, HKJ was a 'project', while for genuine fans like themselves, football was about loyalty to a team. Newcomers were portrayed as nothing more than 'project fans' who 'did not know 'what it means to support a team from birth', and therefore had no right to prevent the merger. In other words, part of the founding members perceived newcomers as a challenge to their definition of identity. They responded to such a challenge with rituals of distinction, and displayed norms of behaviour that set new supporters apart.

Still, this line of argument was rejected by most founding members. Instead, they appealed for solidarity from all HKJ fandom, founders and newcomers alike, with the ideal of a 'united Hapoel team'. The fans also agreed that the united club should continue to be owned by its supporters. When the proposal was brought for approval, more than 90% of the members voted for the formation of a united club, if it were owned and managed by the association.

Eventually, the proposal to reunite the two clubs faded because it was not financially feasible. Nevertheless, the experience of defining a united platform and outlook about fandom was a turning point. The episode tested the validity and endurance of the common values and definitions of identity inscribed in the association's constitution. The process of renegotiating meanings and definitions took place over recurrent encounters, in the online forums, in several general assemblies, and in informal meetings. The eventual outcome was a rejection of a specific definition of 'genuine' fandom based on the distinction from newcomers. In its place, the common core of values and the fans' collective identity were reaffirmed.

Furthermore, participants in the debate on the online forum often stressed their affective ties to the club and its 'project'. They expressed anguish over 'losing what we have built', and recognized that HKJ fandom offered a sense of comfort in a protected space. Therefore, new supporters voted with the founding group, in an expressed effort to 'remain together'.

Moreover, the general assertion that 'football belongs to its fans' meant that 'genuine' supporters displayed their loyalty by joining the association and defending fan ownership. A new autonomous definition of 'authentic fans' emerged from the interactions and debates about the proposed merger with the original club. Thus, HKJ founding supporters adopted norms of behaviour and symbolic categories that did not differentiate them from new supporters. The latter had become, in a short time, 'legitimate' supporters in their eyes and those of the founding fans. Authenticity was constructed through negotiations over meanings during recurrent interactions among supporters from varied backgrounds.

Fandom as 'community': bridging and bonding

Football fandom can ease or hinder the creation of social ties across groups. It can create long-term social relations, if it foments common interests and values and provides an environment that encourages trust and collaboration (Brown 2013). However, fandom can also be a powerful tool of exclusion through the creation of sealed social boundaries. After all, fandom practices not only grant meaning to the idea of 'us', but define 'them' or 'others'. The 'other' is not always a supporter of a rival club; sometimes, he is a fan of the same team from a different background, a different religion or a different ideology.

Studies on football fandom and social policy projects have dealt extensively with questions of inclusion and exclusion (Vermeulen and Verweel 2009). Both practices are part of the process of establishing norms through social interactions in particular contexts. Thus, social links among fans historically developed in urban industrial centres as a response to anonymity (Blackshaw 2008). In such a context, social relations among team supporters were an expression of the geographical proximity of residents of a city, or a sector of it. According to some studies, in modern societies, social connections among supporters stem from the search for stability in a diffuse modernity (Best 2013).

This paper argues that social proximity is crucial in the analysis of the process of inclusion or exclusion. The key question is whether interactions happen between 'similar' people with a perceived common social, economic or cultural background. These types of interactions are often related to the nature of the ties they create through time, whether they are 'strong', frequent, affective, and related to many dimensions of the individual's life, or 'weak', infrequent, and one-dimensional (Granovetter 1973).

The notion of weak and strong ties is of key importance in understanding the character of football fandom. Those ties set the context of interactions and the norms regulating them. Borrowing Putnam's terms, interactions and ties among members of the same social network and the same social background are usually referred as 'bonding', while those among people from diverse social networks are termed 'bridging' (Putnam 2000). Interactions regulated by bonding relations are the basis of exclusion; they are based on the expectation of loyalty to the team and fulfilling obligations to the group (Brown 2013). Interactions among members of ultras groups, holding norms of 'genuine' fandom, are usually associated with this pattern (Kennedy 2013).

Bridging interactions, on the other hand, develop among people from diverse environments usually connected by weak ties. Relations among fans in this pattern of interactions face a double challenge: constructing common meanings, and building expectations based on trust. Without these two elements, bridging as a long-term project becomes impossible. At the same time, bridging is a key to the success of fan-owned clubs, where diversity is the rule. This feature should not be ignored, and the assumption of a homogeneous fandom avoided. Supporters come from diverse backgrounds and hold diverse views about the meanings attached to the support of their club.

When HKJ founders set up their club, they had to create its fandom as well. They had to create ties among various groups of supporters and later attract new fans to the association. The rejection of exclusion as a feasible way of constituting a fandom was therefore a matter of both principle and need. Thus, many interactions occurred between fans barely acquainted with each other. In addition, immediately after the establishment of the club, members volunteered for diverse tasks, despite the weak ties among them, and the uncertain future of the team. The executive board members, internal auditors, and marketing officials are non-paid members. Volunteers manage the club website and podcasts, the sale of merchandize, and the campaigns to recruit new association members.

Explanations of volunteering activities in social organizations emphasize the significance of trust and the importance of social ties as features motivating volunteers (Putnam 2000). The uncertainty about HKJ's continued existence and the initial weak ties between its fans ostensibly did not provide an adequate basis for trust. Nevertheless, in the general framework of HKJ fandom as an instance of reflexive agency, volunteering and trust are deliberate acts of confidence. Since membership in the association is renewed at the end of every season, such confidence is tested yearly.

The developing connections between supporters encouraged cooperation and engagement with the club's projects, even when these were not directly related to football. In addition, once a common set of symbols and values was adopted, the success of the club became the focal point of recurrent interactions. Fans from diverse social networks, economic positions and political beliefs could collaborate, even when the ties between them remained weak. Usually, however, those interactions led to stronger ties.

The encounters among fans, their collaboration and their shared interest in the club led the supporters to use the term 'community' when referring to their fandom. This usage was most prominent during the online debates about the proposed merger with HJ. The symbolic definition of community was widely adopted. Supporters used the term, loaded with positive meanings, when referring to their involvement in the club's activities. The word 'community' was connected to the affective links to the club; it referred to the 'space' they had created secure from the threats and tensions of everyday life.

HKJ fandom is therefore a symbolic community (Cohen 1985), which the fans perceive as continuous and stable. Their encounters are the context in which they reaffirm and update those symbols. In March 2014, during one the most tense weeks in the debate about the proposed merger with HJ, one of the supporters stated his perception of the club on the online forum: 'In Hapoel Katamon, there is love. There is truly a sense of community, a rejection of racism, not only as a response to Beitar Jerusalem, and there is a commitment to society'. The metaphor of space becomes an important element in the analysis of how reflexive agents created through interaction, a location in which the norms of tolerance, inclusion and trustworthiness were reaffirmed.

The case of HKJ illustrates the importance of bridging in the constitution of fandom. Trust and the feeling of a common identity develop during the encounters between supporters, both on match days and at other times. The ties linking the supporters are their social capital – the basis of their perceived power and capacity to react to external pressures.

Our club, our responsibility

A football club is a legal entity, usually working to achieve its goals using business methods and logic. It raises money from sponsors, buys and sells players, sells tickets and sometimes gets money from television broadcasting rights. A handful of mega-clubs have become corporations with a global presence, but most teams in the world act in accordance with local business conditions.

In contrast to club boards and management, supporters base their acts on emotions and shared symbols that define them as a collective entity. Fandom is a voluntary form of enlistment that operates through social ties and networks. Fans regard the symbols that unite them, their cultural capital, as the repository of the team's spirit. They may resist efforts to base club management on the pursuit of financial gain, because they view such behaviour as a threat to their cultural capital (Richardson and Drachan 2006).

Up until the end of the 1980s, owners of football clubs were usually local associations, local councils and municipalities, trade unions, churches, commercial enterprises or local private owners. Since the 1990s, the trend towards commercialization has integrated football into the global market. It has created a global culture of football consumption, and has often shattered existing patterns of ownership (Kennedy and Kennedy 2012).

Parallel to these developments, patterns of fandom have also evolved. Up until the late 1990s, studies of football fandom portrayed supporters as males operating in informal social networks, based to a large extent on geographical and physical proximity. A perceived rise in violence and the emergence of 'hooliganism' were symptoms of the tensions between the supporters' cultural capital and their local traditions on the one hand, and the commercial and financial values embedded in globalized football on the other (Numerato 2015).

However, when examining supporters' response to football's commercialization, it cannot be assumed that they are passive, or merely reacting to club initiatives. The fans are not merely clinging to local traditions and seeking an anchor of stability in a diffuse reality; they are reflexive agents aware of their situation, who can actively choose from a range of possible reactions to commercialization (Williams 2013). Concentrating exclusively on violence and extreme behaviour therefore ignores the variety and complexity of the fans' reaction.

Furthermore, as mentioned above, the analysis of football fandom should not ignore its social dimension. Fandom is a form of collective behaviour conducted within social networks. Therefore, when describing fans' patterns of reaction, it is necessary to take into account their collective dimension, instead of concentrating exclusively on the individual and his everyday life. Fans talk to each other, and sustain a constant dialogue about their situation as supporters of a team. They exchange views about their aspirations and relations with the club owners. Furthermore, by utilizing technology and global communications, they can also learn from the fans' initiatives in other places around the world.

Conversations among supporters may become a recurrent deliberation about the ways to respond to any perceived threat to their values, or traditions. Sometimes, the deliberations become a formal feature, and the fans may set up organizations to advance their interests. In practice, fan organizations have taken diverse forms. They can be one-time efforts or permanent features of engagement; they can be structured flatly or loosely, or conform to a structured hierarchy.

Moreover, there is also great variety in the type of actions adopted by the different groups of fans, depending mostly on the local contexts where they take place and the challenges facing the supporters. This process of 'creative accommodation' to commercialization refers to the character of the relations between the fans' cultural capital, and the club's management of its economic resources (Williams 2013). The range of potential outcomes includes several patterns: all-out confrontation, conflicts over particular issues, cooperation, and, finally, an overlapping of interests when the fans become the owners of the club, like in the case of HKJ.

Fan ownership of football clubs has received less attention than other forms of fandom collective actions, particularly ultras. Specifically, with the exception of some outstanding cases (e.g. FC United of Manchester) (Brown 2008) there is a lack of research regarding the social processes behind it. However, there have been a number of studies on the economic and organizational aspects of supporters' ownership and/or management of their clubs (Working Group Report on Supporter Involvement in Football Clubs 2014).

The path to fan ownership varies according to the club. In some cases, the fans took over after the club imploded financially, while in other cases, fans collaborated with private businessmen to keep the club alive. Finally, there are cases of fans who decided to set up a club that would represent their aspirations, even when their original team was still active, as in the case of FC United of Manchester. HKJ belongs to this last category, since its fans wanted it to embody the 'traditional ideas' of HJ as they defined them. Their basic premise was that a football club morally belongs to its supporters.

However, fan ownership of HKJ did not eliminate the friction between commercial considerations and the principles embedded in the fans' cultural capital; rather, this tension was transferred to the supporters themselves. HKJ fans are compelled to confront the day-to-day management of their club, including its financial needs. The tension between the monetary aspects of club management and their principles led them to include in the association's constitution a clause stipulating that HKJ would be managed on the basis of 'budget responsibility', and would always honour its contractual commitments to its players.

Nonetheless, accommodation to economic needs is ubiquitous in the management of the club. Some of those practices were specific measures dealing with temporary issues. In December 2013, following a report by the board that there was no money for players' wages, the association members launched a special money raising effort, including additional payments from them.

However, when financial issues became recurrent, it was necessary to find formal, even bureaucratic, solutions. This happened when the club was required to set ticket prices – an issue for clubs and followers all over the world. The association appointed several committees, which presented recommendations that were eventually approved by its general assembly. The need to accommodate principles to need was also evident in the case of sponsorships, which are raised mainly by the association members and its board. The need for sponsors has increased with the team's promotions to higher leagues, since the financial needs increased far more than the money coming from members' fees. In an effort to keep the commercial aspect in line with HKJ values, the sponsors are invited to join the community projects and take part in their activities.

Even when sponsors' money has been forthcoming, however, the members are fully aware that long-term financial needs have to be met. In particular, their decision to reach the top division forced them to compromise on one of their main principles: the management of their club. After lengthy deliberations, the members agreed to add to the board representatives of businessmen who donated large sums to the club. The constitution was amended to increase the number of board members to seven, four of whom are association members who are required to vote in accordance with the decisions of the general assembly. While the fans remain the owners of the club and the chairman comes from their ranks, the compromise shows the need for accommodation when fans take the path of ownership of their own club.

These examples illustrate the need for practices capable of managing the inherent friction between financial requirements and the 'spirit of the team'. Fan ownership is a form of engaging and committed fandom, frequently originating with dissent on some of the very issues on which they must compromise when in charge of their team.

Legitimacy and authority

The establishment of HKJ originated from the protest by a group of HJ fans, from one network of friends and acquaintances. They viewed themselves as embodying the spirit of their original team; its symbols and traditions. They staged protests against the way the club was being run, which, in their opinion, jeopardized its future. After becoming increasingly frustrated with the owners, they felt compelled to abandon the club; they would continue their struggle from the outside. In their eyes, their loyalty to HJ justified their acts; legitimacy stemmed from the years they had spent 'following the team wherever it went'.

The fans' campaign against the owners featured, at its onset, similar traits to those of comparable ultras and activist groups around Europe. It involved young men, usually bonded by strong ties, but loosely organized; they came to the rescue of their team, in the name of their 'genuine' love for it; they resisted racism and were attached to local 'traditions' (Doidge 2013). Nevertheless, what started as a grassroots protest, against mismanagement of a football club, grew into an inclusive civil association. The latter is strongly institutionalized; it has a formal constitution, with a defined structure of governance and decision-making procedures, well understood by its members.

HKJ fandom still retains some of the features of a grassroots movement; it promotes resistance to racism and fan ownership of football clubs; the collective adopts and undertakes activities and projects proposed by rank-and-file members. At the same time, HKJ is a civil association that advocates social change through football; it mediates between its members and the community. In addition, HKJ is an inclusive organization, open to all persons who agree to comply with its principles. Finally, the association is a form of formalized fandom; it displays a diversity in views, but has created mechanisms enabling it to reach eventual consensus, when necessary.

This paper has underscored the importance of reflexivity in guiding the fans' choices, and the unintended consequences they had. The process started with a small group of fans, discussing and deciding to open their ranks to other groups of supporters. Their original plan was to raise money in order to buy their team; however, they soon changed course and established HKJ, after the owners of the original club refused to sell it. The new club was meant to embody the fans' values and enable them, in the future, to buy Hapoel Jerusalem. Breaking away from an active club is considered by football fans to be an extreme measure; usually is should be avoided. Thus, HJ rebel fans decided to call 'every supporter that cares about the team' to join them; after failing to buy their team, they raised money to establish a new club. But money was not the only reason behind the call for support from the young fans; they also needed to gain legitimacy for their decision to break away from HJ. Both aims were intertwined, as the commitment to contribute money to the project meant, concurrently, voicing agreement with a radical move.

The concept of fan-ownership was not new to the rebel fans; it had appeared extensively some years earlier, in a fanzine published by some of them. Therefore, when the crisis between the fans and the owners reached a climax, in 2007, the idea of fan-ownership was adopted by the former, without much debate. The initiative offered, to those fans joining it, a powerful vision; the ownership of their football club. It became a focal point of attraction to fans who felt that their team was the victim of mismanagement; it also attracted people who did not support Hapoel Jerusalem.

A wider base of support, beyond 'traditional' HJ supporters, meant that HKJ fandom included persons from diverse economic, social or political backgrounds; 'self-evident' norms and expectations did no longer apply. Witnessing the rise in the number of fans, and their diversity, the founding members drafted, in 2010, the proposed association's principles. According to those principles, the association's general assembly is the source of authority in all matters pertaining to the club's management. The general assembly approved, in 2011, the association's constitution. Since then, it has been amended several times, but it still is the document that defines the principles and values by which the club is managed.

In addition to the formal decision-making mechanisms, the fans online forums are an informal meeting place, where important issues are discussed, and disputes over matters of principle tacitly settled. Thus, in 2009 and 2010, long debates were held on HKJ and its links to party politics. Eventually, the fans agreed that the club should eschew any political identity, but to promote community work. Since then, the issue of politics has only appeared sporadically on the forum.

Through the debates on the forums, norms managing online interactions among fans were defined. This feature was crucial, as practices designed to find common ground among members were routinized. By the time the debates on the proposed merger with HJ began, in 2014, those practices were already firmly established. They were instrumental in reaching a wide consensus, on the association's response to the planned merger. As mentioned above, the online interactions enabled the members to define fan ownership as their primary source of legitimacy.

Conclusions

HKJ fandom was forged, to a large extent, out of a sense of yearning for a team that, in the view of its fans, once existed. The fans of a battered team from the 1990s saw HKJ as embodying the memories of a HJ they never knew, but whose memory they had preserved, through oral traditions; it resisted racism and was rooted in the communities of southern Jerusalem. Their longings were a ` period of time, they created a club with a committed fandom, with a defined common identity.

HKJ fans are reformists, not revolutionaries; they promote the creation of an inclusive community based on a diversity of backgrounds and opinions; they willingly cooperate with state and municipal agencies to promote their projects. Nonetheless, the establishment of a fan owned club was a form of social activism, in response to the commercialization of football. It was also an expression of their opposition to racism, violence and homophobia in Jerusalem's public sphere. The case of HKJ highlights the complexity and diversity of fandom, as a culture of resistance to the conditions defining the fans' everyday life. In this sense, the practices of football fans constantly update fandom itself. Fandom is a process, not an object.

Disclosure statement

No potential conflict of interest was reported by the author.

References

Assmann, Jan, and John Czaplicka. 1995. "Collective Memory and Cultural Identity." *New German Critique, NGC, No.* 65: 125–133.

Ben Porat, Amir. 2012. "From Community to Commodity: The Commodification of Football in Israel." *Soccer & Society* 13 (3): 443–457. doi:10.1080/14660970.2012.655511.

Benkwitz, Adam, and Gyozo Molnar. 2012. "Interpreting and Exploring Football Fan Rivalries: An Overview." *Soccer & Society* 13 (4): 479–494. doi:10.1080/14660970.2012.677224.

Best, Shaun. 2013. "Liquid Fandom: Neo-tribes and Fandom in the Context of Liquid Modernity." *Soccer & Society* 14 (1): 80–92. doi:10.1080/14660970.2012.753534.

Blackshaw, Tony. 2008. "Contemporary Community Theory and Football." *Soccer & Society* 9 (3): 325–345. doi:10.1080/14660970802008959.

Brown, Adam. 2008. "'Our club, our rules': fan communities at FC United of Manchester." *Soccer & Society* 9 (3): 346–358. doi:10.1080/14660970802008967.

Brown, Sean F. 2013. "Epilogue: The Not-so-Hidden Complexity of the Sport-community Connection." *Sport in Society* 17 (1): 134–138. doi:10.1080/17430437.2013.828898.

Clark, Tom. 2006. "'I'm Scunthorpe 'til I Die': Constructing and (Re)negotiating Identity through the Terrace Chant." *Soccer & Society* 7 (4): 494–507. doi:10.1080/14660970600905786.

Cohen, Anthony. 1985. *The Symbolic Construction of Community*. London: Routledge.

Davis, Leon. 2014. "Football Fandom and Authenticity: A Critical Discussion of Historical and Contemporary Perspectives." *Soccer & Society* 16 (2–3): 422–436. doi:10.1080/14660970.2014.9 61381.

Dixon, Kevin. 2011. "A 'Third Way' for Football Fandom Research: Anthony Giddens and Structuration Theory." *Soccer & Society* 12 (2): 279–298. doi:10.1080/14660970.2011.548363.

Dixon, Kevin. 2013. "Learning the Game: Football Fandom Culture and the Origins of Practice." *International Review for the Sociology of Sport* 48 (3): 334–348. doi:10.1177/1012690212441157.

Dixon, Kevin. 2014. "The Role of Lateral Surveillance in the Construction of Authentic Football Fandom Practice." *Surveillance and Society* 11 (4): 424–438.

Doidge, Mark. 2013. "'The Birthplace of Italian Communism': Political Identity and Action Amongst Livorno Fans." *Soccer & Society* 14 (2): 246–261. doi:10.1080/14660970.2013.776471.

Fiske, John. 1992. "The Cultural Economy of Fandom." In *The Adoring Audience*, edited by Lisa A. Lewis, 30–49. London and New York: Routledge.

Fitzpatrick, Colin. 2013. "The Struggle for Grassroots Involvement in Football Club Governance: Experiences of a Supporter-activist." *Soccer & Society* 14 (2): 201–214. doi:10.1080/14660970.2013.776468.

Gibbons, Tom, and Kevin Dixon. 2010. "'Surf's Up!': A Call to Take English Soccer Fan Interactions on the Internet More seriously." *Soccer & Society* 11 (5): 599–613. doi:10.1080/14660970.2010.497359.

Giddens, Anthony. 2013. *The Constitution of Society: Outline of the Theory of Structuration*. Cambridge: Polity.

Giulianotti, Richard, and Roland Robertson. 2004. "The Globalization of Football: A Study in the Glocalization of the 'Serious Life'." *The British Journal of Sociology* 55 (4): 545–568. doi:10.1111/bjos.2004.55.issue-4.

Granovetter, Mark. 1973. "The Strength of Weak Ties." *The American Journal of Sociology* 78: 1360–1380. doi:10.1086/225469.

Kennedy, David. 2013. "A Contextual Analysis of Europe's Ultra Football Supporters Movement." *Soccer & Society* 14 (2): 132–153. doi:10.1080/14660970.2013.776464.

Kennedy, Peter, and David Kennedy. 2012. "Football Supporters and the Commercialisation of Football: Comparative Responses Across Europe." *Soccer & Society* 13 (3): 327–340. doi:10.1080/14660970.2012.655503.

National Insurance Institute. 2015. "Annual Report." Jerusalem: National Insurance Institute.

Numerato, Dino. 2015. "Who Says 'No to Modern Football?' Italian Supporters, Reflexivity, and Neoliberalism." *Journal of Sport and Social Issues* 39 (2): 120–138. doi:10.1177/0193723514530566.

Putnam, Robert D. 2000. *Bowling Alone: The Collapse and Revival of American Community*. New York: Simon and Schuster.

Richardson, Brenden, and Turley Drachan. 2006. "Support Your Local Team: Resistance, Subculture and the Desire for Distinction." *European Advance in Consumer Research* 33: 175–180.

Stone, Chris. 2007. "The Role of Football in Everyday Life." *Soccer & Society* 8 (2–3): 169–184.

The Social Issues Research Center. 2008. "Football Passions." Oxford: The Social Issues Research Center.

Vermeulen, Jeroen, and Paul Verweel. 2009. "Participation in Sport: Bonding and Bridging as Identity Work." *Sport in Society* 12 (9): 1206–1219. doi:10.1080/17430430903137886.

Williams, John. 2013. "Fans: Consumers, Hooligans and Activists." In *The Cambridge Companion to Football*, edited by Rob Steen, Jed Novick and Huw Richards, 198–216. Cambridge: Cambridge University Press.

Working Group Report on Supporter Involvement in Football Clubs. 2014. "Supporter Involvement in Football Clubs." Supporters Direct Scotland.

Ultras in Indonesia: conflict, diversification, activism

Andy Fuller and Fajar Junaedi

ABSTRACT

Ultras play a vital role in the life of Indonesian football. Ultra fandom has emerged as a highly visual, highly spectacular, and frequently violent form of fandom in post-reformasi Indonesia. Ultra fan groups are overwhelmingly made up of young, urban men who dedicate much of the leisure time to supporting their club – whether through being at the stadium, creating on tifos, or through social-media campaigns. Supporter groups such as PSIM's Brajamusti are linked to the cultural and political realities of everyday life in Yogyakarta. While the Surabaya-based Bonek are engaged in an ongoing struggle against FIFA and Indonesia's football federation. The Solo-based Pasoepati are a more recent fan group who have supported several Solo-based teams. This article draws on fieldwork carried out between August and December 2014. The article explores how the different fan groups interact with each other with their city and how they imagine an improved 'soccer-scape' in Indonesia.

Introduction

Indonesia occupies a curious place in global football culture. Football is everywhere in Indonesia: in the streets, in bars, in narrow alleys, in grand and packed stadiums, and in the shabby empty lots of urban decay. The game is a cultural product open to endless varieties of meanings, uses and articulations (Allegri 2010; Wilson 2006, 2014). Football, as the world's game, is sometimes 'the beautiful game', but, it is also a game that produces ugly conflicts, and is thoroughly corrupted by politicians and bureaucrats. Popular non-fiction works have shown how playing the game involves a complicated negotiated with prevailing political orthodoxies as well as placating local mafias through match fixing (Kuper 2011; McGinnis 1999). 'Modern football' is anathema for many football fans; 'modern football', in the eyes of hardcore fans has been corrupted by Sky Sports or Fox Sport while clubs sell out to the highest bidder and disregard the loyal, local fan. At the same time, many kinds of football fans are anathema to the kind of football that is being shaped into an easily consumable product that is produced in a safe, clean, sterile and intricately (and intimately) surveilled space.

Many of the developments in contemporary football culture are strongly protested against by fans, known as ultras. Although, there are fierce rivalries between ultras of different teams, they are united by common styles of clothing, tattoos, values and ways of performing within stadiums. Being ultra is a global culture that takes on local meanings and practices. As such, we continue on from other articles exploring the varieties of ultras in Japan (Doidge and Lieser 2013), The Netherlands (Spaaij 2007) and Spain (Spaaij and Vinas 2006). This article seeks to contribute to the research on football in Indonesia (Colombijn 2000; Dorsey and Sebastian 2013; Flicker 2013; Fuller 2014a, 2014b, 2015b; Junaedi 2012, 2014; Wirawan 2015) and to analyse the rise of ultra fan culture through the examples of three fan groups in Java.

Qualities of performance: going to a football game in Solo

I started reading up on football in Indonesia while living in Leiden, a small town in the area known as the *randstad* region of The Netherlands. The books I read dealt with the administration of the game, its introduction in colonial times, and the participation of Chinese Indonesians in the game. There were also a number of angry and polemical books whose primarily goal was to question the authority of the PSSI – Indonesian Football Association (Fuller 2015a). There was one book on the Bonek of Surabaya (Junaedi 2012), and also an unpublished research report on the same supporters, investigating how the notoriously violent supporters could be pacified in order to make the game more appealing to a broader community. There was very little that could provide an insight into the way the game is watched, consumed and participated in at an everyday level. Rather than rely on the library – which although was up-to-date in its collection – which seemed out-of-date, the official and unofficial websites, Twitter accounts, YouTube videos, blogs and Facebook pages provided the most compelling way into 'football in Indonesia'.

The experiences of reading books on Indonesian football, watching clips on YouTube and that of going to football games in Australia did little to prepare me for the experience of watching games in Solo, Central Java. Regrettably, I have only been to two actual games of Second Division Football (Divisi Utama) – but, I have complemented this by visiting numerous stadiums and meeting with many fans. I have come to the temporary conclusion that it is impossible to distinguish football from the culture of performance and the related urban popular cultures. Football, indeed, makes itself evident on the streets of Indonesian cities, regardless of whether or not an actual game is taking place. Convoys of dozens or hundreds of motorcyclists rev their engines to rent the air with the heavy grunts. Streets are bedecked with flags and murals indicating affiliation to a particular supporter group. Football is urban, highly partisan and easily susceptible to the break out of heavy violence.

My first game of football in Indonesia was at Stadium Manahan in Solo, Central Java. The game was between Persis Solo and PSCS Ciamis. The game was held at 3 pm on a Thursday afternoon. I had arranged my attendance at the game with Ramdhon – a lecturer at one of the universities in Solo and with a strong interest in the city's football history. Ramdhon has positioned himself as a researcher-football activist who is guiding several bachelor-level students through their preliminary researches into Solo's footballing culture and history. Ramdhon and a couple of students were actively forging a new supporter group – known as B7 – which both adopted aspects of ultra-fandom, as well as modifying it to suit their context. One of their primary innovations was the allocation of a reserved section for female Pasoepati fans. At the game I attended, there were between 5 and 7 female students (wearing veils), dressed modestly in red, who somewhat nervously and cautiously joined in the chanting and choreographies.

Ramdhon introduced me to the four main sections of Manahan Stadium: the west side was for the VIPs, the East Side (where we were) was for B7, the new supporter group with a somewhat ultra style and then the two more established supporter groups were at each end. One pocket was appropriated by the surly casuals, who stood and stared and spoke in English throughout the game; the diagonally opposite pocket was reserved for the dozen or so Ciamis fans, who were most likely, students from Ciamis who were studying in Solo or nearby. Given the difficulty of getting to the game from Yogya, where I was living, at the limited time I had to watch games, I had to make the most of attending the game – both as a researcher and as someone who wanted to be able to experience and to enjoy watching football being played. I wanted to be able to participate as a crowd member, to enjoy footballing moments, rather than to be a disinterested and cool researcher, detached from emotions. I decided I would take photographs and record footage for the first half, and then, for the second, I would adopt the role of a fan, albeit a very new fan of Pasoepati.

Ramdhon and I made it to our standing position in B7, moments before the teams came onto the field. As I was setting up my camera, I was hit by a huge wall of sound as the crowd burst into the singing of their anthem, as the teams lined up, facing the Western (VIP) stand (tribune, in Indonesian). The orchestration of this chanting, its synchronization, and of course, its volume was something I had never experienced before. Moreover, I was burdened with the common prejudices of the behaviour of fans at football games: these were young, reckless men and teenagers who were utter laws-unto-themselves. A thundering rendition of a soulful rock ballad was not expected – complete with cheesy gestures and swaying. This was a moment to question the 'machoness', and hyper-masculine nature of ultra fandom; more would become apparent throughout the game and in other interactions with hardcore fans of local football teams. The fans were more than willing to participate in an orderly, conducted manner. Those who didn't respect the ceremonial aspect of the club's anthem (hymn) were admonished by their peers. The conclusion of the song was followed by the hurling of white rolls of paper onto the athletics track that ran around the perimeter of the football field.

The singing of the Persis Solo anthem was seemingly the only moment when the crowd was united as one – except for the moments when goals were scored by Persis Solo. Throughout the rest of the game, the different sections of the tribunes were sang and chanted to the directions of their respective conductors, known as *dirigen*. The dirigen for the B7 section of the Eastern tribune is Andre Jaran. A charismatic, tattooed and muscular man probably in his early 30s. Andre was initially one of the conductors at the north end of the stadium, but, with the effort to make the whole stadium noisy and participative, he was assigned to the Eastern Tribune to enliven it. Throughout the duration of the game, he has his back to the action, except for brief moments to check whether a goal has been scored (or about to be scored) or to check the behaviour of the referee or opposition players. He is armed with a megaphone, aided by an accomplice, but, what serves him most strongly is his domineering personality, his unrelenting energy. Andre implores, admonishes and encourages the crowd before him – probably some 5000 young men – and the few women. He orders the crowd to move closer together and at times singles out individuals who are not paying attention. Andre accepts no copping out: if one comes to a Persis Solo game, one must be active.

I spent the first half photographing the crowd around me. No one paid any attention to me, despite me taking photographs directly of people. I was probably one of very few foreigners (perhaps the only) in stadium: it is common for foreigners to be greeted on streets of Indonesian cities with 'hello Mister', but, on this afternoon, at the game, I was (very happily) anonymous. The young men in the crowd were firmly focused on two far more important matters than a camera-wielding foreigner: the game itself and the orders and instructions coming from Andre. By the end of the first half the score was 1:2 in favour of Ciamis. This was ominous. Persis Solo clearly needed the win to ensure that they would be in the play-offs to be promoted to the Indonesia Super League. But through a combination of dubiously awarded penalties to the home team, dubiously disallowed penalties to the away team, and a few curious given and not-given off-side decisions, Persis Solo were able to emerge the comfortable victors, 5:2.

There is no electronic scoreboard available for replays to clarify the correctness or otherwise of decisions from the referees, but to say the least, Persis Solo were getting the rub of the green. With the worsening violence of the Ciamis players being meted out on the referee, who was no doubt complicit in Persis' victory, the crowd became increasingly angry and disorganized in their yelling and abuse. There were a few tense moments when I thought I might absent myself from the crowd and take the early train back to Yogya. But the game ended soon enough, despite the anger of Ciamis, the Persis fans cheered their team and the anthem was once again played, this time accompanied by flares with their thick smoke. In the short time of 90 min I felt that I had made the transition from neutral researcher–observer to partisan fan on the brink of being unable to contain my anger at the injustices being meted out to *my* team – even though they were clearly being advantaged by refereeing decisions. Ramdhon dropped me back at the train station and warned me several times not to wear the Persis Solo t-shirt he had given me in Yogya, such was the rivalry with the Brajamusti.

Pasoepati: structured fandom and the split between casuals and ultras

The story of the emergence of ultras in the central Javanese city of Solo indicates the instability of Indonesia's footballing infrastructure, and the degree to which the management of football clubs are linked to party political interests. Ultras invest heavily in their sense of regional identity and sense of difference, while at the same time, adopting practices of fandom clearly derived from Europe – in particularly, Italy and the UK. Pasoepati, a supporter group of some 20,000 (overwhelmingly male) youth, are distinct from the Brajamusti of PSIM and the Bonek of Persebaya, in that their allegience has not always been to Persis Solo football club. Pasoepati refer to their fostering of Persis Solo as a point of pride, while their enemies – such as Brajamusti – refer to the changing of teams to indicate that Pasoepati are 'glory hunters' and lack any real and substantial value of loyalty.

The emergence of ultras in Indonesia emerged after the fall of the Suharto-led government in 1998. Football in Solo during the 1990s had strong links to the Suharto family, with the club Arseto Solo being owned by Suharto's oldest son – Sigit Haryojunanto. In the post-reformation era (i.e. after 1998), Pelita Bakrie, a club owned by the Bakrie family, moved its home base from the soon-to-be demolished Lebak Bulus stadium in southern

Jakarta, to the Manahan Stadium in Solo. Aburizal Bakrie, is the current chairman of the political party, Golkar which was and continues to be aligned with New Order interests. Over 15 years, 'Pelita Bakrie' changed its name eight times and is currently based in Bandung and is known as Pelita Bandung Raya.

Arseto Solo, founded in 1978, was one of the founding clubs of the professional league, known as Galatama, and used the Sriwedari Stadium in Solo as its home base. This was a stadium was built between 1932 and 1933 and was used for the national sporting meeting in 1948. These days, it primarily functions for lower level football competitions, athletics competitions and football training. The B7 ultras of Pasoepati held their initial rehearsals at this stadium (Fuller 2015a, 2015b). Arseto Solo disbanded, however, at end of the New Order era, during the financial crisis. The city of Solo also was a site of heavy rioting and looting against Chinese–Indonesian properties and businesses as well as those with apparent links to the Suharto family. Nonetheless, many Solo-based football supporters remember Arseto Solo fondly and remember the Galatama era (i.e. the first professional league) as being relatively stable and productive.

Pasoepati was founded by Mayor Haristanto – the owner of an advertising agency in Solo. The founders of Pasoepati agreed that it would be a structured supporters group with a clear budget. The Pasoepati supporters, however, saw their team transferred to the town of Cilegon, however, they quickly adopted the new team, Persijatim Solo FC, which had moved to Solo from East Jakarta. This club only stayed in Solo for two seasons (2002–2003, 2003–2004), before moving to Palembang, after having been sold to a new investor. The club then adopted the name of Sriwijaya FC, where it remains as a team in the top division of Indonesian football. After being promoted to the second division (Divisi Utama), the Pasoepati fans adopted Persis Solo as their team. Their adoption of this team strengthened their links with the city's identity as Persis Solo is the city's oldest club, having been founded in 1923. The club's heritage and its age, being a vital factor in creating a sense of a glorious past – so central to the formation of club and supporter identity. Although Persis Solo had a small group of supporters prior to the arrival of Pasoepati, known as *Alap-Alap Sambernyawa*, this group was essentially taken over by Pasoepati who were more organized and systematic in their fandom (Laily 2016).

The rise of Solo-based ultras and their incorporation into Pasoepati

The post-New Order era saw a great opening up of political and cultural freedoms. There were many new developments in the fields of literature and film and the visual arts. Censorship and ideological conformism had been the dominant mood of the 30-year New Order era and its decline saw an often euphoric embracing of youth subcultures, often mashed together in curious ways. The 2000s saw a great rise in punk and hip hop culture and new artistic modes of production. The 2000s also saw an increasing awareness of the importance of 'history' and archives, just as much of Indonesia's recent history was being deliberately forgotten. Pasoepati fans – and particularly those in the B7 group – have been active in researching the football history of Solo: football, for these fans, becomes not only a means for accessing, interacting with and borrowing from global subcultures, but is also a means into the history of one's own city as a part of strengthening the sense of one's local identity.

Although the rise of ultras in Indonesia is specifically a post-New Order phenomenon, the live-broadcasting of Italian Serie A in the 1990s laid the foundations for an introduction into ultra fan culture. The main reference point being the supporters of AC Milan and Juventus – incidentally – both clubs continue to have strong support in Indonesia; with Juventus having an official Indonesian language website. The increasingly ease of access to the internet in the 2000s and the popularity of You Tube gave football fans opportunities to learn the rituals, styles and performances of ultras from Italy and elsewhere. Learning the art of ultra support was mediated, rather than from fans witnessing directly the presence of foreign ultras. Nonetheless, through the travelling of fans for domestic games is an opportunity for learning and imitating styles. The Pasoepati ultras were among the first ultras in Indonesia to heavily use the large flags, flares (and smoke bombs) and choreographies so ubiquitous in global football culture.

The first Solo-based ultras, positioned themselves behind the southern goals at Manahan Stadium; this was a replication of ultra practice elsewhere. This group named themselves as the Ultras 1923, referencing the year of Persis Solo's birth, and simultaneously indicating the independence from the Pasoepati supporter group. Their imagery relying heavily on the incorporation of the *totenkopf* (borrowed from Nazi symoblism), an appropriation of the Fred Perry-logo, and the primary use of red, white and black. Their initial use of flares and smoke bombs were protested against by other fans, but, after the increasing coverage of their displays on the Pasoepati.Net website, the Ultras 1923 gained credibility and more members. The difficulty in accessing flares and smoke bombs led to the Ultras 1923 to start making their own flares or smoke bombs; often resulting in rather toxic products. The ability to make such essential equipment for ultra fandom is a means for establishing one's credibility within the group, which relies very much upon the amateur skills of its members who create artefacts in the name of supporting their team. There is a strong-quality of 'home-made', 'collaboration', 'working-together' within the ultras: learning much from YouTube. Although this is a strongly macho culture, the male-youth work conscientiously in the otherwise female-gendered activities of craftsmanship – such as sewing (flags), designing, dancing (choreography) and singing (chanting).

The success of the Ultras 1923 led to tension with the Central Leadership Committee of Pasoepati. The tension was, in part caused by the Ultras 1923's decision to travel to away games by themselves as well as their reluctance to use the name 'Pasoepati' as part of their designation. They relented however and became a sub-section of the Pasoepati Pasar Kliwon Kota Solo. Nonetheless, the Ultras 1923, or, officially the Pasoepati Ultras 1923, were more strident in the promotion of the club, Persis Solo, rather than the supporter group, Pasoepati. The ultras style of the Ultras 1923, was subsequently taken up by the Pasoepati supporters in the northern terrace, as well as those in the B7, eastern tribune.

The Brajamusti of Yogyakarta: Loyalis Mataram

The Brajamusti supporter group emerged in the early 2000s after the disbanding of an earlier incarnation, the PTLM. The Brajamusti was founded as a means to modernising PSIM's supporter base and providing a structured organization in order to more professionally support the football club. Although PSIM is not – and has never been particularly successful – the Club is well-loved within the city of Yogyakarta and its stadium is in (relatively) central Yogyakarta. The Club's identity is inextricably linked with the city of Yogyakarta; the

Club's emblem, that of the Tugu, is borrowed from one of the city's landmarks. The Sultan of Yogyakarta, however, has not always taken a favourable position to the club. During the periods of relative success in the early 1990s, the Sultan was closely linked to the Club's management. Over the last decade, however, the Sultan has increasingly distanced himself from PSIM. Brajamusti members claim that this is because there are three teams from the province of Yogyakarta in the Divisi Utama and that the Sultan doesn't want to offend any particular fans. Others have said that it is because the fans of PSIM (primarily the Brajamusti and The Maident supporter groups) have a reputation for causing trouble.

Rivalries are a key aspect of supporter groups and ultras in particular. Rivalries not only maintain antagonisms which perpetuate the sense of a distinctive group, but are used to shape alliances with other groups of ultras. The Brajamusti supporter group is characterized by two main rivalries; first, the internal rivalry with The Maident, and secondly, the external rivalry with Pasoepati – the supporter group to be discussed in the next section. Although relations between Brajamusti and The Maident have been officially smoothed over, tensions remain between the broad masses of supporters. The split between Brajamusti and The Maident is evident in the occupation of the grandstands at Mandala Krida Stadium as well the cultural geography of the city of Yogyakarta. The streets of Yogyakarta are marked with flags indicating affiliation with one of the supporter groups. The blue and white flags indicate Brajamusti, while the black and blue (and occasionally other colours) indicate affiliation to The Maident. The various *laskars* (smaller sub-groups) of Brajamusti or The Maident adorn the flags or murals. As such, the supporter groups remain active throughout the year, regardless of whether or not there is any football taking place.

The split between the Brajamusti and The Maident emerged in the wake of the 2004 election for the president of Brajamusti. During the tense ballot, which saw many police deployed to prevent any serious violence from breaking out, Eko Satrio Pringgodani emerged victorious after making several emotive speeches and accepting his supporters requests to remain as a candidate. The result was tight, and the losing candidate refused to accept the legitimacy of the outcome. As a result, he and several close confidantes soon formed a new group – The Maident, an abbreviation for Mataram Independent. The Maident and Brajamusti subsequently became engaged in an intense and violent rivalry. Members of both groups would abuse each other and throw rocks at each other while games were taking place inside Mandala Krida. This resulted in games being stopped and security forces being deployed to, apparently, contain the fighting. But, the most intense fighting took place on the streets of Yogyakarta; resulting not only in street battles and sweeping, but, also the death of a member of The Maident, seventeen year old Nurul Huda. It is his unsolved killing, that has remained as one of the main sources of the continual tensions between the two groups.

External rivalries

Brajamusti and soccer supporters are generally considered 'violent', 'troublemakers' and disturbers of civil, public order. Violence, *tawuran* (street battles) (Simone 2014) amongst soccer supporters has become so normalized, that it is rarely covered in the local and national press. This is not simply a crisis affecting semi-professional teams: supporters attending high-school futsal competitions are also required to be chaperoned by a police convoy.[1] Brajamusti reject the condemnation that they are simply a group of supporters who like to fight with other supporters – particularly Pasoepati but also those from Malang and its team, Arema. Yet, upon being asked 'what were the great games that you remember watching, being a part of' one respondent Adnan D. Kusuma mentioned only games which involved violent street battles and riots at the stadium. He said, 'it is these moments that make me love PSIM even more. I can't stop being involved with PSIM because of these events'. This respondent is required as relatively neutral and on the periphery of Brajamusti, yet, he is well-respected amongst Brajamusti and is close with its affiliates.

Three days after the Brajamusti futsal competition, buses and cars transporting Pasoepati to Ciamis, West Java were attacked in Yogyakarta and at the city's eastern and western periphery. Ari and Unyil recounted the night of stone-throwing with relish. They stated that it was unorganized, spontaneous and done out of their love for PSIM. They knew of Pasoepati's trajectory through following their statements sent out through Twitter. Pasoepati, apparently, sent tweets saying that they were in Yogyakarta. For these two members of Brajamusti, such statements were too provocative and broke the ethics of supporter conduct. Buses and cars with Solo number plates (indicated by the letters AD) were attacked from Sleman in the north and inner east to Kulon Progo in the west. Ari and Unyil recounted gleefully, humorously, that Brajamusti had come out of their houses in the middle of the night to join in the stone throwing without *any co-ordination*. They stated that they were already 'ready to great Pasoepati' as they arrived in Yogyakarta. Pasoepati's tweeting of their journey was a step too far for the Brajamusti to tolerate. Ari and Unyil, instead, gave the counter example of their methods of travelling through Solo on their 'awaydays'. That is, to take a general bus, rather than a hired bus, or to use fake number plates to disguise where the vehicle is travelling from.

Ramdhon of *Universitas Sebelas Maret* (11th March University, Solo) argued that Pasoepati's brazen movement through Yogyakarta was not a sign of the supporter group's arrogance, but, instead a sign of their unity. He stated that Brajamusti and PSIM fans more generally are not brave enough to travel through Solo as they are a fragmented supporter group. This sense of fragmentation is also emphasized by Fajar Junaedi who argues that PSIM fans' loyalty is split between political faction, laskar and affiliation (Brajamusti or The Maident). Ari and Unyil, however, argue that they are able to travel through Solo undetected because of their superior methods at remaining incognito. Brajamusti have a severe trauma of being attacked in Solo in 2003. This incident became known as Kandang Menjangan. after the Brajamusti were locked up in one of Solo's army barracks as a means to protect them and to prevent further rioting. Brajamusti condemn the degree of organization of the violence, rather than the violence itself. They claim that the Solo branch of *Radio Republik Indonesia* was announcing their arrival into Solo and thus residents were ready to pelt them with stones as they made their way into town. This indicates that although soccer violence can be articulated and directed at specific supporter groups, it can also easily spread to residents who may have little direct involvement with soccer itself.

Tensions within football fandom in Yogyakarta (the city and the province) have intensified over the past decade with the emergence of the northern-Yogyakarta team, PSS Sleman. The emergence of the team as a powerful club within the Divisi Utama (second division) occurred in the wake of the reformasi movement and the implementation of decentralization policies. Suddenly, the resource-rich kabupaten of Sleman was able to use its income for itself, without the money being syphoned off to the central government of the province of Yogyakarta. Moreover, PSS Sleman had a new stadium built for it, by the bupati (regional head) of Sleman,. Despite the bupati being eventually coming under suspicion for corruption (hardly uncommon), the PSS Sleman supporter groups of Slemania and BCS (Brigade Curva Sud) have been able to enjoy a stadium designed as a mini-San Siro. The BCS and Slemania fans quickly established themselves as some of the most co-ordinated, active and fashionable ultras in Indonesian football. Their choreographies and chanting achieving huge numbers of views on You Tube and most games being as good-as-sold out. Their rise, however, was less appreciated by PSIM supporters, both Brajamusti and The Maident, who not only saw their own fans switch alliances, but, also faced the overwhelming support for PSS Sleman in their own stadium.

The supporter base of PSIM has also come under threat from the south with the relative success of Persiba Bantul. Despite being unsuccessful during the amateur era, Persiba became champions of the Divisi Utama (Second Division) in 2009, leading to their participation in the ISL. They would be relegated back to the Divisi Utama at the end of the 2014 season, after finishing last. The presence of these two younger and more recently successful teams intensified fan-rivalry at local derbies and clearly threatened PSIM's status as the primary football club in Yogyakarta. The Sultan of Yogyakarta, Hamengkubuwono X, also gave the reason for the presence of rival clubs in the same league as the reason for his withdrawal of support (financial and symbolic) for PSIM.

A journey through the streets of Yogyakarta quickly reveals the scope and range of the three teams supporter groups. The main streets of the city, and many of the smaller back-streets, are decorated with football murals or simple graffitied statements of supporter-group affiliation. Yogyakarta's inner south, for example, is home to numerous laskars (sub-groups within a larger supporter group) from Brajamusti. The different laskars, generally consisting of a minimum of 50 male youth, set up a base at a street-side road-stall or relatively open public green space, such as Lapangan Minggiran football field. The murals are a means not only to claim space and thus territory for the larger supporter group (it seems that Brajamusti are far more active than The Maident in the production of murals), but, also for establishing their own reputation amongst the different laskars. The murals are often complemented by the placement of massive flags which hangover the roads. These flags, usually a combination of blue and white (for Brajamusti) and blue, black and white (for The Maident) also feature writing indicating their affiliation. The flags indicate which supporter group controls the informal economy, covering costs such as motor-cycle and car-parking fees, as well as rent that is paid for use of footpath or road-side space. Members of laskars patrol these streets, collecting funds which are then given to the leaders of the relevant supporter group.

Bonek and the rise of Green Nord 27

> GreenNord27 belongs to all of us. It doesn't belong to a particular community. No one [group] dominates and no one has a monopoly on it. No one feels the most heroic; no one takes credit for having given the most service or having the rights to it. Everyone, One Heart, One Attitude and One Action. Green Nord 27 is a collective, owned by us all, together. Conviction makes as stronger. One Heart, One Attitude, One Action. Against Politics in Football!!

It is a damp Thursday night and I am driven on the back of a motorbike along slippery and busy roads to Airlangga University, where I meet up with Arif, a researcher and football activist. He makes some phone calls, speaking in Javanese (with an East Javanese dialect and strong accent) and soon five of his mates have arrived. He orders a tarpaulin from one of the nearby street-stall operators and we sit down and order our drinks of coffees (with condensed milk) or varieties of herb drinks. Arif and his mates withdraw their packs of thick clove cigarettes – the classic macho brands of Dji Sam Soe, Gudang Garam and Djarum – one of the former main sponsors of the Indonesian domestic football league. These are simple and egalitarian circumstances: all are welcome here – with only one condition, that one is a supporter or sympathiser with the cause of the Bonek 1927. This gathering, however, is one of the meeting places for the sub-group of Bonek, known as the Green Nord 27. And out of deference to one of its most fervent activists, the meeting place is near his university, where he is finishing his Bachelor's thesis on women's football in Indonesia. His fellow-Green Nord 27 mates tease him about the length of time that it is taking him. Arif, it emerges, devotes most of his time to the cause of Persebaya 1927, Bonek 1927 and his own Green Nord 27.

Back in the town of Yogyakarta, I meet with another Bonek 1927/Persebaya 1927 activist, Cak Tulus. After introducing himself he says, 'I am a ronin. Do you know what a ronin is? It is a samurai without a master. I am a ronin, because I am a supporter [ultra, football activist] without a team.' His full-name is never given and he is only ever addressed as 'Cak Tulus'. 'Tulus' could be his name or his nick-name (meaning 'sincere'), either way, the Cak (an honorific appellation meaning 'brother') is never separated from his name. Cak Tulus carries with him a backpack seemingly always filled with Bonek 1927 t-shirts, while also seemingly always wearing one variety of Bonek 1927 t-shirt or another under a heavy jacket. His hat, pulled down low over his forehead is also adorned with Bonek and Persebaya pins. Cak Tulus, a long-time Persebaya fan and Bonek activist, spends his time going back and forth between Yogyakarta and Surabaya as well as visiting other cities where the 'Bonek diaspora' are active. Cak Tulus has made a name for himself within the Bonek fraternity not only as having astute entrepreneurial acumen, but also as a negotiator and mediator between conflicting groups of ultras. His role is particularly important with the absence of a Persebaya 1927 team in either the ISL (first division) or Divisi Utama. Cak Tulus, and other Bonek, particularly those based outside of the city of Surabaya are charged with galvanising support for a broad movement against the PSSI – Football Federation of Indonesia. This means attempts to forge alliances with previously bitter rivals such as the ultras from Malang (Arema), Solo (Pasoepati) and Jakarta (Jakmania).

The Bonek of Surabaya, i.e. supporters of Persebaya, are considered to be the oldest and largest supporter group in Indonesia, having emerged in the 1980s with the support of Dahlan Iskan, owner of the Jawa Pos newspaper group (Junaedi 2012). The Bonek earned a reputation as lawless (male) youth who would travel by train from Surabaya to wherever their team played, without taking any money with them. They would ride on the roofs of trains, or jump on the backs of trucks, hitching from one town to the next. For food, they would ransack the stalls at train stations or bus stops. The term 'Bonek' was coined to describe their brazen, lawless, courage and their undying support for their team. After a conflict between Persebaya and PSSI, Persebaya formed a break-away league, Liga Primer Indonesia in 2011. After the unification of the two leagues in 2013, the original Persebaya was replaced with Persebaya Surabaya, which was a team that had been moved from East Kalimantan. The majority of Bonek fans rejected this team, even though it had been filled with stars and would prove successful. In order to differentiate themselves from the Bonek who followed this team, they added the affix 1927 to their designation of Bonek.

The Bonek 1927, of which Green Nord forms a significant sub-group, has transformed into a football-protest movement which seeks to confront the various political and footballing hierarchies which continue to corrupt and compromise the domestic league (and thus the national team, too) and their club in particular. Their protests carried out in the streets of Surabaya do not engender much public sympathy; for the protests only entrench their image as troublemakers. The Bonek 1927 have a multitude of grievances: against the PSSI, against the Minister of Sport (Imam Nahrawi), against the Persebaya Surabaya (regarded as the Persebaya palsu or Persebaya gadungan), against the Bonek Persikubar (derogatory name given to those supporters who support Persebaya Surabaya) and against the managers of any league or competition that permits the participation of Persebaya Surabaya. The imagery and slogans adopted by the Bonek 1927 and Green Noord clearly invoke some of the mainstays of ultra fandom. The fashion artefacts such as hooded jumpers, scarves pulled up over faces (leaving nothing visible except for the eyes), an appropriation of the Fred Perry logo, the use of a pair of hammers and the ubiquitous imagery of silhouettes of capos and megaphones. The slogans include 'Love Persebaya Hate Management' and All Cops Are Bastards (often abbreviated to ACAB). Green Nord and Bonek 1927 use the hashtags of 'Surabaya Melawan' (Surabaya resists), 'wani' and 'respect' in their twitter campaigns.

The Bonek 1927 persist as a barometer of football fandom in Indonesia. Being a bonek has shifted from being loosely affiliated with the team of Persebaya and the city of Surabaya to being an indication of one's attitude of contempt for the status quo of Indonesian football. Bonek 1927 and their activists condemn the PSSI and the corruption of football management by politicians who seek to use football as a means for gaining (illegitimate) wealth and access to a mass of potential supporters. The last fifteen years has seen the Bonek (and subsequently the Bonek 1927) supporter group increasingly identify with practices of global ultra fandom. Bonek 1927 remains the heart and soul of Indonesian football; it is not possible for Indonesian football to progress without the reconciliation of Bonek 1927 with a completely reformed PSSI. Until that happens, the protests will only grow and spread further amongst ultra groups throughout Indonesia.

Conclusion

Ultra-fandom exhibits similarities and differences across cultures. Indonesia's football culture, is not separate from the processes of globalized fandom. Yet, the interests and practices of ultras in Indonesian cities are closely related to local political interests. The cases of Pasoepati, Brajamusti and the Bonek follow on from Doidge's statement that 'the ultras style of support is translated in various ways depending on the specific pre-existing local and national cultures' (Doidge and Lieser 2013). This article has aimed to provide a starting point for research on a particular kind of fan of football in Indonesia. While ultras attract much attention through their well-rehearsed and choreographed performances, are not the only types of fan: many fans, too, resist the highly exclusive process of becoming and being accepted as a true and real fan. In the Indonesian context, being an 'ultra' could arguably be extended to those fans who are diehard, loyal and serious fans of EPL or other European league teams. One might not need to be present at the game to be an ultra. This kind of globalized fandom also has much scope for exploration within this context.

The three groups of ultras studied in this article share similarities while also being indicative of different trends in football culture in Indonesia. Pasoepati is a relatively united supporter group that has supported different Solo-based teams in the post-1998 era. Their flexibility in supporting different teams is something that rankles with other fans, while they take claim for fostering the rise of Persis Solo. The potential divisions within Pasoepati, have until now, been reconciled by such means as the Ultras 1923 adopting 'Pasoepati' as a prefix for their title. The highly organized style of Pasoepati, however, imposes a rigidity that many of their fans – particularly the 'casuals' and the 'hooligans' seek to oppose. PSIM's supporter groups of the Brajamusti and The Maident split along party-political lines. Brajamusti is aligned with the conservative Islamic party, PPP (United Development Party), while The Maident is aligned with the nationalist and secular, PDI-P (Democratic Party of Struggle). The Bonek of Surabaya are the most legendary supporter group, yet they too find themselves afflicted by ongoing division. The divisions within the Bonek supporter mass were brought about by the instability of Indonesia's football infrastructure and the deep involvement of corrupt politicians in the administration of the domestic football leagues. The Bonek 1927, ultras without a team, epitomize global ultra football fandom and its credo of being 'against modern football'.

Note

1. Yogyakarta, long known as being a student city, is also known for its tawuran (street battles) between high school students. The two main groups being Joxzin in the south and Q-zruh a.k.a QZR in the north. Divisions are also based along religious lines.

Disclosure statement

No potential conflict of interest was reported by the authors.

References

Allegri, Peter. 2010. *African Soccerscapes*. Athens, OH: Ohio University Press. doi:10.1353/book.598.

Colombijn, Freek. 2000. "The Politics of Indonesian Football." *Archipel* 59: 171–200. doi:10.3406/arch.2000.3557.

Doidge, Mark, and Martin Lieser. 2013. "The Globalisation of Ultras Culture: An International Comparison of Japanese and Italian Fan-Groups." Global Research Project on Fan Communities and Fandom Conference, Harris Manchester College, University of Oxford, March 22–23.

Dorsey, James M., and Leonard Sebastian. 2013. "The Politics of Indonesian and Turkish Soccer: A Comparative Analysis." *Soccer and Society* 14 (5): 614–635. doi:10.1080/14660970.2013.792482.

Flicker, Tim. 2013. "Framing, Corruption and Nationalism in Indonesian Soccer: A Case Study of Media Reporting". Bachelor of Arts Honors thesis. Monash University.

Fuller, Andy. 2014a. *Playing Cities, Making Sport*. Yogyakarta: Tan Kinira Press.

Fuller, Andy. 2014b. *The Struggle for Soccer in Indonesia: Fandom, Archives and Urban Identity*. Yogyakarta: Tan Kinira Press.

Fuller, Andy. 2015a. "Approaching Football in Indonesia." *Soccer and Society* 16 (1): 140–148. doi:10.1080/14660970.2014.954387.

Fuller, Andy. 2015b. "Sriwedari Stadium." *Reading Sideways*. March 6. http://readingsideways.net/sriwedari-stadium/. doi:10.1080/14660970.2014.954387.

Junaedi, Fajar. 2012. *Bonek: Komunitas Suporter Pertama dan Terbesar di Indonesia*. Yogyakarta: Buku Litera.

Junaedi, Fajar. 2014. "Rusuh Suporter Sepakbola vs. Polisi dalam Bingkai Berita: Mempersoalkan Akurasi dan Verifikasi Berita."[Football Supporters Riots against the Police in Media Framing: Questioning Accuracy and News Verification] Paper presented at Airlangga University, Surabaya, December 6.

Kuper, Simon. 2011. *Ajax, the Dutch, the War*. London: Orion.

Laily, Devi Fitroh. 2016. *Kota, Klub dan Pasoepati* [The City, Club and Pasoepati]. Yogyakarta: Buku Litera.

McGinnis, Joe. 1999. *The Miracle of Castel di Sangro*. New York: Little Brown and Company.

Simone, Abdoul Maliq. 2014. *Jakarta: Drawing the City Near*. Minneapolis, MN: University of Minnesota Press. doi:10.5749/minnesota/9780816693351.001.0001.

Spaaij, Ramon. 2007. "Football Hooliganism in the Netherlands: Patterns of Continuity and Change." *Soccer and Society* 8 (2–3): 316–334. doi:10.1080/14660970701224566.

Spaaij, Ramon, and Carles Vinas. 2006. "Passion, Politics and Violence: A Socio-historical Analysis of Spanish Ultras." *Soccer and Society* 6 (1): 79–96. doi:10.1080/1466097052000337034.

Wilson, Jonathan. 2006. *Football Behind the Curtain*. London: Orion.

Wilson, Jonathan. 2014. *Angels with Dirty Faces: The Footballing History of Argentina*. London: Orion.

Wirawan, Oryza. 2015. *Imagined Persebaya: Persebaya, Bonek dan Sepak Bola Indonesia* [Imagined Persebaya: Persebaya, the Bonek and Football in Indonesia]. Yogyakarta: Buku Litera.

'Supporters, not consumers.' Grassroots supporters' culture and sports entertainment in the US

Markus Gerke

ABSTRACT
Based on ethnographic research with supporters' groups in the US, this article explores how Ultra and other global models of fandom are being appropriated by soccer fans in the US and Canada. I argue that these fans enact more than stylistic expressions of fandom but instead contest the boundaries of locally accepted models fandom. Most notably, organized soccer supporters in the US reject the notion of being simply consumers of sports entertainment and see themselves instead as stakeholders in the teams they follow and as de facto constituents that the clubs need to be accountable to. At the same time, the global and local organizational structures and histories of professional soccer confront these fans with specific restrictions in how they are able to articulate their interest as fans.

Introduction

The US and Canada are typically not thought of as possessing any meaningful soccer fan cultures. Yet, over the past years a soccer supporters' culture of groups following virtually all professional men's teams – as well as some women's and semi-professional men's teams – has emerged. These supporters' groups draw on European Ultras as well as South American Barra Bravas, Torcidas and Porras in their performances and conceptions of fandom. Beyond mere stylistic mimicry, however, these supporters' groups challenge traditional local modes of fandom and the relationship between fans and professional sports teams as they presently exist (not only) in North American professional sports. Rather than being content with being consumers of a sports entertainment product, these supporters see themselves as stakeholders in the clubs they support and demand accountability from them. Yet, the history of professional soccer leagues going out of business as well as the current organizational structures of soccer in the US and Canada also give rise to a sentiment among (often the same) supporters that embraces the very market-logic European Ultras are typically thought to reject. In other words, the hyper-commercialized and globalized 'modern football' is both empowering and disempowering for these supporters.

Scholars of soccer fandom around the globe have pointed to parallel processes. For instance, Sandvoss (2003) focuses precisely on the relationship between consumption and fandom, arguing that fandom consists of a series of consumptive acts through which taste – and thereby difference – can be communicated. Moreover, increasingly soccer clubs lack a clear link to particular social classes or other demographic markers, become global in nature and try to foster an image that allows them to connect with audiences across the world. Nevertheless, they remain objects onto which fans project their own meanings, values and ideological commitments, with fans thus engaging in a type of 'DIY citizenship'.

In this article, based on ethnographic research with soccer supporters' groups in the New York City area and an analysis of online media of the wider North American supporters' subculture,[1] I argue that organized supporters appropriate and adapt more than a stylistic way of expressing fandom. Beyond the adaptation of styles to form collective identities and communities, appropriating notions of Ultra fandom also empowers these supporters to engage in collective action and to lobby for their interests as fans.

Background: the Ultras

Research on the politics of Ultra fandom has investigated the subculture in many different locales across the world – from Italy (Doidge 2015; Testa and Armstrong 2010) and Spain (Llopis-Goig 2015; Spaaij and Viñas 2013) to Germany (Gabler 2011) and Turkey (Battini 2012; Batuman 2012; McManus 2013; Nuhrat 2013) and from Mexico (Magazine 2007) to Egypt (El-Zatmah 2012; Woltering 2013) and Israel (Porat 2012). Apart from a handful of studies (Brown 2007; Wagner 2012), the US and Canada have, maybe unsurprisingly, not been taken seriously as spaces where Ultra-like fan subcultures exist. Yet, supporters' groups in the US make for an interesting case study of how Ultra is translated, precisely because of the (re-)emergence of professional soccer as a spectator sport relatively recently and because of the ways in which the professional game is organized there.

Like other youth and subcultures, Ultras are notoriously hard to define in precise terms, both for scholars of the phenomenon and even among those involved in the subculture themselves (Gabler 2011). Most broadly, the term Ultra refers to groups of soccer fans that are (and see themselves as) the most passionate and loyal supporters of a soccer club, and who employ a certain style of support in the stadium. Beyond, Ultras have shared in a common philosophy or ethos about relationships between supporters and clubs as well as the state of contemporary professional soccer in general.

Ultra subculture can be traced to 1970s Italy and was initially connected to the political youth movements of its time, which accounts for the style and symbols employed by Ultras until today (Doidge 2013). Ultras are known for their constant singing during the game, and for the display of banners, flags and visual choreographies in the supporters' section of the stadium, all reflecting the imagery and tactics of social movements. Over the past decades, this style of support has spread to other European countries and beyond.[2] In addition to these stylistic expressions of fandom and the passionate devotion to the club, Ultras also share in a specific ethos: they see themselves as stakeholders in the professional club and as the embodied spirit of the club itself, with management, coaches and players merely serving as the current stewards of the club. As such, they demand accountability from the professional clubs and perceive themselves as the voice of fans more broadly. In recent years, the Ultras have become a major source of critique against the hyper-commercialism of professional football, uniting under the slogan of 'Against Modern Football' (Kennedy 2013). However, this shared unease with 'modern football' does not necessarily mean that

Ultras agree in their political and ideological beliefs. Instead, this sentiment lends itself to both right-wing and left-wing interpretations. For instance, whilst many Italian Ultra groups have been dominated by neofascist ideologies since the 1990s – with notable exceptions, such as the supporters of A.S Livorno who define themselves as antifascist and communist – the Ultra subculture in Spain is divided into right-wing, left-wing and supposedly apolitical groups (Doidge 2013; Spaaij and Viñas 2013; Testa and Armstrong 2010). In contrast, some argue that Ultras in Germany tend to hold a left-wing critique of 'modern football', whilst others caution that the slogan also lends itself to neofascist interpretations (Merkel 2012). No matter the political commitments, however, Testa's and Armstrong's (2010) observation that the Italian neofascist Ultras they studied conceived of themselves as a 'rebellious' movement seems to hold true for Ultras more generally regardless of political affiliation. Despite their unrelenting support for the clubs they follow, their performance of fandom is one that stresses an anti-establishment identity and an alternative vision of the sport.

Numerato (2014) argues that the protests against 'modern football' point to an increased reflexivity among soccer supporters who are aware of how neo-liberalism impacts soccer and who see themselves as potential agents for change. Yet, groups and individuals embracing this slogan are not uniform in their outlooks but subscribe to different ideas and values. Thus, the social action undertaken with reference to this slogan does not automatically constitute a transformation of the status quo but may at times result in preserving it, calling into question clear dichotomies of hegemony vs. resistance. This argument mirrors findings by King (1997) in his study of organized Manchester United supporters, although he relies on a more classed-based analysis than Numerato: The 'lads' in King's study, who on the surface seem to express distaste for the neo-liberalization of soccer, ultimately are neither unambiguously resistant nor compliant towards 'modern football' but instead maintain a complicated and contradictory relationship with their soccer club, embracing some aspects of the business of soccer whilst rejecting others. It is processes similar to these that are very much at play in the ways in which soccer supporters in the US relate to their objects of fandom, complicated by the specific history, economic model and cultural place of professional soccer in the US.

'We embrace the best from around the world ... and leave all the other nonsense behind' (ISC 2015). An emerging soccer supporters' culture in North America

The revival of professional soccer in North America since the mid-1990s that was marked by the founding of Major League Soccer (MLS) in 1996 has taken the form of soccer as a sports entertainment product. Unlike in Europe where teams have been based in local communities for decades, where some team are owned by their fans, and where teams outside major metropolitan areas have established themselves in the first divisions through sustained success on the field, current teams in the US and Canada have been businesses from their inception, established in cities that promised to be financially beneficial for the respective team owners or the league. Thus, fans possess no formal input into the operation of the clubs they support. Yet, despite professional soccer re-emerging in the US and Canada in the form of 'modern football' and sports entertainment, supporters have not been content with being relegated to the role of consumers. Instead, global modes of soccer fandom, histories of community involvement in soccer clubs and the Ultras' anti-commercialist rhetoric have served as templates for soccer supporters in North America in formulating their version of fandom.

The influence of European fan culture on US and Canadian organized supporters is obvious even by simply looking at the names supporters' groups have given themselves. For instance, as of September 2015, at least seven out of the 20 MLS teams feature supporters' groups explicitly called 'Ultras', and at least five other groups have chosen the monikers of 'Hooligans', 'Firm', or 'Casual' as their group names.[3] In addition, amongst the more popular names for supporters' groups are 'Boys', 'Army' or 'Brigade', mirroring supporters' group names from Britain and Italy.[4] At the very least, these group names reflect how US and Canadian supporters are aware of and seek to associate themselves with the style and culture of soccer support in other countries. Yet, the mere appropriation of the label of 'Ultra' or 'Casual' does not automatically settle the question of whether these fans should be considered as part of the wider Ultra subculture, as two of my informants themselves are quick to point out:

> People over here who decide to call themselves 'Ultras' or 'Hooligans' or 'Firm' or whatever is usually pretty laughable. They are there to portray this image of tough guy and whatever. (Andres)

Andres, himself member of a supporters' section that takes pride in singing for the duration of the game and that combines continental European, British and South American styles of support, sees the appropriation of the label of 'Ultra' as purely a type of performance and not necessarily as based in the group's actions. Jeff, a member of the same supporters' group, holds a similar view:

> [The terms 'Ultra', 'Casual', 'Firm'] are all just stylistic terms. But in the United States they just get overused as umbrella terms for anything. (Jeff)

Speaking about one specific group that calls themselves 'Casuals', he adds:

> I have seen photos of them, and they all wear team colors, and it's like: This is not what a casual does. The whole point of being a casual is that ... you wear specifically designer street clothes. And they would do that in England, so that when the fight broke out, you could just run away and just hide in the crowd. (Jeff)

For Andres and Jeff – who prefer to self-identify as 'supporter' or 'hardcore fan', respectively – calling themselves 'Ultra', 'Casual', 'Hooligan' or 'Firm' lacks authenticity or, as Jeff puts it: 'They have seen "Green Street" [a 2005 drama movie about soccer hooliganism in England], so they decide they are going to call themselves "casuals"'. According to Jeff, the 'stylistic terms' of 'Ultra', 'Casual' or 'Firm' are being used by fans in the US as markers of soccer-fandom more generally and without any actual knowledge of their meaning.[5] In contrast, both Andres and Jeff are less dismissive of some fans in their supporters' section self-identifying as 'Barra Bravas':

> I think a portion of our section ... are 'Barra Brava'. And that is just their style of support. And that is what they brought with them from South America. And that is what they do here. (Andres)

What makes this term more acceptable in the eyes of Andres then is the fact that it is rooted in cultural tradition and social practice. Most of those in the group that conceive of themselves as 'Barra Brava' are not only first- or second-generation immigrants from countries in which Barra Bravas are part of the fabric of soccer fandom but some have even been members of Barra Brava groups themselves before their migration to the US. Thus, unlike Americans who self-identify as 'Ultras' and 'Casuals' but who do not have first-hand experience within these respective supporters' cultures, the label of 'Barra Brava' is not perceived as an inauthentic appropriation, as long as it is applied only to those who can claim personal or cultural connections to the respective subculture.

The concerns raised by Jeff and Andres are certainly valid and speak to the appropriation of subcultural identities within a foreign locale and to the desire by US and Canadian soccer fans to associate themselves with iconic subcultures of soccer fandom from around the globe. Yet, this is only part of the story. Despite the reluctance of my informants to embrace the identity of Ultra, I argue that Ultra has been appropriated by supporters in the US and Canada as more than a mere label. Although arguably originally a stylistic choice, the model of Ultra – as well as Barra Brava – fandom has heavily influenced the structures and philosophies of supporters of US and Canadian clubs. What may appear as a simple matter of style, has, in fact, challenged the boundaries of notions of the fan-as-consumer in the US context itself.

'We are consumers, too, but ... in a much different way'.[6] Contesting the boundaries of accepted models of fandom

US sports entertainment has generally (and increasingly) treated fans at sporting events exclusively as spectators who are to be entertained; fans are encouraged to consume both the game as well as the merchandise, food and drinks that are readily available at major sports stadiums. Although fans do engage in some spontaneous chants and cheers, these tend to be reserved for specific situations or especially high-profile games. This tendency to treat spectators as passive consumers is reflected in the ubiquitous merchandise as well as the constant audio-visual entertainment during game breaks. Moreover, the opportunities for expression on the side of fans are severely restricted in all stadiums of the major leagues. Fans are typically banned from bringing in flags and flag poles, banners, musical instruments and other items. In 2013, the National Football League (NFL) even introduced a policy of banning all bags and back packs from the stadium; instead, fans are only allowed to bring in clear plastic bags. These measures ultimately serve to discipline fans in a specific practice of fandom: They are supposed to be customers whose only activities inside the stadium are restricted to consuming the amenities, providing a colourful backdrop for the TV broadcast and promoting the sports entertainment product on social media platforms via their smartphones. In other words, stadiums "employ the neoliberal tactic of offering a mirage of publicness" (Guschwan 2014, 897) but are controlled by corporations, making them "anything but open for public dissent" (897).

The experience within a supporters section in US and Canadian soccer stadiums stands in stark contrast to the unilaterally regulated space of American football, basketball, baseball and hockey stadiums in the US and Canada. Today, designated supporters' sections exist in virtually all stadiums in professional soccer and supporters' groups have been able to negotiate and lobby for certain privileges that differ substantively from those afforded to fans in the stadium of the big four spectator sports. Supporters' groups across the US and Canada have adopted expressions of fandom in the stadium that is reminiscent of the support style prevalent in continental Europe – and, to a lesser extent, of that of South America as well as Britain. Fans stand for 90 min, wave flags, chant and sing, use drums, and decorate their sections with self-made banners. Many of the supporters' sections feature a 'capo', a member of the group at the front of the section who faces the crowd rather than the field and who directs the supporters in their chants and songs.

Beyond this resemblance in the style of support, the supporters' groups are also highly organized, which is one decisive factor in enabling them to carve out this space for Ultra-like support in the first place. Supporters' groups are more than ad hoc crowds of fans that only exist during match day. Instead, they communicate via the internet or in person on a regular basis, employ email listservs, social media groups and closed internet message boards to share thoughts and ideas or hold planning meetings during the week. They feature varying membership models, from paid membership schemes – that often come with benefits such as access to discounted trips to away matches or members-only merchandise – to open models of membership by affiliation, and from elected leadership boards to participatory-democratic as well as less transparent decision-making models.

Regardless of the specific group structure, however, the formation of supporters' groups has enabled these fans to engage in collective action vis-à-vis the professional clubs they follow, and has allowed them to negotiate for varying levels of self-determination within the supporters' sections. For instance, supporters of the New York Red Bulls as well as the New York Cosmos have reached agreements with the respective clubs that grant a limited number of supporters early access to the supporters' section, in order to set-up flags and banners prior to each game. In the case of the Red Bulls, supporters are even allowed to use the stadium premises at designated days in order to paint so-called tifos (large-scale banners that are displayed before important matches or to celebrate important achievements). The stadium has also installed pulleys for the displays of these tifos, and Red Bulls fans are granted the right to self-police their supporters' section to a certain degree; security personnel are typically not positioned within the section as long as fans abide by the stadium policies. Whilst the terms negotiated by fans of the Red Bulls may be more extensive than those found at other stadiums, they are by no means an exception, and similar arrangements can be found across the country.

That these supporters' privileges that allow supporters' groups to express themselves in the way they choose are of crucial importance for the self-concept of these supporters and are seen not as a concession but as a de facto right is reflected in the fans' reaction to losing these privileges. For instance, in response to alleged misbehaviour during the 2014 MLS Cup Final, MLS temporarily stripped Los Angeles Galaxy supporters' group Angel City Brigade of all supporters' privileges (including the use of drums, banners, flags, capos, etc.). This sanction was heavily criticized by the Independent Supporters Council (ISC), an umbrella organization of supporters' groups across the US and Canada. An open letter, signed by more than 25 supporters' groups, criticized the collective punishment of the group and discussed various precedents of (less severe) MLS sanctions against supporters to argue that the ban was 'unprecedented, arbitrary, unilateral and unnecessary' (ISC 2015). Additionally, supporters' groups across the US expressed their solidarity with Angel City Brigade on social media as well as on banners in stadiums across the league. Lastly, Angel City Brigade itself drew on additional social movement tactics, calling on fans to boycott merchandise and concessions in their home stadium (ACB 2015). Ultimately, these tactics proved successful, as the sanctions against Angel City Brigade were lifted early during the 2015 season.

This example of fans lobbying for their rights to express themselves according to Ultra- and Barra-Brava-influenced modes of fandoms shows that the soccer supporters' subculture transcends the model of the fan-as-consumer. The ability to engage in forms of collective actions presupposes a consciousness of having collective interests as supporters – of being a community for itself – and the conception of being stakeholders in the game. In this sense, soccer supporters can be classified as forming 'serious leisure' (Stebbins 2005) communities that form a sense of identity around their leisure activities and potentially engage in collective actions to further their interests as participants in such communities, similar to members of other leisure-based groupings (Haenfler 2004; Rosenbaum 2013).

Moreover, the templates for fandom from across the globe enable these supporters to draw on not only the modes of expression but also the tactics utilized by these fan groups (which in turn are inspired by social movement approaches). Thus, appropriating the style of Ultra becomes more than a fashion choice. Instead, simply by enacting this style, these supporters fundamentally change their relationship to the 'product' of sports entertainment and become active participants rather than just passive consumers. That criticism against the league's decision inside the stadiums – in the form of banners and signs – was possible in the first place and that the pushback against sanctions against supporters was ultimately successful also testifies to the fact that these supporters have managed to establish themselves as collective agents with at least some power to impact the professional game.

'You can have a dialogue with the club and not be the club's punk': holding the club accountable between dialogue and protest

The role of supporters as active participants rather than customers not only plays out in supporters standing up for their ability to express their fandom according to styles they prefer but also in the relationship between supporters' groups and the professional clubs they follow. Rather than simply conceiving of themselves as paying customers whose only avenue for expressing disapproval over poor results on the field or unpopular decisions by the front office would be to not spend their money on tickets, supporters utilize the same tactics and practices mentioned earlier to make their voices heard in an attempt to hold the clubs accountable, as an example from MLS's 2015 season illustrates.

The start of the 2015, New York Red Bulls season was marked by controversy and fan protests. During the offseason, the front office had made the decision to fire popular manager Michael Petke, despite his two-year tenure being arguably the most successful time in club history, with a win of the Supporters Shield – the trophy for the best regular season team – in 2013 and a narrow loss in the playoff semifinals in 2014.[7] What made the sacking especially unpopular in the eyes of many fans was the status of Petke as a club legend who had played for the team and who had earned the manager position after serving as an assistant coach. The decision to fire him was seen by some fans as the latest and most blatant example of Red Bulls' front office being out of touch with the perspective of fans. In response, some fans tried to utilize their economic power as individual customers and threatened to cancel their season tickets, whilst other organized supporters took to collective responses to protest against the firing. On the one hand, a small group of supporters united under the moniker of #RedBullOut, calling for the Red Bull company to sell the team to new ownership. They argued, Red Bull had treated the soccer team exclusively as an advertising tool for their soft drink company, treating both the success of the team and the needs of the fans as afterthoughts. Members of this #RedBullOut initiative distributed information at the bars frequented by fans before games and launched a website to disseminate their message. In addition to these outreach campaigns, #RedBullOut managed to raise more than $5,000 to fund a billboard sign in the vicinity of the stadium in order to protest against the firing of Petke.

Whilst the #RedBullOut initiative has been the most explicit and sustained fan reaction to the situation, other supporters voiced their dissatisfaction inside the stadium at the beginning of the season. The oldest and largest New York Red Bulls supporters' group Empire Supporters Club (ESC) opted to express their opposition by unfurling a large banner that read 'Legends deserve better' at the beginning of the first home game of the season. Moreover, instead of engaging in their typical songs, they chanted Petke's name for the first minutes of the game.

The unrest and protest among some factions of New York Red Bull supporters speak to the degree to which these fans have transcended the status of being simply consumers of soccer as sports entertainment. Voicing their displeasure as a group both on the internet and in the stadium, these fans employed collective strategies reminiscent of both Ultra fans in Europe and social movements more broadly, rather than simply reverting to individualistic responses such as refusing to watch the games. Moreover, the fact that these fans engaged in this protest, not narrowly to defend their perceived rights as supporter but to hold the club accountable for its decisions shows how much these fans see themselves as constituents of the club.

The protests surrounding Petke's firing and their aftermath also reflect both the relative power some supporters' groups have built as stakeholders in the professional clubs as well as the limits of such influence. In response to the criticism by the fan base, the New York Red Bulls held a 'town hall' meeting at which club leadership addressed 300 season ticket holders. Whilst this can be interpreted as reflective of the supporters' increased power, insofar as the club at least felt the need to justify its decisions, it ultimately also exemplifies the relative powerlessness of the supporters. Without a formal democratic input into the club's decisions or the composition of the club's leadership – as is the case in supporter-owned clubs or clubs that operate as membership organizations in some parts of the world – the fans are left with few mechanisms of influence beyond symbolic or monetary (eg. boycotts) protests. Although the supporters spoke out in the stadium and during the 'town hall' event, this ultimately did not impact the direction of the Red Bulls front office in any meaningful way. Instead, Red Bulls' response in the form of staging an event that simulated dialogue may even have served as a successful image campaign by the club, as they were able to portray themselves as attentive and responsive to the concerns of their fans. For instance, despite the 2015 Red Bulls season starting with controversy and protests against club leadership, the ISC recognized the New York Bulls front office as the 'Front Office of the Year' because of its responsiveness to fans and its treatment of away fans at the stadium at the end of the very same season (ISC 2016).

'That's the limits of what the fans here can do'. Supporters between resistance and compromises

The ESC activism and their overall philosophy in supporting the Red Bulls can be taken to reflect the compromises supporters are faced with in the context of professional soccer in the US more broadly. Whilst ESC employ a style of support that is reminiscent of European Ultras and British supporters, and whilst they make attempts to hold the club accountable to the vision of the supporters, they also remain fans of a team that is named after an energy drink company and whose European sister clubs are highly controversial among local soccer fans. In addition to the New York Red Bulls, the Red Bull company also owns teams in Salzburg (Red Bull Salzburg, Austrian first division), Leipzig (RasenBallsport[8] Leipzig, German second division and likely to be promoted to the Bundesliga at the time of writing) as well as in Ghana and Brazil, all of whom feature virtually identical branding, including a club crest that is a variation of the Red Bull energy drink logo. In Europe, Red Bull Salzburg and RasenBallsport Leipzig have become the exemplars of what is wrong with 'modern football' in the eyes of many fans. Both teams are seen as utilizing soccer purely for financial and marketing reasons with no real interest in the sport itself. Moreover, in the eyes of the fans, the teams' emergence marks the replacement of teams rooted in local communities by new teams that lack any tradition. This sentiment is especially fuelled by the origin of both teams, with the case of Salzburg bearing some parallels to the history of the New York Red Bulls.[9] In 2005, Red Bull acquired Austrian club Austria Salzburg and subsequently renamed and rebranded the team, changing the club's colours from violet and white to Red Bull's corporate colour scheme. For some fans of Austria Salzburg this marked the virtual death of their club, to which a group of fans reacted by founding a new club by the original name of SV Austria Salzburg; as of 2015, the team has gained promotion into the Austrian second division.[10]

Whilst the situation faced by fans of the New York Red Bulls has important parallels to the case of Red Bull Salzburg, the reaction among the respective supporters also points to the limits of power and self-determination among fans in the US. The New York Red Bulls were known as the MetroStars until 2006 when they were sold to the Red Bull company who changed the team's name and crest, and altered the club colours from red and black to white, red, blue and yellow. Mirroring the situation faced by supporters of Austria Salzburg, some MetroStars fans abandoned the team in response to the rebrand, precisely because they felt that the club they supported had ceased to exist. However, other supporters, including the oldest supporters' group ESC, have continued to support the team, despite a critique of the name change and a nostalgia for the original identity of the club. To this day, ESC members tend to refer to the team as the 'Metros' as opposed to calling them team by its actual 'Red Bulls' name, both in conversations and in their songs and chants in the stadium. Moreover, the part of the supporters' section inhabited by ESC features few people wearing official Red Bull jerseys and merchandise. Instead, the majority of ESC members – especially the core of the group – are typically dressed either in merchandise from the MetroStars era or in clothing produced by ESC themselves, which in turn predominantly features the colours red and black. The fact that this supporters' group is continuing to follow a club whilst at the same time being deeply conflicted about its ownership, colours and crest – to the point of not officially recognizing its current identity – reflects the tensions supporters face in US professional soccer and the compromises they are forced to make. In a league system without promotion and relegation, the option of abandoning the club after its rebrand in order to form a new club and see it rise to relevancy again – as done by fans of Austria Salzburg – simply does not appear as a realistic option. The impossibility of achieving promotion to the top leagues via success on the field (as the professional leagues operate as closed-shop systems without promotion and relegation), league rules that mandate team owners must prove a net worth of millions of dollars, and not least the status of soccer as a marginal spectator sport that is virtually unsustainable in the lower leagues, makes the alternative to staying with the team even less desirable than supporting it despite its name. That Red Bulls fans faced an impossible choice after the team was bought by the soft drink company is even conceded by Jeff, fan of the rival New York Cosmos:

> When Metrostars was gone, it was just gone, you know, it was either fuck off or get onboard with supporting the beverage.[11] They didn't have the choice because that's the structure of American soccer. That is what we are stuck with. Unfortunately. I'd like to think we are not, that we could change it but this is the way things are and that's the limits of what the fans here can do. (Jeff)

In other words, the realities of soccer as a professional sports business delimit the options for action on the side of the supporters in the US, resulting in pragmatic compromises that may contradict the overall philosophies.

Conclusion: between transformative soccer politics, pragmatism and Ultra as style

As I have argued, the appropriation of Ultra – and other global – modes of fandom in the North American context transcends matters of style. Instead it has empowered supporters to build active fan subcultures in which they can express themselves as more than mere consumers of sports entertainment. At the same time, the economic and political structures of globalized professional soccer and their specific shapes in the US and Canadian context, coupled with the local history of soccer repeatedly failing as a spectator sport also restrict supporters in the scope of their demands. Unlike Ultras in European countries who are confident in lobbying for their interests as fans even if their demands contradict the economic interests of the professional leagues, supporters in the US tend to be more cautious and often pragmatically accept supposed economic imperatives. For instance, in our interview Andres acknowledged the reality that fans today are faced with a situation in which 'every major team is owned by some sort of big business … But the difference here is, who does the team serve?' In other words, the prospect that truly supporter-owned soccer clubs may become a reality seems so far-fetched that the most promising vision is one where corporate owners prioritize the team's success over ulterior motives and remain accountable to the fan base. King (1997) found similar attitudes among the group of organized Manchester United supporters he studied. On the one hand, these fans were able to compartmentalize the business of soccer from the meaning projected onto the club name and logo. And on the other hand, the very nature of sporting competition and the rivalries with other clubs led them to tacitly agree with the economic imperatives in club decisions as long as they led to success on the field.

A similar sentiment is even reflected in #RedBullOut's demands. Despite the group's far-reaching criticism against the corporation that owns the club and despite the arguments they present on their website that, at least in their eyes, document the failure of the club to prioritize the team and its fans, the demands and solutions presented by the group remain trapped within the existing framework of how professional soccer is organized; a pragmatic, rather than a systemic critique. Amongst other things – such as the dismissal of the new sporting director and a reversal of the firing of head coach Petke – their main demand reads: 'The expedited sale of New York's original MLS club to a new investor. Our club is not to be used as a branding experiment' (RedBullOut 2015a). In a separate article, the group clarified its position as being an effort 'to push Red Bull to sell the club to a local investor' (RedBullOut 2015b). Whilst the explicit dismissal of soccer clubs being used as 'branding experiments' speaks to the group's vision of seeing soccer prioritized over economic interests, the solution they propose ultimately must be a pragmatic one that is restricted by what is perceived as the economic realities of soccer as a business. Instead of demanding transformative changes in how soccer operates, the fans project their hopes of the club being attentive to them onto the notion of a future investor being 'local'; a committed and benevolent multi-millionaire owner who puts the fans and the success of the team first is supposed to replace an allegedly disinterested and absent one who supposedly prioritizes monetary interests regardless of success on the pitch.

Claussen (2007) has argued that soccer is always intertwined with the societal conditions under which it is played, whilst at the same time containing the potentiality of transcending the restrictions of a given society. The situation soccer supporters in the US and Canada face exemplifies this dialectic perfectly in multiple ways. The re-emergence of soccer as a spectator sport in the US and its current incarnation as a globalized and hyper-commercialized form of sports entertainment both empowers and disempowers fans at the same time. On the one hand, by exposing fans to modes of fandom practiced elsewhere around the world, supporters are able to enact versions of fandom that transcend their roles as customers, whilst at the same time, it is paradoxically the re-emergence of professional, commercial soccer in the US in the first place that gave rise to their formation as organized groups with similar identities and interests. On the other hand, the status of soccer as a sports entertainment business and its imperative of being financially successful severely restricts the ability of supporters to articulate truly alternative visions of how to make clubs and leagues accountable to their fans and communities. Especially the perceived threat of soccer disappearing as a viable spectator sport, rooted in the memory of the NASL folding in the 1980s, often results in fans pragmatically agreeing with the argument that what is beneficial for the professional clubs and leagues is ultimately in the fans' interest as well, as it ensures the continued existence of professional soccer and by extension the existence of them as supporters' groups. It remains to be seen whether supporters in the US and Canada in the future will grow confident to express more fundamental critiques of commercialized soccer or whether they will accept the notion that their interests as fans are automatically identical to the interests of those running professional leagues and clubs for their financial benefit.

Notes

1. This article is based on ethnographic research with three rival clubs in the New York City area. More specifically, I have conducted participant observation, informal and formal qualitative interviews with fans of the New York Cosmos of the division 2 North American Soccer League (NASL), as well as with supporters of both the MLS (division 1) teams New York Red Bulls and New York City FC (for a discussion of how research with rival supporters is possible see: Spaaij and Geilenkirchen 2011. These data are supplemented by analyses of online media (twitter, public message boards, blogs, websites, etc.) of the wider US and Canadian soccer supporters' subculture, since online interactions are increasingly important in order to understand soccer fan identities, especially in a country with few rivalries based on geographic proximity (an argument for the importance of online research in the study of fan cultures see: Gibbons and Dixon 2012.
2. While the Ultra subculture is often traced to 1970s Italy, from which it spread to other European countries and beyond, it is important to note that South American Barra Brava (Argentina and other Spanish speaking countries), Torcida (Brazil) and Porra (Mexico) groups share many similarities with Ultra culture.

3. This count is based on the official listing of supporters' groups on MLS's website, supplemented by groups personally know to be currently in existence to the author.
4. 'Barra' and 'Banda' are also popular, reflecting South American influences on fan culture.
5. Jeff himself, in contrast, is highly knowledgeable about the histories of various supporters' cultures around the world, as he demonstrates during multiple conversations with me. A white, college-educated professional in his early 20s, he has no deep first-hand experience with Ultra subculture in Europe himself. Yet, through media and research – he admits to religiously watching videos of supporters' groups on the internet, with a preference for smaller and more obscure groups – as well as through the networks he has formed through his fandom, he has become an autodidact of soccer culture. It is this specialized knowledge that enables him to call out other supporters' groups on their names.
6. Unless otherwise noted, quotations in section headings are quotes from interviews with my informants.
7. The MLS league champion is decided by a playoff tournament following the regular season. Meanwhile, the team with the most points during the regular season is awarded the Supporters Shield, a trophy originally lobbied for and funded by a network of MLS fans advocating for a recognition of the regular season champion.
8. German league rules prevent clubs being named after their sponsors. For this reason, the club officially bears the name RasenBallsport in order to leave the abbreviation of 'RB' intact. The neologism 'RasenBallsport' loosely translates to 'Lawn Ballsports'.
9. Red Bull bought a lower league club from the suburbs of Leipzig in 2009. The team has been promoted to Germany's second division as of 2015 and is likely to win promotion to the German Bundesliga in the 2015/2016 season. In the case of Leipzig, criticism towards Red Bulls' involvement in soccer centers on a number of factors. First, there exists a more general dissatisfaction with a newly formed club achieving success and replacing traditionally established clubs by virtue of their financial resources, especially in light of formerly well-known Leipzig-based clubs having been unable to make their way up from the lower leagues. On a more substantive level, RB Leipzig's approach has also challenged Germany's model of clubs being membership organizations, as the franchise has been able to circumvent league requirements.
10. This effort was in part inspired by similar initiatives of supporter ownership in England, where fans have established supporter-owned clubs in response to the corporate takeover or relocation of the club they cheered for.
11. Opposing fans call the Red Bulls dismissively 'the beverage', 'fizzy drink', 'dead bulls', 'pink cows' and other monikers based on their name being that of an energy drink company.

Disclosure statement

No potential conflict of interest was reported by the author.

References

ACB (Angel City Brigade). 2015. "ACB Financial Sanctions against MLS, Galaxy and Stub Hub Center." March 02. http://angelcitybrigade.net/2015/03/acb-financial-sanctions-against-mls-galaxy-and-stub-hub-center/.

Battini, Adrien. 2012. "Reshaping the National Bounds through Fandom: The UltrAslan of Galatasaray." *Soccer & Society* 13 (5): 701–719. doi:10.1080/14660970.2012.730771.

Batuman, Elif. 2012. "The View from the Stands: Life among Istanbul's Soccer Fanatics." *Soccer & Society* 13 (5): 687–700. doi:10.1080/14660970.2012.730770.

Brown, Sean. 2007. "Fleet Feet: The USSF and the Peculiarities of Soccer Fandom in America." *Soccer & Society* 8 (2): 366–380. doi:10.1080/14660970701224640.

Claussen, Detlev. 2007. "On Stupidity in Football." *Soccer & Society* 8 (4): 654–662.

Doidge, Mark. 2013. "'The Birthplace of Italian Communism': Political Identity and Action amongst Livorno Fans." *Soccer & Society* 14 (2): 246–261. doi:10.1080/14660970.2013.776471.

Doidge, Mark. 2015. *Football Italia. Italian Football in an Age of Globalization*. London: Bloomsbury.

El-Zatmah, Shawki. 2012. "From Terso into Ultras: The 2011 Egyptian Revolution and the Radicalization of the Soccer's Ultra-fans." *Soccer & Society* 13 (5): 801–813. doi:10.1080/14660970.2013.766030.

Gabler, Jonas. 2011. *Die Ultras: Fußballfans und Fußballkulturen in Deutschland* [The Ultras: Football Fans and Football Cultures in Germany]. Köln: Papyrossa.

Gibbons, Tom, and Kevin Dixon. 2012. "Surf's Up! A Call to Take English Soccer Fan Interactions on the Internet More Seriously." *Soccer & Society* 11 (5): 599–613.

Guschwan, Matthew. 2014. "Stadium as Public Sphere." *Sport in Society* 17 (7): 884–900. doi:10.1080/17430437.2013.806036.

Haenfler, Ross. 2004. "Rethinking Subcultural Resistance: Core Values of the Straight Edge Movement." *Journal of Contemporary Ethnography* 33 (4): 406–436.

ISC (Independent Supporters Council). 2015. "Open Letter to Don Garber and Mark Abbot Calling for an Immediate Removal of ACB Sanctions." March 06. http://independentsupporterscouncil.com/acb-sanctions/.

ISC (Independent Supporters Council). 2016. "Independent Supporters Council Holds 8th Annual Independent Supporters Conference." February 23. http://independentsupporterscouncil.com/independent-supporters-council-holds-8th-annual-independent-supporters-conference/.

Kennedy, David. 2013. "A Contextual Analysis of Europe's Ultra Football Supporters Movement." *Soccer & Society* 14 (2): 132–153. doi:10.1080/14660970.2013.776464.

King, Anthony. 1997. "The Lads: Masculinity and the New Consumption of Football." *Sociology* 31 (2): 329–346. doi:10.1177/0038038597031002008.

Llopis-Goig, Ramón. 2015. *Spanish Football and Social Change: Sociological Investigations*. Basingstoke: Palgrave Macmillan. doi:10.1057/9781137467959.

Magazine, Roger. 2007. *Golden and Blue like My Heart: Masculinity, Youth, and Power among Soccer Fans in Mexico City*. Tucson, AZ: University of Arizona Press.

McManus, John. 2013. "Been There, Done That, Bought the T-Shirt: Besiktas Fans and the Commodification of Football in Turkey." *International Journal of Middle East Studies* 45: 3–24. doi:10.1017/S0020743812001237.

Merkel, Udo. 2012. "Football Fans and Clubs in Germany: Conflicts, Crises and Compromises." *Soccer & Society* 13 (3): 359–376. doi:10.1080/14660970.2012.655505.

Nuhrat, Yagmur. 2013. "Playing by the Book(S): The Unwritten Rules of Football in Turkey." *FairPlay, Revista de Filosofia, Ética y Derecho del Deporte* 1 (1): 89–111.

Numerato, Dino. 2014. "Who Says 'No to Modern Football?' Italian Supporters, Reflexivity, and Neo-Liberalism." *Journal of Sport & Social Issues* 39 (2): 1–19.

Porat, Amir Ben. 2012. "From Community to Commodity: The Commodification of Football in Israel." *Soccer & Society* 13 (3): 443–457. doi:10.1080/14660970.2012.655511.

RedBullOut. 2015a. "The Demands: #RedBullOut." January 09. http://redbullout.blogspot.com/2015/01/the-demands-redbullout.html.

RedBullOut. 2015b. "Voicing Our Displeasure: The Town Hall: #RedBullOut." January 13. http://redbullout.blogspot.com/2015/01/voicing-our-displeasure-town-hall.html.

Rosenbaum, Michael S. 2013. "Maintaining the Trail: Collective Action in a Serious-Leisure Community." *Journal of Contemporary Ethnography* 42: 639–667. doi:10.1177/0891241613483560.

Sandvoss, Cornel. 2003. *A Game of Two Halves: Football, Television, and Globalisation*. London: Routledge.

Spaaij, Ramón, and Matthijs Geilenkirchen. 2011. "Ta(l)king Sides: Ethical and Methodological Challenges in Comparative Fieldwork on Avid Football Rivalries." *Soccer & Society* 12 (5): 633–651. doi:10.1080/14660970.2011.599583.

Spaaij, Ramón, and Carles Viñas. 2013. "Political Ideology and Activism in Football Fan Culture in Spain: A View from the Far Left." *Soccer & Society* 14 (2): 183–200. doi:10.1080/14660970.2013.776467.

Stebbins, Robert A. 2005. *Serious Leisure: A Perspective for Our Time*. New Brunswick: Aldine.

Testa, Alberto, and Gary Armstrong. 2010. *Football, Fascism and Fandom the UltraS of Italian Football*. London: A & C Black.

Wagner, Jesse. 2012. "Cultural Hybridization, Glocalization and American Soccer Supporters: The Case of the Timbers Army." Unpublished MA Thesis, Portland State University.

Woltering, Robbert. 2013. "Unusual Suspects: 'Ultras' as Political Actors in the Egyptian Revolution." *Arab Studies Quarterly* 35 (3): 290–304. doi:10.13169/arabstudquar.35.3.0290.

Social agency and football fandom: the cultural pedagogies of the Western Sydney ultras

Jorge Knijnik 🆔

ABSTRACT

This article addresses key questions of social agency and cultural pedagogy within the neoliberal structures of 'modern football' in the Australian context. It reports on a two-year ethnographic study of the Red and Black Bloc, an Australian ultras group in Western Sydney, one of the most culturally diverse areas in Australia. The origins of the Western Sydney ultras are described, along with their struggles to build their own cultural identity and to fight for social agency within a commodified football league. By combining a multifaceted theoretical model with a range of ethnographic data – including document analysis and in-depth interviews – this study reveals the processes by which the Western Sydney ultras enhance members' social cohesion towards an increased social consciousness. The paper acknowledges the role that ultras, as authentic cultural formations, may have in the propagation of new cultural pedagogies that have the potential to enhance citizenship, communal life and participatory democracy.

Fans without a team

The Western Sydney football *ultras* emerged on the mainstream Australian sports scene in 2012, when their team, the newly formed Western Sydney Wanderers FC (WSW) participated in the A-League (the country's major football competition) for the first time. However, uniquely, WSW fans came into existence before the team itself.

Western Sydney has always been known as *the heartland of Australian football* (Pennington 2012) due to its multiple football communities and clubs. Also, while attempts in 2010 to constitute a professional team in the region failed, they left emotional traces in the fans' imaginary[1] for a football team. As one of my informants declared, 'before the first game, we [Western Sydney football-lovers] were already passionate for a club which hadn't been named yet' (RBB/HC).[2]

Since 2012 'westies', as people from Western Sydney are called, have caught the attention of the *sports nation* of Australia (Adair 2009) due to successes on the pitch: WSW made it to two consecutive A-League finals and is the first (and so far the only) Australian side to have won the Asian Champions League – in the 2014 season. However, what has definitely helped to put the Westies on the football map and drawn the attention of the sports media are the new – from an Australian perspective – forms of fandom brought to the stadia by the *Red and Black Bloc* (RBB).

The RBB calls itself the true representative of *ultras* culture in Australia. Unlike other Australian groups of organized supporters, and like their global partners, the RBB never stops dancing and singing – they are 'noise-makers' (The Daily Telegraph, 30 October 2014). They meet in pubs to cheer and chant at pre-game festivities and march to stadia in carnivalesque street celebrations. Inside stadia, they use chants, musical instruments and banners, not only to have a good time and support their beloved team but also to display political messages of protest against 'modern football'.

'Modern football' is a commodified profit-oriented operation that is attempting to convert a genuine passion into a disheartening neoliberal trade (Numerato 2015). Since the 1980s modern football organizations have pushed for the commercialization of every sphere of the game. The core gatekeepers of this football business – mainstream media, police, security and football authorities – act to keep a sterile atmosphere inside the stadia, which often opposes fans' desires to promote their own cultural traditions within the football realm (Kennedy and Kennedy 2012). In opposition to modern football, ultras football groups have been uniting thousands of youth around the world (Kennedy and Kennedy 2012) to argue for the preservation of traditional football culture as a form of social identity.

As authentic cultural formations, ultras provide youth a rare educational space for civic training that prioritizes citizenship values over commercial interests and human relationships over business transactions. Education is seen here as a 'cultural pedagogical practice that takes place in multiple sites' (Giroux 2011, 141). These cultural pedagogical practices – things like debates, dialogue and creative processes – raise the most fundamental questions of public life in order to enhance social consciousness and produce more cohesive communities. These cultural pedagogies are political in that they prepare young people to live in and to understand their culture, and also to engage with and to transform their world if necessary (Giroux 2011).

As open learning spaces, ultras groups can create and foster cultural pedagogies that 'extend, if not supersede, institutionalized education as the most important educational force in developed societies' (Giroux 2011, 137). The cultural pedagogies of the ultras go beyond the mere transmission of conventional knowledge, as they are sustained by the emotional investments that youth bring to this social space. Such pedagogies are not pre-given techniques, but an outcome of present social struggles; they try to make 'visible the operations of power and authority as part of its processes of disruption and unsettlement' (Giroux 2011, 147).

Rationale for the study

International studies on football fandom and culture have questioned the lack of research on fans' daily practices (Dixon 2013). These investigations have pointed out that empirical data on the origins of fandom is scarce, preventing social researchers from understanding how such an important aspect of society operates (Crawford 2004).[3] Within the Australian context, previous research on sport fandom has also called for more qualitative studies on Australian fan culture, to produce a deeper understanding of its social significance (Melnick and Wann 2011).

This paper reports on a two-year ethnographic data collection amongst members of the RBB, the Western Sydney ultras. My aim is to uncover the social interactions that make the construction of a new communal identity possible. Furthermore, I want to portray how the social agency promoted by the RBB is lived in the modern football context of the A-League (Numerato 2015). Ultimately, I want to bring attention to what I call the 'cultural pedagogies' of the RBB that have the capacity to enhance social cohesion and democratic citizenship in Western Sydney.

In my search to address these aims, I undertook, during the 2013–2014 and 2014–2015 Australian football seasons, a two-year ethnographic venture which provided a rich range of empirical data (Silverman 2013) on the Western Sydney ultras. Using a snowball technique and an in-depth interview method (Hesse-Biber 2007), I interviewed 12 RBB members. During this period, I also collected ultras' opinions from online and social media forums. I kept a detailed diary of the hundreds of hours I spent on the stands, in pubs and at street marches, travelling, cheering and talking with ultras. I also participated in club forums and, while 'becoming one of them', I observed fans' performances from diverse points of the stadia so I could grasp the reactions of other fans towards the group (Knijnik 2015a). I collected secondary data from the Australian media, as well as official communiqués from the clubs, the FFA and the RBB itself. In addition, I developed a close relationship with a core RBB member, who in the past two years has shared key information with me about the group's development, helping me to complete this ethnographic puzzle (Atkinson 2013). The triangulation of this array of data offers a multifaceted view of the diverse social realities that frequently remain unknown and unvoiced in Western Sydney (Hesse-Biber 2007).

I start by giving a sense of the social uniqueness and relevance of Western Sydney in the Australian social and football context. Next, after briefly discussing the ultras phenomenon in today's football, I outline the theoretical inspiration I use to interpret my data. I argue that Toledo's (2010) concept of football fandom as the metaphysic of the ordinary people can help to explain the Western Sydney ultras and their commitment to their team; I use Giroux's (2011) notions of the role of cultural pedagogies in the construction of community resistance and social agency; and I introduce Numerato's (2015) recent attempts to discuss the ambiguities and complexities that permeate the potential for social change within contemporary football fandom.

These theoretical approaches are then employed to discuss the ways RBB cultural practices can lead to an enhancement of individual and communal social agency in football. I conclude by discussing the potential of these cultural pedagogies for citizenship, communal life and participatory democracy.

Some aspects of the RBB culture could not be covered in this study. Fandom gender dimensions and the role of women on the stands deserve a deeper look in future studies. Also, I have just briefly addressed the subgroups that exist within the RBB and the consequent political divisions that can block social change and threaten the viability of a group in the long term.

Westies and *wogs*

A brief socio-geographic description of the Western Sydney area is central to understandings of the Western Sydney ultras' challenges and ambiguities. Greater Western Sydney is one of the most cosmopolitan cities on the planet: 58% of its inhabitants comprise first or second generation migrants from every part of the world (Collins, Reid, and Fabiansson 2007) and the majority of Sydney's recently arrived migrant groups settle in Western Sydney, the area of Australia in which the largest immigrant population can be found.[4]

Western Sydney comprises 14 city councils in a vast area that is distant from famous Sydney icons such as the Opera House or Bondi Beach. Transport disadvantage, lack of public services, social exclusion, discrimination, urban violence and criminality are all components of the region's profile (Arthurson 2004).

On the other hand, the mix of refugees, Indigenous Australians and migrants from all over the world has brought a distinctive and super-diverse cultural profile to Western Sydney (Collins and Poynting 2000). Amongst the many cultural traditions of the different ethnic groups that live in the area, there has always been something in common: a passion for football. Football has been described as a 'key dimension of the social experience of certain migrant groups in Australia' (Hallinan, Hughson, and Burke 2007, 295).

The strong link between football and ethnic communities has resulted in the game being stigmatized. Migrants have suffered from considerable prejudice and social discrimination throughout Australia's history, being targeted and labelled as second-class citizens, as 'westies' and 'wogs' (a derogatory term for immigrants) (Warren 2003). Hence, if you played 'wogball', you would be considered one of 'them', even if you were a sixth-generation Australian as in the case of John Warren, former Socceroos captain.

Ultras: a 'metaphysic of the ordinary people'

The celebratory atmosphere created by ultras is entirely different from the ambience of everyday life. In durkheimian terms, it can be seen as a collective sacred experience that promotes 'ecstatic enthusiasm' (Durkheim 1995, 214). This atmosphere entails an unconventional and spirited socialization (Toledo 2010) and is passionate and festive (Spaaij and Viñas 2005). Insofar as it takes fans to a non-mundane dimension, it cannot be quantified; neither can it be lived alone. In this sense, it is a collective embodied transcendental experience, a 'metaphysic of the ordinary people' (Toledo 2010, 176). This metaphysic exists in the ultras' bodies and relates to their sensibility. Most important, though, it can only be intuited and lived by those who are there in the moment, not only participating but essentially creating the atmosphere with their voices, instruments, gestures and bodies.

This collective embodied transcendental experience, or metaphysic, is concomitant with emotional attachment, to the club and its fan group (Numerato 2015). The emotional connections boost the bonds between group members, leading over time to a strong sense of social cohesion that empowers fans to express their views on the neoliberal apparatuses that underlie modern football. These indications of an increased consciousness of their social situation within modern football have been present in the conversations, displays, chants, manifestos and demonstrations of ultras groups (Kennedy and Kennedy 2012). The link between the ultras' metaphysic experience and the potential for questioning neoliberal modern football has led to the claim that 'there is likely no better space to train protests than the space of football terraces' (Numerato 2015, 131). In this paper, I want to examine the truth of this claim.

Ultras: social agency and cultural pedagogies

With their festive but tense explosion of desires, meanings, bodies and languages, ultras can be seen as organized cultural workers who transmit lessons on how to live a communal life (Giroux 2011). These lessons, which I call the ultras' cultural pedagogies, 'comprehend the value of sentiments, emotions and desires as part of the learning process' (Freire 1998, 41). Created and experienced within a vibrant and political public sphere, the ultras cultural pedagogies support their struggle to reclaim the football stadia and their surroundings as common spaces filled with more than commercial displays and shopping malls; but occupied by the ultras' mix of unruled bodies, chants and tifos – by ultras culture. Ultimately, the ultras' cultural pedagogies have the potential to challenge the oppressive commodified context of their daily lives and can generate 'the conditions of their own agency through dialogue, community participation, resistance and political struggle' (Giroux 2011, 111).

To paraphrase Giroux (2011), ultras groups may be one of the few places currently remaining for young people to learn how to critically address the tensions between the possibilities of civic participation and the constraints of their everyday lives 'within a social order dominated by market principles' (Giroux 2011, 121). Ultras groups offer one of the rare inclusive public spheres in which young citizens can learn how to exercise some sort of social agency and critical leadership in public life. The cultural pedagogies in place there promote much more than job training: they enhance public responsibility, critique and imaginative inquiry 'through social relations which foster a mix of compassion, hope and ethics' (Giroux 2011, 89). In this sense, the ultras cultural pedagogies may help the formation not only of critical individuals but also of social collectivities.

'We're from the streets of Western Sydney'[5]: the origins of the RBB

The RBB has been proudly displaying their love for the Western Sydney area since the group's first meeting in 2012. The forty or so supporters who responded to an advertisement on a local website for supporters to 'gather to discuss active support' (WestSydneyFootball 2013, 21) formed the original core group of the RBB; they committed to a 100% devotion to their yet-to-be named team with the aim of creating a fervent world-class atmosphere in the stadium. During this primary meeting, as the club's formal identity was still being planned elsewhere, these ultras in-the-making came up with their first ever chant: 'Western Sydney Ole Ole Ole'.[6]

For them, though, Western Sydney is not only a location in the map, but also, in light of the stigmatization of the area discussed above, a cause to fight for. Hence, when the RBB sing that they 'are from the streets of Western Sydney', they are claiming that, despite their tough lives and the associated social and cultural stigma, they are not second class citizens: 'we fight for our pride of Western Sydney being number one not only on the field and terraces but on the streets' (RBB/HC).

Other factors that help unite Western Sydney residents are an emphasis on a 'Westie accent' and the working class origins of many. The idea that 'we're all hard-workers here in the West' (RBB/HC) is commonly expressed by RBB members. These ties have created a new cultural representation that plays a powerful role in modelling self and group identities, as well as in reinforcing residents' sense of belonging to this particular community (Giroux 2011); as a member says 'we represent[…] RBB, we represent our area which is […] Western Sydney' (RBB/HC).

The creation of a 'we' through this intense communal identification is one level of a multilayered cultural construction. Next, I look at the way the metaphysic, the embodied transcendental dimension of football, reinforces RBB members' identity and sense of belonging to their community (Doidge 2013).

'We as one': embodied metaphysics on the stands

Being a football ultras fan is an experience which escapes superficial or easy analysis. The identity of the supporter exists as s/he shares her/his experiences in a collective sphere (Toledo 2010). It is a socio-political process of creating a 'we' that transforms all supporters into a single living body.

This sense of 'we' permeates RBB cultural productions. In chants, the idea of 'we' not only resonates loudly but is also embodied. The performance of 'Call to arms', one of the earliest RBB chants, illustrates this. After chanting the words of the last verse 'stand together and fight as one', fans embrace each other, making long lines as if they were a single organism, and jump to the left and to the right, screaming 'tererererere', while 'La Banda' creates the perfect dance atmosphere. Everyone – men and women from diverse ethnic groups, children, the young and the elderly – is embraced, laughs, jumps and sings non-stop for at least ten minutes. RBB members love it:

> I'm like yeah I won't ever experience something like this before. It's just something different that makes me thrilled, you don't experience this normally, it's unbelievable you know. I woke up singing the RBB chants (SOM).

> The atmosphere was crazy. My hairs on my arm we going up, I couldn't think, people were singing, you don't see that here nowhere, that made me homesick. (RBB/HC)

This sharing of emotional connections, this dancing and singing, and these embraces create a new collective identity, made not only by individuals, but also by their jerseys, chants, gestures, flags and displays (Toledo 2010). This collective identity strengthens fans' sense of community (Doidge 2013); in a time of civic fragmentation and in a racist era, these embodied performances enhance union and promote social inclusion (Giroux 2011).

These corporeal performances also act in contrast to the increasing tendency towards individualization that permeates contemporary society (Giroux 2011). In the era of digital social nets, the fans' embodied act of collective dancing, chanting and cheering reinforce the sense of 'we' of the group, and works against the:

> elitist need to individualize […] the football fan's behaviour, altering their [collective] dynamics, trying to push the epicentre of feeling from immanent body sensations to the rational brain (Toledo 2010, 110)

Hence, on one side, the commodified modern football structure of the A-League (Numerato 2015) pushes for an individualized passive supporter who remains seated and who consumes the spectacle and the products within the stadia (Cleland 2010); on the other side, is the RBB organic experience of standing for the whole game and of jumping, singing, dancing, screaming, clapping – a collective experience that has, within the same modern football structures, the potential to reinforce social change.

This collective experience should not be seen as a utopian exercise where everyone displays equal power. There are hierarchies and divisions amongst the RBB. No woman has ever occupied the RBB 'capo' position (the leader who stands in the front stage of the group coordinating the chants) and most of the leadership roles within the group are held by young men. A few homophobic remarks – usually in a joking format – appear on online interactions, but are always rejected by most of the members. Small subgroups within the main active group have already been formed and proclaim a different agenda. This agenda is focused more on the team's performances than the active support group efforts. However, none of these facts has been relevant enough to break the production of the collective identity on the stands.

'We unite as one'[7]: cultural diversity and social cohesion

The Western Sydney ultras are proud of the unity they can achieve within their culturally diverse group. RBB members celebrate the implications of Westie cultural diversity as evidence of the moral superiority of a lifestyle that promotes cultural dialogue and peace:

> In the past the Croatians just wanted the Croatians, the Serbians stick to their own. Now it's just all mixed. It's a mishmash of everything. You know everyone is like a family. I put another example, the leaders of the RBB are a Bosnian guy, a Serbian and a Croatian. They're like brothers here; they look after each other's kids. (RBB/HC)

The lesson here is that the RBB is capable of promoting reconciliation where earlier there was only animosity. This social cohesion can also be seen in the several initiatives that RBB has launched, inside and outside the stadia, to support vulnerable and socially disadvantaged people in the west – such as raising money for charities as well as for those who were severely affected by the 2014 summer fires in Western Sydney.

This diverse community has the capacity to provide its members with the skills, empowerment, agency and social cohesion, 'through which individuals recognize themselves as social and political agents' (Giroux 2011, 141). The group's cultural pedagogies – learning how to chant and dance while embracing the social and cultural diversity of the terrace; respecting group decisions over protests and actions against police brutality, and helping vulnerable people, for example – provide a singular space for civic life. Furthermore, in this sense the production of unlikely friendships between people from several and even 'antagonist' ethnicities (such as Serbian, Croatians and Bosnians) makes this new culture a probable terrain for producing more critical identities in the establishment of social subjects that can reclaim the centrality of social justice rights (Giroux 2011).

'Fuck off Sydney FC'[8]: reinforcing social ties

The social cohesion created by the RBB collective experience is reinforced through their fierce antagonism to Eastern Sydney and its football representative, Sydney Football Club (SFC). SFC has been in the A-League since the inaugural season (2005–2006). Originally intended to be the only team for the whole city of Sydney, it clearly failed to include people from the west, who have never felt represented by the 'sky blues':

> Western Sydney has been distant from the city, 'they' have the Sydney FC team. It was like we weren't included, we weren't a part of that, and then when a team was created and developed in Western Sydney, we owned it (RBB/PA).

As soon as WSW was born, so too was club rivalry and banter between fans. SFC's supporter group, 'The Cove', was seen by the RBB as not having the authenticity of real fans; they were no more than childish teenagers who did not know how to cheer properly or be a loyal football fan. 'Plastic fans', 'fake and pet supporters' are some of the adjectives RBB has used to describe Cove members.

> Mate, when I used to go to SFC games, 50 guys with acne on their face would turn up in the cove. The only drum they would bring was a wheelie bin[9] that they would smash (OF).

The challenge for the title of 'best supporters' group' is an everyday topic on RBB SOM and online discussions. Posted photos of RBB members cheering and chanting under heavy rain are compared with The Cove's empty sector in rainy weather conditions. The comments reveal the ongoing social class dispute: 'they' are teenagers who live on parents' savings while 'we' are hard working men and women.

In the 2014–2015 season, just a week before the Sydney Derby, the big game that opposes Western Sydney Wanderers FC and Sydney FC, the RBB launched a statement titled 'We are different' in which they called on all fans for the upcoming battle on the stands:

> In three years we've gained worldwide recognition. Conquered a continent. Moved masses all over the country … They've had 10 years yet still fail to match us … They take out their frustrations at rival fans using knives. Put more effort into creating memes and taking selfies instead of chanting for 90 minutes … Passion cannot be bought. This city is ours (Red and Black Bloc, Social Media, 2015).

During the Sydney derbies, the RBB displays heightened levels of passion, aggressiveness and energy. Their sector is crowded and it is nearly impossible to find a ticket to stand with them; RBB ultras should never sit. Tifos from both sides typically dispute who 'owns this city', and even if The Cove does better with its more elaborate displays, the RBB is unbeatable with its very loud drumming and chanting throughout the whole 90 minutes of play – which continues after the match, if the team wins.

'We're better': East vs. West and social consciousness beyond the football realm

The passionate investment during a Derby day helps the RBB to reaffirm its collective identity. However, this battle puts at stake much more than a classic football rivalry that reinforces the collective character of the Western Sydney ultras; this opposition carries the potential to build the group's own social consciousness and political agency (Giroux 2011). The dispute to see whether 'Sydney is red and black or sky blue' exposes conflicting social practices, identities and cultural values, as well as diverse understandings of community building and belonging. Furthermore, it reveals political and socio-economic power struggles between the two groups.

The rise of the Western Sydney football culture and its 'takeover' of the eastern side of the city are permeated by a growth of social consciousness. Themes such as social class tensions and stereotypes are constant in the RBB chants, online forums and interviews.

> I was at the finals in the first season in the city, that was amazing, like you had something to fight for, because like I said, there was stereotype we didn't deserve to be in the A-League and it was like proving a point and actually fighting to be there you know, proving why we should be in the A-League. I was just remembering while you were talking about the Grand Final, when yeh, the RBB invaded the Allianz stadium, I was just thinking about the SFC fans what they were thinking, seeing these 'westies' there instead of them (RBB/PA).[10]

As this informant elaborates her thoughts about a sports and territorial dispute, she clarifies the social class issue: 'Sydney FC, apparently their supporters think they have really high status. They think they're above us. They say we're on Centrelink and we are all dole bludgers'.[11]

The same theme is prevalent in dozens of online posts:

And they call us bogans[12] out west, some of the crap I heard coming out of some Sydney FC supporters after the match was disgusting, dole bludgers,[13] get off the meth, bunch of housos,[14] etc. Some people need to grow up. I'm so sick of people from the east thinking they are better than us (SOM);

I am proud to live out west and am sick of the stereotypes that we are thugs, dole bludgers etc. Sledging and banter are different; it's the full on discrimination that is taking place (SOM)

The list goes on and shows that the East–West opposition offers a space for the Westies to acknowledge their own social circumstances and claim political fairness and action.

'They will never understand us'[15]: political agency in a commodified modern football context

A social consciousness also develops in RBB members as they interact with the gatekeepers of Australian modern football structures: police, private and public sports bodies, and their own club board. This section discusses data that reveal the RBB's relationship with the neo-liberal powers that govern modern football; although the collective experiences of the ultras builds emotional energy 'primarily related to passion and sport rivalries', it is also associated with 'anger [towards] the "juggernaut of modern football"' (Numerato 2015, 128). In this section, I present some histories that show how the RBB as an organic group reflects and acts on the boundaries imposed daily by the modern football institutions of the A-League.

RBB chants and choreographies are consistently highlighted as one of the main assets of the A-League by WSW management, the FFA and TV sports channels. 'You empower the game', the advertisements say, when showing the RBB performing their choreographies in the background. At the same time though, and confirming the prejudice against migrant culture, the mainstream view – from the media, sport bodies and the police – is of an extremely stereotyped image of Western Sydney ultras. Numerato's (2015, 129) description of Italian ultras 'as potentially violent social actors that must be kept under strict observation and control' accurately captures the way the RBB are seen.

The number of police officers, including 'anti-riot' squads with dogs and horses around the stadium and during RBB marches, is incredibly high. As supporters approach the gates of the RBB sector, they are submitted to pat-down searches and as soon as they enter the sector, they face an overbearing presence of police with sniffer dogs. This type of police surveillance and these kinds of searches are not seen anywhere else in the stadium. Harassment from police officers is a constant theme in RBB discussions; several RBB members who have enacted some sort of 'anti-social behaviour' have already been banned by police or security staff; these bans involve monetary fines, court processes and interdictions of from one to five years on going to any football stadium. These state institutions do not exist to solve social problems or create a civic conviviality; on the contrary, they are punitive organizations exerting social control over the public (Giroux 2011).

RBB leadership tries to work with the police command and the club to minimize the persistent incidents and clashes between their members and police officers. However, these leaders constantly complain about their 'criminalization' by police ('passion is not a crime', RBB signs declare). At least on three occasions in just two years, in a similar way to what has already happened with ultras in Europe (Numerato 2015), RBB members have protested and gone on a 'supporters' strike', demonstrating, as their banners stated, 'a silent stand for our brothers banned'; the RBB has even walked away from the stadium when police officers, after a flare was lit by a fan, arbitrarily invaded its sector and pepper-sprayed everyone, including children (Knijnik 2015b).

This amounts to a political struggle that ultimately has a pedagogical aspect for RBB members, as it opens a space where the 'complexity of knowledge, culture, values and social issues can be explored in open and critical dialogue, through which individuals recognize themselves as social and political agents' (Giroux 2011, 174). The RBB cultural and social practices are a constant challenge to the aspiration of the football bodies and the state security apparatus to ensure a normative order within their commodified league. The clash of views between the RBB and the gatekeepers of modern football generates not only physical but also ideological confrontations:

> That was […] the last straw in a never ending tirade of attacks against not only our freedom as football supporters but as citizens of a country with apparently laws that protect us. I myself have been pepper sprayed by police indiscriminately, my phone searched by police unlawfully etc. If we do not take a stand as one, we might as well bend over for the FFA and police to take away all our freedoms (SOM).

This quote articulates how RBB members can take advantage of this cultural space to create the circumstances of their own agency.

Mainstream media is another modern football gatekeeper that Western Sydney ultras treat with suspicion. The ultras comments on the media coverage of their group reveal a critical and social consciousness of the role that mainstream media play in constructing negative social images of them. Alongside the accusation made in online forums that influential media channels will do anything to undermine football in the country because of commercial interests in other sports codes (Skinner, Zakus, and Edwards 2008), the ultras also complain of a never-ending negative labelling of the people from the west.

> Fans are staying home because they are sick of being treated like criminals for loving their team. The media are painting our supporters as criminals, and we all know they have underlying financial interests with the NRL [National Rugby League]. They want to tarnish the sports reputation so to stop people attending. (SOM)

This discriminatory process became visible when a major TV channel reported the flare/pepper spray incident that occurred during the 2014–2015 season. The images of the RBB clash with police outside the stadium were immediately followed by screening of a major brawl that had happened in Serbian football. The manipulation of viewers and the stereotyping of 'wogball fans' could not be clearer (Knijnik 2015b). The video circulated amongst RBB members and their responses demonstrate their rage against mainstream media and the neoliberal sports business:

> This is the same sensationalism that the media perpetrated during the NSL [National Soccer League] era. This is the new football but still slaves to the same media-inspired bullshit. (SOM)

There are instances, though, when the cultural pedagogies of the RBB cannot be claimed as practices moving towards social agency. Next, I discuss another layer of this culture that shows a certain level of belligerence that may affect the ability of the group to battle for a better cultural understanding within modern football (Numerato 2015).

'No pyro no party'[16]: the smoke screen that may obliterate social agency

Numerato (2015) emphasizes that not all acts of supporter groups can be seen as emancipatory; they may instead lead to an inhibition of the capacity to fight for social change. This is clearly seen in the flares issue. Flares are unlawful in Australian stadiums. Ultras argue that flares are inseparable from the worldwide 'football culture'. Flare demonstrations at South American and European matches are glorified within SOM, with explicit statements wishing that the 'real football atmosphere' could soon arrive in the A-League. Despite the searches to which they are submitted when entering the stadia, ultras are often successful in smuggling these artefacts in and lighting them.

The topic of flares is an ongoing debate amongst fans. Many love them, as several online posts and signs express: 'no pyro no party' and 'if you don't like flares and if you don't like the support in the real football; fuck off this page and go back to your fucking cricket' (SOM). Other fans, though, acknowledge that some defiant acts can lead to even tougher hostility and to the strengthening of neoliberal doctrines of social control (Numerato 2015).

> This is exactly the reaction police wants [sic] in order to lift heavier bans and fines. Their goal is to get rid of the RBB. Don't be silly and throw flares but be smart and record all these incidences, have a fundraiser to get a team of lawyers and fight the law with law … Time to get smart, not even!!! (SOM).

Hence, some defiant acts perpetrated by football fans, despite being considered part of their culture, can 'risk losing their transcendental – and therefore transformative – character and becoming ends in themselves' (Numerato 2015, 128). The flares topic is emblematic of the current cultural tension within the Western Sydney ultras context. It means RBB leaders walk a narrow tightrope, avoiding either publicly condoning or condemning flares as they can bring consequences that weaken the potential of the group to act as a place of social agency, worsening governance and police repression, and inhibiting the potential cultural and social change brought by this new fandom culture (Numerato 2015).

'Fans control the game': towards a new understanding of ultras culture as a civic pedagogical space

Cultural sites serve as spaces for youth to learn and experiment. They can also be political spaces where youth learn to question what is taken for granted in their communities and societies (Giroux 2011); to pay attention to the manoeuvres of power; to construct narratives about their social and physical environment, themselves and others; and to develop a consciousness of those 'forces that sometimes prevent people from speaking openly and critically' (124). The cultural site of the RBB is such a space.

This ethnography of the RBB has presented data that confirmed ultras groups as potential sites for the enhancement of social agency and communal participation. Through their embodied metaphysic experiences, members can increase their social cohesion, may become more conscious of the social constraints within modern football structures, and have the chance to increase their community participation. This paper has also shown the connections between this social agency and the Western Sydney ultras' cultural pedagogies, confirming that the pedagogical is part of political life. This insight can be used in future studies that compare the Western Sydney ultras with other Australian or international ultras groups. This would be a valid effort in the search for a better understanding of the global ultras movement as a cultural pedagogical social sphere and of football stands as sites for enhancing or obstructing social agency.

The data analyzed here reassert Giroux's notion of culture as a pedagogical site where identities are created and performed as well as social and political agencies negotiated and configured through conflicting forces. Through their embodied actions and a cultural mix of art, music and performance; through the sarcasm, criticism and aggression used to antagonize both rivals and neoliberal powers that want to undermine their social agency and control all aspects of football culture in Australia; through ongoing conversations over their civil and social struggles, the Western Sydney ultras have, in just a few years, been able to transform the cultural panorama of football not only in the Western Sydney region but in Australian football generally.

Claiming their right to demonstrate and recreate their culture in the public domain, Western Sydney ultras confront the powers of modern football that push for the individualization and commercialization of all spheres of the game. This process does not come without its risks. On the contrary, as in any living culture, the Western Sydney ultras face difficulties and contradictions. They advance but also retreat. They make and receive criticism. They craft their own ways of life by producing cultural pedagogies that may inspire their young participants and their communities with new forms of common cooperation that can lead to the enhancement of democratic life. There are civic lessons to be learnt within and from this group that have the potential to show communities new ways to reconfigure democracy not via individual consumerism, but through communal involvement.

Notes

1. The failed attempt by the Football Federation Australia (FFA) and a group of investors to constitute the Western Sydney Rovers did not pass unperceived by local football lovers, as one of my informants recalls:

    Well, in 2010 there was a team called Western Sydney Rovers and they played Sydney FC, a competition game in Parramatta stadium. There were 20 or so Rovers' supporters – because they thought the new Western Sydney team would be born next year – with red and black signs. Basically there was something already building there, without a team: 20 or so, the leaders of the RBB. (RBB/HC)

2. For this research, my informants are identified as follows: Red and Black Hard Core members (RBB/HC), those who are leaders or 100% committed to the group, and who spend days working on displays, creating and rehearsing chants, building websites and social media posts, and so on; RBB/PA, those whose participation, despite being intense, is more likely to occur on match days; and RBB/IF, the informant within the core group with whom I have over time developed a special and deep relationship. This connection started through RBB social media channels (SOM), expanded to a few face to face formal interviews, and has developed as a football friendship, through chats and phone calls about RBB, football fandom, football tactics and politics. I also quote some opinions from fans' SOM and from fans' online forums (OF). These quotations use original words as much as possible.

3. Crawford,. *Consuming sport*.

4. The 2011 Australian census reported that nearly two million people live in Western Sydney in approximately 700,000 dwellings. Within 50% of these residences, people speak a language other than English.

5. 'We're from the streets of Western Sydney' is the first line of one of the most popular RBB chants

6. 'Ole Ole Ole' later became one of the fans' favourite chants across the different sections of the WSW home stadium as well as through the main streets of Western Sydney.

7. 'We unite as one', title of another RBB chant.

8. A chant in Derby days: 'Sha la la la la la la la. Fuck off east Sydney Sha la la la la la la la. We run this city'.

9. Australian idiom for a trashcan with wheels.

10. The grand final referred to here is the one WSW played in its first A-League season (2012–2013) against Central Coast Mariners FC; the Allianz stadium is Sydney FC's home ground, a major sports facility in the city used for that final event.
11. Centrelink is the Australian government agency that pays social benefits to the unemployed, families and socially vulnerable people.
12. Australian idiom for lower-class people.
13. Australian idiom for someone who receives unemployment benefits (the dole) from the government but are too lazy to look for work.
14. Australian idiom for a person who lives in housing commission/ Government assigned low budget housing.
15. Banner in the RBB section of the stadium. 'They' refers to the control apparatus of modern football.
16. 'No pyro no party' is the motto that runs around ultras social media forums, displaying a profusion of flares around stadia and ultras groups around the world.

Acknowledgements

The author would like to acknowledge Dr. Constance Ellwood for the English editing of this paper, as well as Mrs. Catherine Myson and Mrs. Nikolina Mabic Oricchio for their outstanding research assistance during the data collection phase of this project. Finally I thank Mr Jawed Gebrael for his assistance with the final formatting of the paper.

Disclosure statement

No potential conflict of interest was reported by the author.

Funding

This work was supported by the 2013 School of Education (WSU) small research grants scheme.

ORCID

Jorge Knijnik ⓘ http://orcid.org/0000-0003-2578-8909

References

Adair, Daryl. 2009. "Australian Sport History: From the Founding Years to Today." *Sport in History* 29 (3): 405–436. doi:10.1080/17460260903043351.

Arthurson, Kathy. 2004. "From Stigma to Demolition: Australian Debates about Housing and Social Exclusion." *Journal of Housing and the Built Environment* 19 (3): 255–270. doi:10.1007/s10901-004-0692-1.

Atkinson, Paul Anthony. 2013. "Ethnography and Craft Knowledge." *Qualitative Sociology Review* 9 (2): 56–63.

Cleland, Jamie A. 2010. "From Passive to Active: The Changing Relationship Between Supporters and Football Clubs." *Soccer & Society* 11 (5): 537–552. doi:10.1080/14660970.2010.497348.

Collins, Jock, and Scott Poynting. 2000. "Introduction: Communities, Identities and Inequalities in Western Sydney." In *The Other Sydney: Communities, Identities and Inequalities in Western Sydney*, edited by Scott Poynting and Jock Collins, 19–33. Melbourne: Common Ground Publishing.

Collins, Jock, Carol Reid, and Charlotte Fabiansson. 2007. *Tapping the Pulse of Youth in Cosmopolitan South-Western and Western Sydney: Report for The Department of Immigration and Citizenship.* www.immi.gov.au/media/publications/multicultural.

Crawford, Garry. 2004. *Consuming Sport: Fans, Sport and Culture*. London: Routledge.

Dixon, Kevin. 2013. "Learning the Game: Football Fandom Culture and the Origins of Practice." *International Review for the Sociology of Sport* 48 (3): 334–348. doi:10.1177/1012690212441157.

Doidge, Mark. 2013. "'The Birthplace of Italian Communism': Political Identity and Action Amongst Livorno Fans." *Soccer & Society* 14 (2): 246–261. doi:10.1080/14660970.2013.776471.

Durkheim, Emile. 1995. *The Elementary Forms of Religious Life*. New York: Free Press.

Freire, Paulo. 1998. *Pedagogy of Freedom: Ethics, Democracy and Civic Courage*. New York: Rowman & Littlefield.

Giroux, Henry A. 2011. *On Critical Pedagogy*. London: Continuum.

Hallinan, Christopher J., John E. Hughson, and Michael Burke. 2007. "Supporting the 'World Game' in Australia: A Case Study of Fandom at National and Club Level." *Soccer & Society* 8 (2–3): 283–297. doi:10.1080/14660970701224541.

Hesse-Biber, Sharlene Nagy. 2007. "The Practice of Feminist In-depth Interviewing." In *Feminist Research Practice: A Primer*, edited by Sharlene Nagy Hesse-Biber and Patricia L. Leavy, 111–148. London: Sage.

Kennedy, Peter, and David Kennedy. 2012. "Football Supporters and the Commercialisation of Football: Comparative Responses Across Europe." *Soccer & Society* 13 (3): 327–340. doi:10.1080/14660970.2012.655503.

Knijnik, Jorge. 2015a. "Feeling at Home: an Autoethnographic Account of an Immigrant Football Fan in Western Sydney." *Leisure Studies* 34 (1): 34–41. doi:10.1080/02614367.2014.939991.

Knijnik, Jorge. 2015b. *Brazilians All Let Us Rejoice: FIFA Arrests and A New Era for World Football?* http://www.theroar.com.au/2015/06/03/brazilians-all-let-us-rejoice-fifa-marin-in-jail-and-a-new-era-for-world-football/.

Melnick, Merrill J., and Daniel L. Wann. 2011. "An Examination of Sport Fandom in Australia: Socialization, Team Identification, and Fan Behavior." *International Review for the Sociology of Sport* 46 (4): 456–470. doi:10.1177/1012690210380582.

Numerato, Dino. 2015. "Who Says 'No to Modern Football?' Italian Supporters, Reflexivity, and Neo-liberalism." *Journal of Sport & Social Issues* 39 (2): 120–138. doi:10.1177/0193723514530566.

Pennington, James. 2012. "Western Sydney Wanderers: Australia's Newest, Oldest Club." In *A Football Report*, edited by Eric Beard. Los Angeles, CA: A Football Report.

Red and Black Bloc. 2015. Post on "Red and Black Bloc's Facebook Page." *Facebook.com*, February 26. https://www.facebook.com/RedAndBlackBloc/posts/608180639283691.

Silverman, David. 2013. "What Counts as Qualitative Research? Some Cautionary Comments." *Qualitative Sociology Review* 9 (2): 48–55.

Skinner, James, Dwight H. Zakus, and Allan Edwards. 2008. "Coming in From the Margins: Ethnicity, Community Support and the Rebranding of Australian Soccer." *Soccer & Society* 9 (3): 394–404. doi:10.1080/14660970802009007.

Spaaij, Ramón, and Carles Viñas. 2005. "Passion, Politics and violence: A socio-historical Analysis of Spanish Ultras." *Soccer & Society* 6 (1): 79–96. doi:10.1080/1466097052000337034.

Toledo, Luiz Henrique De. 2010. "Torcer: a metafísica do homem comum." [Football fandom: the metaphysic of the ordinary people.] *Revista de História* 163: 175–189. doi:10.11606/issn.2316-9141.v0i163p175-189.

Warren, Johnny. 2003. *Sheilas, Wogs and Poofters*. Sydney: Random House Australia.

WestSydneyFootball. 2013. *Football Comes Home: The Early Days of Western Sydney Wanderers FC*. http://www.westsydneyfootball.com/sitefiles/fch/football_comes_home.pdf.

Carnival supporters, hooligans, and the 'Against Modern Football' movement: life within the ultras subculture in the Croatian context

Benjamin Perasović and Marko Mustapić

ABSTRACT
This paper is based on sociological research on Torcida, football supporters of Hajduk Football Club from Split (Croatia). We used ethnographic methodology throughout 37 months of fieldwork (from July 2012 to August 2015) and conducted 23 in-depth interviews with hardcore members of Torcida. Although our research included the distinction between carnival supporters and hooligans, these elements are much more interconnected within the hard core of Torcida than they are separate. Because of various social efforts (sometimes coordinated with other Ultras groups) against the local and global football establishment – especially against the Croatian Football Federation and UEFA – we consider Torcida part of a wide, heterogeneous social movement against modern football. This corresponds to the self-reflection and self-perception of the core group of Torcida. Ultras subculture in the Croatian context represents a key (although not the only) social actor in bearing the AMF movement.

Introduction and key concepts

The accelerated commercialization of football began in the 1960s, and took its current shape as a part of corporate business in the 1990 (King 2003; Millward 2011; Sandvoss 2003). Football supporters reacted to this commodification process in different ways, and their reactions were determined by local economic, legal and cultural contexts (Kennedy and Kennedy 2012). This in turn affected the football supporter scene in Europe, which has been the subject of sociological research since the 1960s. Although there were some signs of the use of ethnographic and qualitative approaches in the 1970s and into the 1980s (Marsh, Rosser, and Harré 1978; Williams, Dunning, and Murphy 1989), a great deal more ethnographic and other qualitative insights into the world of football supporters have been gained in the last two decades (Armstrong 1998; Brown 1993; Giulianotti 1991, 1995; King 2003; Millward 2011; Spaaij 2006; Stott and Pearson 2007; Testa 2009). Research on football supporters in Croatia began in the second half of the 1980s. After some papers and books on the subject were published, it became clear that it was a fertile and inspirational time for Croatian sociology (Lalić 1993). However, after a period of extensive research on football supporters in the 1990s, a series of significant social changes began to occur in Croatia, including war (1991–1995), and research on football supporters stopped almost completely. No ethnographic research of football supporter subculture has been done in Croatia since then (Perasović and Mustapić 2013). On the other hand, the phenomenon of 'football hooliganism' is a frequent and important subject in the Croatian media. The goal of this paper is to analyse what the concepts of carnival, hooligan and AMF mean to the actors themselves on the basis of ethnographic research already conducted on the Ultras group Torcida (Croatia). This is also the first empirical research on the role of the Croatian football supporter subculture in the AMF movement.

After the first year of sociological research (Perasović and Mustapić 2013), it seemed important to describe relevant aspects, such as the group's core and its extensions, social class, age and education, identity, gender, and organization, and to explain the role of banners, away matches, chanting, choreography, pyrotechnics, organized social events and the struggle against enemies (who, in addition to rival supporters, consist of the police force and the Croatian Football Federation), etc. After three years of ethnographic research, we asked ourselves by key terms we could use to describe our experience, especially in relation to the long history of research on the phenomena of football hooliganism. In this paper, we have decided to analyse those terms we deem crucial to an understanding of contemporary football hooliganism and the Ultras movement in Croatia. In doing so, the role and significance of violence in relationships within the supporter group itself, in relationships with other supporter groups, and in activities related to the AMF movement are of key importance.

The few decades of discussion on football hooliganism have been marked by the analysis of violence and behavioural patterns connected to violence. Because of this, our analysis focuses on the term 'carnival' as opposed to the term 'hooligan', so that we can describe the awareness of the differences and similarities between these terms we have gained through our research. Unlike previous research on football supporters that began in Croatia in the mid-1980s, this research reveals a widespread sense of belonging to the Ultras movement that is often connected to the AMF movement on both the global and local level. In the 1980s, the core groups shared a sense of belonging to a wider (international) tribe of football supporters, as well as of the joint creation of an international subcultural style of football hooliganism. Today, the sense of belonging to a social movement that opposes the commodification of football and police repression – and corruption in the Croatian context – is much clearer and more articulate.

Ultras subculture

The concept of 'Ultras' describes fanatical support offered by supporters to their club regardless of the club's results, weather, quality of play, etc. The roots of this type of support are found in Brazil, and later spread to Europe after the World Cup in 1950. The concept is tied to Italy, where numerous Ultras groups began to form in the 1950s (such as Fedelissimi Granata in Torino in 1951), whose support for their clubs included, in addition to the traditional chanting, singing and occasional violent conflicts with rival supporters, the use of flares, drums, banners and anything else that might contribute to an atmosphere of fanatical support. Supporters who consider themselves Ultras consider their club an important life orientation, and will support it and follow it regardless of when and where their matches are held. This style of support spread throughout the remainder of Europe in the 1970s, and especially in the 1980s.

The term 'subculture' is defined as a social actor and symbolic structure whose values and norms contrast in part with that of their broader social environment. The concept of social class as a world of socialization, inherited from the American functionalists in the 1950s and British Marxists in the 1970s, was crucial during one period of subcultural theory, however it is not something we insist upon. In other words, the term subculture is not strictly connected to social class, nor is social class considered the main source of subcultural style. Social class can play a significant role in the subculturalization process of a certain actor, but we endeavour to avoid the class determinism that characterized the sociology of youth subcultures in the 1970s. In this case, 'Ultras subculture' refers to actors that base their lifestyles and identities on specific behaviour patterns influenced by the continuous following of a chosen football club. The identity of Ultras is not limited to football matches, leisure time or similar isolated segments of time/space – it is a well-rounded identity that manifests in various ways in everyday life. Despite the fact that their identity is becoming more and more fragmented and fluid in today's society, the identity of Torcida's core members seems rather firm, with clearly defined and visible lifestyle and group identity boundaries. The theoretic legacy related to subculture was heavily criticized in sociology by the post-subculturalists (Bennett 1999, 2000; Muggleton 2000, 2005; Redhead 1990, 1993; Thornton 1995). However, parallel to the 'post-subculturalist' stream, authors like Hodkinson (2002) or Pilkington (2004, 2010) reclaimed the notion of subculture (and part of the previous theoretic legacy) directing our attention not to 'paradigm wars' but to 'thick description' and the content of research on youth (sub)cultures. The notion of subculture has also survived in recent studies on football supporters; for example, Geoff Pearson (2012) argued that 'carnival supporters' are a distinct subculture within the wider body of football supporters.[1]

The 'Against Modern Football' movement

Various football supporter actors have been expressing their discontent with the intense commodification of football ever since the process began roughly two decades ago. The academic community noticed this rather young phenomenon and began to study it (Gonda 2013; Kennedy 2013; Kennedy and Kennedy 2012; Numerato 2015; Webber 2014). This also included studies on football clubs founded by supporters themselves (Brown 2008; Porter 2011; Shafto 2013).

We think that, through the variety of reactions to commodification, the emergence of football supporters as social actors is creating a common denominator, a covenant, a symbolic field – or expressed in sociological terms – a social movement. Against Modern Football is the common denominator of a worldwide, heterogeneous social movement comprised of various actors and the methods of conflict: simple, symbolic actions like slogans written on flags, banners or walls; boycotts, petitions, demonstrations, direct actions and the foundation of new football clubs by supporters, such as FCUM, AFC Wimbledon, Austria Salzburg, Varteks Varaždin. This movement exists globally in networked society (Castells 1996), but is embodied mostly in the local community. The movement is primarily focused on the fight against the rigid commercialization of football and against turning supporters into 'consumers of football merchandise'. AMF is also against the ever-stricter surveillance system and control of supporter activities during football matches in stadiums and surrounding areas, ie against laws concerning supporters that are becoming more and more restrictive and rigorous in most European countries.[2]

Carnival supporters and hooligans

During the 1990s, it was common for sociological and cultural studies to reinterpret and reaffirm Bakhtin's notion of carnival as a transgression and inversion of social norms and behavioural patterns. Even though research on football hooliganism has been present for quite some time, the notion of carnival used by Giulianotti (1991, 1995) in his description of Scottish football supporters (Tartan army) marked a new phase in the differentiation of football supporters as social actors. There were other attempts at describing fervent and loyal football supporters who travel to away matches and cheer for their team, but are not inclined to brawl with rival supporters, however, the term carnival became common both in sociology and the wider academic community. It would seem that the self-perception of Scottish supporters, aided greatly by the Scottish media, influenced the use of the term, which is why differentiation between carnival supporters and hooligans has become commonplace in the sociology of sport and is also frequently used by sports journalists.

After Giulianotti's contribution (to both the conceptual framework and the description of supporter behaviour), it was accepted that the specific difference between the behaviour of carnival supporters and that of hooligans is violence. Contrary to Bakhtin's original study (Bakhtin 1984) in which carnival transgression included violence, the term 'carnivalesque' in discourse on football supporters has begun to signify a celebratory quality, an orgiastic hedonism based on alcohol that does not contain true transgression against or inversion of social norms. Thus, the presentation of our findings will focus on the attitude towards violence as crucial to the understanding of a different, interconnected relationship between the terms 'carnival' and 'hooligan'.

Methods, key actors and social context of research

Ethnography

This paper is based on sociological research on Torcida, football supporters of Hajduk Football Club from Split (Croatia). This research was conducted as part of a large international EU funded FP7 project entitled MYPLACE (Memory, Youth, Political Legacy and Civic Engagement). We used ethnographic methods throughout 37 months of fieldwork (from July 2012 to August 2015). The ethnographic research diary contained 154 extensive diary entries. Of these, 87 entries refer to football matches we attended (50 home matches and 35 away matches, and 2 matches of the Croatian national team). We always attended matches with Torcida core members. The remainder of the entries relate to socializing, celebrations, aid gathering for supporters in need and other group activities. We conducted 23 in-depth interviews with our respondents, who are hard-core members of Torcida. The field diary entries and interview transcripts were coded using Nvivo 9.2. It should also be noted that both authors of this paper are supporters of Hajduk, and, in accordance with their respectable age, have had the experience of being Torcida members in the past. This made communication with the group's core members easier and aided in the research. Before the

MYPLACE project began in the summer of 2011, both authors of this text renewed their involvement in actively supporting Hajduk for private, non-academic reasons. Considering the perspective of insider/outsider, the researchers in this case are insiders as concerns knowing the people, slang, symbols and rituals of Torcida. However, they found themselves in the positions of outsiders as concerns the younger generation, which took over leadership shortly before research began in 2012. The specific distance that existed in the early stages of research faded after a few months of field research. Initially, only a few key supporters knew that we had academic motivations in addition to our motivations as supporters, and after a few months many other members of the hard core knew about our research, some of who later assented to in-depth interviews.

Hajduk and Torcida

Despite numerous political events and social changes, Hajduk is one of the rare football clubs on the territory of the former Yugoslavia that has not changed its name ever since it was founded in 1911.[3] One of the oldest banners of Torcida is one bearing the message '*Hajduk živi vječno*' [Hajduk Lives Forever]. Throughout its 105 years of existence, Hajduk has won a total of 18 national championships and 15 cups, and its greatest European successes have been three quarterfinal matches at the Champions Cup/Champions League (1976, 1980, 1995) and one semi-final match at the UEFA Cup (1984) and Cup Winners' Cup (1973). Hajduk is, alongside Dinamo Zagreb, the most popular football club in Croatia. Since 2008, Hajduk has functioned as a sport joint stock company, and its majority owner is the City of Split (56.1%). Since the mid-2000s, Hajduk has been burdened by both poor results and financial problems, including a brush with bankruptcy in 2012. Despite these issues and poor results, Hajduk matches are still the best-attended in Croatia, with an average of 11,600 people having attending matches in Split during the 2013/2014 season, while the average of all Croatian Football League matches in the same season was only 3200.

Torcida, the staunchest supporters of Hajduk, is the oldest supporters' (Ultras) group in Europe, founded in 1950. Immediately after its foundation, the repressive apparatus of socialist Yugoslavia banned the further action of Torcida, arresting its leading members and sentencing some of them to prison terms. Despite this, memory of the foundation of Torcida remained, as did all of its supporting activities, which were still carried out without banners bearing the name 'Torcida'. During the liberalization of society in Yugoslavia in the late 1970s, a new generation began the subculturalization process, and Torcida was renewed (Lalić 1993; Perasović 1995). From that point on, it was the most influential subcultural actor in the City of Split and the region of Dalmatia. Apart from various informal group-ings and its friendship-based structure, Torcida as an Ultras group has also been an NGO with a formal structure and hierarchy since the mid-1990s. Torcida mobilizes thousands of young people, providing a framework for the identification process and the creation of a distinct subcultural style – Ultras subculture. Perasović and Mustapić (2013) stressed that the hard core of contemporary Torcida numbers between 300 and 500 members, however this number easily grows to between 1000 and 1500 people who regularly travel to even minor away matches. This number grows to between 3000 and 4000 when more important away matches are played, such as matches against Dinamo in Zagreb or European matches. When important matches are held in Split, during which the entire northern stands of the stadium are filled (6000–7000 people, or as many as 9000) Torcida plays the role of conductor for the entire stadium. Torcida has undoubtedly been the most numerous at home and away matches in Croatia in recent seasons. One part of contemporary identity of Torcida is its strong, 20 year friendship with No Name Boys (supporters of Benfica) and two other passionate and official friendships with Magic Fans (St.Ettienne) and Torcida Górnik (Górnik Zabrze).

Social context and Croatian football establishment

After the fall of the socialist regime, Croatia underwent 'tectonic' social changes – specifically, the conversion from a totalitarian society to a democratic one. Since then, Croatia has been in transition, which, unlike most other post-socialist countries, was additionally burdened with the tragic consequences of the Croatian Homeland War (1991–1995). Županov (1995) has noted the controversy of the simultaneous strengthening of individual utilitarianism (at the individual level), nationalism and the heroic code (at the national level), and radical egalitarianism (at the societal level), which outlined the framework ('re-traditionalisation') of Croatian society and articulated its basic values in the first decade of transition in the 1990s. Croatian citizens witnessed this transition as an unequal race for positions of power and control over accumulated public resources. Franičević (2002, 5) points out: 'The institutional structure that developed in Croatia during the 1990s was ineffective, the credibility of formal institutions was low, law enforcement was weak, and uncertainty was very high, and all these facts have strongly contributed to the emergence of crony capitalism instead of an effective economy and a truly democratic society'. During the 1990s, the successes of Croatian athletes, and especially of its football players, played a great role in forming the modern Croatian national identity (Bartoluci 2013), in which football supporters often played the role of emphasizing and disseminating nationalist discourse (Brentin 2016; Hodges 2016a, 2016b; Vrcan 2003; Vrcan and Lalić 1999).

The socio-economic processes of the 1990s, paired with political centralization, created entirely new relations in Croatian professional sports, specifically in Zagreb's clubs' success in monopolizing national sporting events due to the fact that Zagreb had become the strongest centre of political and economic power, as opposed to the economically atrophied and war-torn centres of regions in eastern and southern Croatia (Slavonia and Dalmatia, respectively). Our focus on the city of Split (Dalmatia) due to our research on Torcida allows us to describe the special position of Split and Dalmatia as a double periphery – Croatia is on the periphery regarding European centres of power, and Split (with its population of 178,000) is on the periphery as compared to Zagreb (with its population of 792,000) as the Croatian centre of power. The Croatian Football Federation is an extremely important sports organization both in the political and the economic sense. Unlike local clubs or the weak national league, the Croatian national team has become an icon of national identity, and is thus important to various political actors.[4] Considering how often regulations on football are broken, especially by key actors in the Croatian Football Federation (Hrvatski nogometni savez – HNS) and its judicial organization, this is paradoxical indeed. For example, in 2010, 22 football players and citizens were arrested under suspicion of match fixing in the First Croatian Football Division, and were later convicted. Fifteen players were found guilty after a seven-month trial in 2011. Željko Širić (former vice-president of the Croatian Football Federation) and Stjepan Djedović (the president of the Referee Commission) were arrested in 2011 for seeking and accepting a bribe for so-called 'fair refereeing'. Djedović pleaded guilty and was given a suspended sentence, while Širić received a four-year prison sentence in 2014. At the beginning of July in 2015, Zdravko Mamić (executive vice president of HNS and GNK Dinamo), Damir Vrbanović (executive vice president of HNS and vice president of the UEFA Club Competitions Committee) and Zoran Mamić (coach of GNK Dinamo) were arrested on suspicion of the embezzlement of GNK Dinamo funds (€15 million) and tax evasion. A large part of the Croatian public, and especially members of the Ultras subculture, considers Zdravko Mamić the very symbol of modern football in the Croatian context, burdened with criminality and corruption.

Key findings

Carnival & hooligan: differentiation or integration in the case of Torcida's core members?

One of the goals of our research was to determine how the differentiation between the carnival and hooligan type of supporter functions in the case of Torcida. Although our respondents do not use the distinction between carnival and hooligan in their speech, they do use numerous other terms to describe differentiation among supporters. One of the most frequently used differences is that between true supporters, Ultras, and 'derby supporters'.[5] As is to be expected, those who go to every match, both home and away, are mistrustful of those who go only to derbies or other 'important' matches. There is also a distinction between 'real' supporters, ie Ultras, and 'alealeština' – a Croatian slang term derived from supporter chants of 'ale-ale'. This refers not only to 'derby supporters', but also to a cultural type whose aesthetic and stylistic preferences reveal a mainstream, traditionalist orientation that does not understand contemporary urban forms of supporter expression. This is revealed through poor knowledge of Torcida songs and the wearing of several shawls, flags, jerseys and similar club accessories that are considered kitsch. Under the influence of excitement and alcohol, these supporters catch only the echo of chants of 'ale-ale' and other recognizable chants and songs. Our research has also noted differences between segments of Torcida as a supporters' group. Fans consider this both natural and legitimate. As conflicts with rival supporters are a part of life in the Ultras subculture, just like pyrotechnics, choreography, banners, and so on, it is also natural that some supporters are more active than others, and are thus recognized as specialists for one of the mentioned areas of supporter activity.

The segment that covers conflicts with rival supporters is referred to as the 'street' (*ulica*). There are groups within Torcida that are dedicated to the 'street' more than to choreography or pyrotechnics, for example. However, those dedicated to the 'street' and those dedicated to other segments of supporter activity travel together and stand together in stadiums, just like those who are not especially immersed in any of these specific activities. All supporters will, if need be, participate in various activities together. This specifically relates to the hard core of Torcida, which includes 300–500 people. Therefore, 'street', choreography, banners, song writing, declaration writing and similar activities can be understood as the basis for a segmentation that differs from the notion of fragmentation. These segments comprise a single whole (Torcida), which is not weakened by its partitions. During research between 2012 and 2015, we witnessed situations in which 'street' became the dominant behaviour of most of the supporters present, regardless of whether the violence was initiated by the police (eg Sveti Ivan Zelina 2012), Torcida (boycott of the match between Split and Hajduk in 2013), or the mutual desire of Torcida and other Ultras (mass brawls with supporters of GNK Dinamo Zagreb (Bad Blue Boys – BBB) and supporters of HNK Rijeka (Armada) that occurred several times on the highway). In these situations, it was easy to see that some supporters were more eager to fight than others, who did not push and shove to get to the front lines. Nevertheless, solidarity prevails, and the group as a whole subsists despite differences in willingness to commit violence. They still all gather, either at away matches or in the northern stands of Poljud (Hajduk's stadium), forgetting that those in the front lines were too emotional in their judgement of those who kept a safe distance, and that those in the back were critical of the hard-core faction that wanted to fight rival supporters they had met on the highway. Situations like this rarely pass without conflict, however the segmentation of supporter activity in Torcida has never led to a fragmentation into 'hooligan' and 'carnival' factions. One of the reasons for this may be the size of the group, ie the conviction that Ultras groups such as Torcida cannot allow differentiation, which might lead to dissipation. Another reason is the notion held by most Ultras (the hard core of Torcida) that hooliganism, riots and chaos are a legitimate part of the football carnival, a kind of hedonism equivalent to drinking beer and singing. For them, the possibility of riots is an 'added value' to the drinking and singing – in other words, the adrenaline rush and excitement at the thought of possible riots adds a carnival atmosphere of excitement to the drinking and singing without which the occasion would be no different than a private party. Our conclusion as to the thin line between what could be called the 'carnival' and the 'hooligan' orientation within Torcida corresponds with the opinions held by many of our respondents. Here is an example taken from our conversation with OSP,[6] who never belonged to the 'street', nor did he participate in ambushes organized by others. OSP belongs to the hard core of Torcida and has been at every single Hajduk home and away match in the past 10 years. Here, he expounds upon his thesis on the two types of supporters as concerns hooliganism:

> We could divide hooligans into two groups; hooligans who like to be hooligans and fight, and those who become hooligans because they are attacked by hooligans … Both groups go to matches non-stop. For example, I belong to the second group, and I won't attack the other group, or will rarely do so; my approach is to go primarily to see the match, not to attack someone. I go to see Hajduk, I don't want to attack other groups, but there is a rule in the Ultras world that the other group is always waiting for you, so you come to them, naturally, and you also become a hooligan for a moment because you have to defend yourself, and if you have a chance to attack them, since you know they will attack you, then you attack them, why the fuck not … (OSP)

This statement clearly demonstrates that those actors who are not primarily involved in action planning or ambush planning, ie actors for whom the 'street' is not the first choice of activity within the supporter world and a given supporters' group, do accept a certain type of violence as a constituent part of Ultras scene. In our interviews with the hard-core members of Torcida during the past three seasons, we often encountered people who were not primarily active in the 'street', but who nevertheless expressed group solidarity in various situations. Some of them participated in ambushes, even though they were not personally interested in such activities:

> I participated in ambushes several times, but nothing happened. We used to sit in a car for a few hours, then a friend would call and say 'they took the highway, the other route', so nothing happened … I decided to go because I felt all right, although I don't usually like to go. In fact, when I see that there are enough guys, I would rather stay at home. I'm not really a fighter,

look at me, I'm small and thin, if someone who weighs 100 kg hits me in the head, I'm done for ... But I did go several times, in order to help the group ... (Ekstrem)

The violence that is considered as a normal part of the Ultras subculture is not without limits. There are clear rules and there is a willingness to obey the unwritten code of conduct. An ideal fight is one in which hands and feet are used and no weapons are allowed. Many of our respondents clearly defined fair play in fighting and abhorred weapons, especially knives and guns, which are not considered a part of the Ultras world. However, no matter how clearly they distanced themselves from using bats and stones in fights, we have noted a few situations in which supporters used bats, brass knuckles, flares and other means of fighting. One frequent statement shows a tendency towards the ideal fight (in which no weapons are allowed) and an acceptance of a reality in which anything close at hand can be used for self-defence:

> ... in a fight, hands and feet, that's it ... weapons, knives, that's rock bottom. The very word 'weapons' does not belong to the supporters' world ... but, you know, if you're in a café bar and you're attacked by a group of rival supporters, it's normal that bottles and ashtrays will fly, chairs as well ... it's normal in self-defence ... (Sokol_St)

Some respondents, wishing to stress fair play rules, showed understanding for the reality of street fight in which rules are not always followed. Even then, however, they made a clear distinction between that which can be tolerated and that which is never allowed:

> I think there has to be a boundary. Rocks for example, I don't like that. It would be ideal to fight only with fists, but to tell you the truth, it's impossible in a street fight, it's not realistic, people would use anything ... So no rocks, but flares could be all right, not in the face but as a psychological weapon, to throw a flare at them, that's all right. Knives or guns are completely out of the question, it's not a part of the Ultras style ... (Nessuno)

Torcida and the AMF movement: values, issues, methods of struggle

'Against Modern Football' is a widespread and heterogeneous social movement that exists all over the world. Most of the Ultras groups belong to this movement at least symbolically, and they express their solidarity with other actors in the movement in various ways. Various Ultras groups, each in their own environment, apply different methods and nurture different discourses about the movement depending on their local context. Our research has shown the existence of two main and interconnected dimensions of activism. First, symbolic actions that carry universal meaning, most often related to the 'Against Modern Football' slogan itself, messages relating solidarity with other Ultras groups, R.I.P. messages, etc. Second, a set of various actions based on the principles of the AMF movement, which in the Croatian context includes the fight against the football establishment, surveillance, control and commercialization. There is also a strong wish for Hajduk, as a public company, to remain a 'people's club' (a public good of the city of Split) without a private majority owner.

As relates to the first dimension, we have noted that Torcida uses numerous flags and banners with the slogan 'Against Modern Football' written on them, one-off messages in stadiums (also connected to the movement or expressing solidarity with other actors in the Ultras movement), graffiti on walls, messages on t-shirts and stickers, etc. Slogans and motifs inspired by AMF can also be found on the Internet, ranging from individual activities (icons, symbols, photos, nicknames or other representations) to group Internet activities. All of the Torcida members interviewed believe that they, as an Ultras group, are a part of a large supporters' movement that shares a common set of ideals and fights for a common goal. Although Torcida did bring banners and flags bearing the message 'Against Modern Football' to several important international matches (against Skonto Riga, Inter, etc.), the most quoted banner slogan is one Torcida members brought to the match between Croatia and Turkey during Euro 2008 in Vienna.[7] The death of young Torcida member Marko Azapović in 2013 caused distress among Ultras who, like Azapović's family, believed that his death was a consequence of police brutality. In May 2013, Ultras all over the world (Croatia, Slovenia, Bosnia and Herzegovina, Macedonia, Kosovo, Portugal, Spain, France, Germany, Bulgaria, Australia, etc.) raised banners of solidarity during matches of their respective clubs bearing messages ranging from R.I.P. messages to anti-police slogans. Similarly, Torcida members expressed their compassion for the police murder of Polish supporter Dawid Dziedzic in May 2015. Messages like these are common in the Ultras world. The Internet enables supporters to communication quickly and offers them the feeling of a shared public space (both a material and local space, such as the one in their own stadium, and a virtual and global space on the Internet). There are other known symbols of the AMF movement in Torcida, such as the nostalgic image of an old leather football and other 'retro' creations displayed on shawls, hats and small banners held on two poles reminiscent of the period before the rapid global commodification of football and increasing surveillance and control. The spirit of nostalgia fits the significance Torcida applies to its history as well – all Torcida members are proud of the fact that Torcida was founded in 1950. Considering the significance that tradition has in the contemporary supporters' movement, it is not surprising that the slogan 'Against Modern Football Since 1950' has appeared on items of clothing made and sold by Torcida.

Besides the form of expression it shares with other Ultras and with members of the greater AMF movement, Torcida is one of the main social actors in the fight against modern football in Croatia. In this fight, Torcida uses most of the known methods of struggle that can be found in the rich tradition of social movements: petitions, boycotts, demonstrations, direct actions, various forms of pressure, physical conflict. The boycott of an exhibition match between the national teams of Croatia and Switzerland in Split in 2012 was a complete success despite not having been publicly announced. A boycott of the city derby against RNK Split in 2013 was announced, caused by a price hike in tickets for visiting supporters, however as it coincided with the case of Marko Azapović, the boycott of the match and a gathering of Torcida members in front of the stadium ended in a violent confrontation with police. The boycott of Hajdučko Beer in the summer of 2013 was a successful form of pressure on Koprivnica Brewery to pay its dues to Hajduk. Following news that the majority owner of Hajduk (the City Council of Split) refused to act as a guarantor for a loan to the club, demonstrations held in October 2012 managed to put so much pressure on city council members that they changed their vote and saved Hajduk from bankruptcy.

One of the clearest examples of supporter action in accordance with shared values took place between October 2013 and March 2014, during which time all Croatian Ultras groups proclaimed a truce and broke off conflict in order to share in the fight against the Croatian Football Federation. On 17 October 2013, the Federation decided to ban organized trips of supporters' groups to away games unless their clubs supplied the police and the home team with a list containing personal data on all supporters expected to come. Every visiting supporter was to be provided with a 'voucher'. During the fight against these vouchers, members of Torcida carried banners bearing the text 'Higher Goal', broke off conflict with their most hated rivals such as supporters of Dinamo (Bad Blue Boys), and showed numerous forms of supporter solidarity in this battle, frequently even purchasing tickets to home matches for their greatest rivals. The police were confused by this manner of behaviour from supporters, and the general public saw their first examples of behaviour that deviated from the stereotype of hooligans constantly reinforced and reproduced by the media. On 25 February 2014, a Croatian Football Federation Executive Committee session was held where it was decided that vouchers had not provided the desired results. In fact, it turned out that they had harmed the Federation, clubs and supporters, for which reason they were withdrawn immediately. Only a few hours after this decision was announced, Torcida reacted on its Facebook page (https://www.facebook.com/torcida.split.1950), saying that supporters had no cause to celebrate, because the war 'against the football mafia will continue until its final defeat'.

More than 30,000 citizens attended demonstrations against the Federation held in Split in November 2014, thus proving that football supporters were able to initiate a social movement against corruption in Croatian football. It should be stressed that, in this particular case, Hajduk Football Club refused to play in the biggest Croatian derby. Hajduk's management decided to boycott the match because its organizers (Dinamo Zagreb) had denied stadium access to Torcida members that had not been officially banned from matches by the police.[8] During 2013, Torcida played an important role in opposition to the Split city government's attempt to sell its majority stake in Hajduk, thus preventing the transfer of ownership to a US company. At the outset of our ethnographic research in 2012, Torcida's pressure against the city government had already existed for some time – Torcida members founded a supporters' association called *Naš Hajduk* [Our Hajduk] through which they managed to prevent the sale. In 2011 and 2015, the *Naš Hajduk* association, acting on behalf of the club's owner, managed to organize an election for seven of nine members of the Hajduk's supervisory board.[9] Thus, it is clear that Torcida directly influences the governance of the club. In their fight against police repression and increasingly restrictive laws, supporters use public announcements and media space to reach their goals, and in certain situations, do not shy from attacking police or burning police vehicles to do so as well.

All the interviewed members of the Torcida hard core feel like they belong to the wider, international football supporters' movement known as Against Modern Football. Many supporters describe the difference between the past and present, stressing the seriousness of the present situation in which supporters are dealing with the survival of the club, ownership relations and laws. The Against Modern Football movement is considered as an obligation and the duty of every true Ultras supporter.

> I also started as part of the old school in a way. I used to a wear bomber jacket as a kid. I understand the old school. Maybe it was the best for that time and for the people who were at the top then, because they didn't care at all. For them it was like: take drugs, get loaded, go crazy, drink, smoke, wander about, and everything's great. I think the contemporary supporters' movement also brings elements you would rather not have, but that you have to accept. In fact, it's like a burden or something. It's like you're living another life, whether you want it or not, which isn't so easy. It's not just like 'go out there, get loaded, and go crazy'. It's something else and you have to adjust, and I am glad that I managed to adjust, although I also had my phases. I had to understand that it's not that simple, it's not just the madness and the great times, especially when you're not 15 or 16 anymore. The notion of Against Modern Football also just means a kind of duty for real supporters, real Ultras in modern times. Yes, simply put, I support that notion 100%. (Paul Gascoigne)

Regardless of complex operations like the election of the Supervisory Board members or the organization of mass demonstrations against the Croatian Football Federation, supporters stress that simple, symbolic expressions are important and effective. That is why many of our respondents commented on the importance of the big AMF banner at UEFA EURO 2008 in Vienna:

> Regarding AMF, the most significant moment specifically regarding Torcida took place at Euro 2008, when we were playing against Turkey in Vienna. There were about 100 of us, all gathered around the 'Against Modern Football' banner. In my opinion, it was the supporters' most positive moment, not only when it comes to chanting and so on, but I think that at that very moment everyone connected to Torcida, to the entire supporters movement. They had to think about it, use their head, and see the direction football was taking and what we wanted to say with that message. It means football is literally reduced to production and money making, so we have to add two and two together. These things are good for FIFA, UEFA, and football federations making money from it. Having this kind of supporters around definitely doesn't suit them – supporters who care about their own tradition. In Torcida, it's about flares, flags, and chanting as only we can, so to speak. In that sense, supporters as supporters aren't good for them, they presents an obstacle that makes it much harder for them to sell their story. And, thank God, we have the means for that struggle, and that's it. (Adobe)

While respecting symbolic actions (in the second part of his statement, Adobe hints at other means, such as flares, which have become a universal symbol of resistance in the Ultras world), many Torcida members are aware of the significance of new clubs that are being founded by supporters in order to help the AMF movement.

> FCUM – that is one of the most impressive things regarding the entire football supporters' story. They've reached the most fundamental question: what does football mean to them, what is their football club, what is their name? They evidently have to play their part radically, so that they can take back and enjoy everything that has been trampled and destroyed … This isn't so much an issue of repression kicking them out of the stadium, or the managers of the club – they were kicked out by expensive tickets, overpriced players, crowds of tourists in the stadium … In fact, they [supporters, the FCUM founders] were kicked out by money. They've reached the essence, the conclusion, so, our club has mutated into something that has nothing to do with us anymore, let's go and make our own club and show people what Manchester really is. They even brought back the traditional uniform of Manchester United – the original uniform is black socks, black shorts, and a red shirt, while today's United plays in white socks and white shorts … They really succeeded and that's great. We have a similar example in Varaždin, with Varteks FC. So, it's a fucking great thing and I think it's one of the most impressive steps within the Against Modern Football movement. (Vikar)

Croatian mainstream media discourse often stresses the idea of a wealthy owner as the only true solution for the club's financial crisis. In the past few years, Torcida members have struggled to prove that a private owner, regardless of their wealth, is not compatible with the concept of a people's club. Regardless of the youth of the actors and their wish to engage in the usual supporter's activities, there are priorities. The following supporters' quote clearly states what these priorities are:

> We are all football supporters. A supporter is someone who lights the flares, fights in the street, who is a part of this subculture – we all know that. Recently, however, as we're talking about AMF, it's a fact that more of my energy goes to explaining why not to sell Hajduk … I lead the struggle more on that level than on the hooligan level. I have to explain to people that the club should not be sold to an American guy (or any other guy) … That has been more important lately than everything regarding supporting, chanting, away matches. So, energy goes in that direction and not in the other direction … (Zeus)

Concluding remarks

Violence as part of the carnival

Considering the issue of violence, which is crucial to definitions of football hooliganism, members of Torcida represent an Ultras subculture in which a certain dose of violence has always been a constituent part of the scene, at least for its core group. In fact, the Ultras movement never excluded violence – it simply included more activities (choreography, flags, pyrotechnics, chanting, songs, organization, etc.) than the hooligan type of supporting. A portion of the Ultras have always felt an almost ritual intolerance of rival supporters, the expression of which included violence, but because of the wide variety of other activities – including hedonistically oriented activities that would later be reductionistically proclaimed to be carnivalesque – this was not always obvious. The Ultras scene and the phenomenon of football hooliganism are far more alike than was initially suspected. The revival of casual style is strong in the contemporary Ultras scene, both in fashion and behaviour. In fact, the contemporary Ultras movement nurtures both traditions equally – both the loud and fanatical cheering and rituals in and around the stadium, and the English tradition of 'casuals'. Torcida is a good example of this process.

The carnival supporters in Pearson's ethnographic research (2012), as opposed to tourist supporters, have a style of dress similar to that of European Ultras, who do not want to wear official jerseys or look like contemporary football consumers or tourists. They do care about supporting their club and they are hedonistically oriented, but they do not participate in conflicts as often as members of the hooligan faction do.

The connection between violence, riots and other characteristics of hooliganism on one hand and the 'non-violent' meaning of carnivalesque in the hard core of Torcida on the other hand does not mean that the core is mostly hooligan oriented; if we observe the segments of Torcida carefully (choreography, songs, pyrotechnics, 'street', organization, etc.), it becomes clear that only a small part of the hard core is dedicated to the 'street'. Most of the Ultras within Torcida are not focused on planning conflicts with other supporters, however they will not run from conflict if they find themselves in a situation that sparks it. There is a form of solidarity that allows for some differences in levels of dedication to this or that segment of a supporters' life, but which unites supporters in most situations, especially during away matches and regardless of different approaches to violence and conflict. The term 'carnivalesque' is doubtlessly a good metaphor for a great portion of supporters' rituals, but in this case, notions of violence, riots, conflict, vandalism and other similar behaviours should not be excluded from the term, as that would be congruent neither with our findings nor with Bakhtin's original interpretation. Hughson (2002) reached similar conclusions. Although it is evident that a certain process has begun – a process that could hypothetically grow into a differentiation process regarding the approach to violence – there is an intertwining of forms of transgression within the Torcida hard core that does not allow differentiation between hooligan and carnival. Internal cohesion is aided by the mainstream media's complete misunderstanding of the supporter lifestyle, frequent moral panic campaigns and external pressure, which strengthens the movement internally.

AMF – 'the higher goal'

Life in the Ultras subculture (at least as concerns Torcida) is extremely dynamic, and includes the complex world of football games, choreography, away matches, conflict, emotions and passion. Besides the usual supporter activities and the specific relationship to other supporters' groups, together with a strong animosity towards the police, members of Torcida are characterized by the sense of belonging to the wider social movement known as Against Modern Football. Contempt for the pompous spectacle of contemporary corporate football and its television/theatre elements, and resistance against the football establishment, which is perceived as a mafia, connects Torcida with numerous other actors in the Ultras subculture in various countries. In Croatia, this fight has taken the shape of a fight against corruption, against rule by the sole big boss of Croatian football (Zdravko Mamić) and his followers. In order to remove the mafia from Croatian football, Torcida sometimes cooperates with its fiercest rivals (like BBB) because they share a common goal – a 'higher goal' towards which not only Torcida members strive, but other actors in the Croatian Ultras subculture as well. Dedication to their own subcultural style and participation in numerous rituals, the creation of their own style and identity (which may contain slang, visual expression, gestures, clothing style, values, etc.) proves the existence of subculturalization patterns similar to those that can be found in psy-trance, goth, punk or any other subcultural scene.

Because of their patriotism and a tendency to commemorate important events from the period of the Homeland War, some media discourse has branded Torcida as far-right. Even though political orientation is not what we focus on in this paper, this stereotype should be noted. Our findings show that Torcida is an actor that cannot be unambiguously described as left or right. If patriotism is associated with nationalism, machoism and homophobia, the result will be a stereotypical image that will be partly reinforced in the stands during each match. However, knowledge of all other discourses used within the hard core of Torcida prevents a shallow stereotype. For Torcida members, the fight against modern football as a fight against mafia in both the national and international football establishment is more important than cheap calls for patriotic unity where the 'sacred' national team is concerned. Regardless of their own (strong) patriotism, Torcida members are prepared to risk the anger of society at large in cases like Milan (Italy – Croatia, 17 Nov 2014 – qualifications for EURO 2016) in which Croatian Ultras disrupted a national team match by throwing flares onto the pitch in a fight against an incomparably stronger opponent (the Croatian Football Federation). Political orientation within Torcida is limited by consensus on patriotism on one hand, and by participation in the AMF movement on the other hand, both on the general level of symbolic solidarity with other Ultras groups and on the local level of fighting for the concept of Hajduk as an honourable people's club without a private owner. An emphasis on political orientation aside from these two discourses is not allowed. Moreover, all of the respondents interviewed abhorred political parties, seeing the differences between them as less significant than their similarities – which is why they grouped seemingly opposing politicians into the same corrupted political class.

Considering the values present among supporters from the hard core, belonging to the AMF movement represents a kind of common denominator, and points to a specific social environment that joins individual themes and methods of struggle (against commodification or police repression) into one recognizable sensibility (AMF). As a typical Ultras subculture, Torcida represents one of the main social actors bearing the AMF movement in the Croatian context, and it does not exclude violence from its carnivalesque approach and methods of struggle. Considering the existing literature on the AMF movement, we can conclude that AMF in the Croatian context – and especially in the context of Torcida – is similar to that identified by Kennedy (2013) and Webber (2014) concerning resistance to commodification, including a modicum of the self-reflection described by Numerato (2015) and the AMF movement in Poland as described by Gonda (2013). As opposed to Poland, where the AMF movement among supporters is mainly a fight against the repression and control of supporters, Torcida represents an example of an AMF movement in the Croatian context that includes resistance against the commercialization of football and resistance against repressive laws, forming the core of a broader social movement against corruption in Croatian society, symbolized by corruption in the football establishment.

Notes

1. The 'Ultras tribe' sounds just as good as 'Ultras subculture', and both terms are sociologically valid. However, reclaiming Maffesoli (1996) into the sociology of youth subcultures would demand more space than we have here. In short, our interpretation of the term 'tribe' as reintroduced by Michel Maffesoli (1996) is different than the usual interpretation found in the works of the post-subculturalists (Bennett 1999; Muggleton 2000, 2005), where inconsistency, fluidity, superficiality, and mutability are overemphasized while the consistent new structures of the postmodern tribe are often neglected. In spite of being based on the instinctive, the emotional, and the symbolic, as Maffesoli (1996) points out, these structures are nevertheless not devoid of firmness and power.
2. The dominant media discourse in Croatia presents Margaret Thatcher's solution to football hooliganism as an example to be followed – ie similar laws and measures should be adopted and implemented to solve the problem. We dare to claim that media campaigns against Ultras and hooliganism are textbook examples of the sociological concept of moral panic.
3. For more on the construction of the official memory of Hajduk's history, see Perasović and Mustapić (2014).
4. At the moment, out of 17 members of the CFF Executive Comitte (the 'football government'), 11 are notable members of a political party, and the president and vice president of CFF are members of the same party. It has been a consistent occurrence for years that, whenever the Croatian Football Federation breaks the law, the actors involved explain to the media that they have been subjected to 'political pressure'. In such cases, they seek (and receive) protection from umbrella organizations like FIFA and UEFA each time the state attempts to sanction their illegal behaviour.
5. It is important to note that the term 'derby' in Croatia refers to matches played between traditional rivals – such as a match between Dinamo and Hajduk – regardless of whether they are local clubs or not.
6. In order to stay anonymous, every one of our respondents chose a pseudonym. In this case, OSP is an acronym of the well-known phrase 'o svom poslu', which loosely translates as 'doing our own thing', connoting freedom and independence among football supporters.
7. The term 'quoting' here means the frequent use of photographs of this banner for academic presentations, book covers (Kennedy and Kennedy 2012), in the media etc. As our field research began long after 2008, the respondents, many of whom were active at the time, often mentioned this occasion.
8. This decision cost Hajduk the anger of a part of the public and the official penalty, but it also strengthened its connection to its supporters and drew attention to the deeper problems of Croatian football, such as corruption and autocratic rule of a single man and his followers. After the boycotted derby in Zagreb, Hajduk was upon coming home to Split greeted by 8000 fans that celebrated the gesture of the club. A week after, during the demonstration against CFF which gathered 30,000 people, the players and management of Hajduk showed their support by joining in.
9. In 2016 more than 43,000 supporters had joined *Naš Hajduk*.

Disclosure statement

No potential conflict of interest was reported by the authors.

References

Armstrong, Gary. 1998. *Football Hooligans: Knowing the Score*. Oxford: Berg.

Bakhtin, Mikhail. 1984. *Rabelais and his World*. Bloomington: Midland Books; Indiana University Press.

Bartoluci, Sunčica. 2013. *Uloga vrhunskog sporta u oblikovanju nacionalnog identiteta u Republici Hrvatskoj: usporedba devedesetih i dvijetisućitih: doktorski rad* [The Role of High-performance Sport in Shaping of National Identity in the Republic of Croatia: The Comparison of the 1990s and the 2000s: Doctoral Thesis]. Zagreb: Sveučilište u Zagrebu, Filozofski fakultet.

Bennett, Andy. 1999. "Subcultures or Neo-tribes? Rethinking the Relationship Between Youth, Style and Musical Taste." *Sociology* 33 (3): 599–617.

Bennett, Andy. 2000. *Popular Music and Youth Culture: Music, Identity and Place*. London: Macmillan.

Brentin, Dario. 2016. "Ready for the Homeland? Ritual, Remembrance, and Political Extremism in Croatian Football." *Nationalities Papers* 44 (6): 860–876. doi:10.1080/00905992.2015.1136996.

Brown, Adam. 1993. "Ratfink Reds: Montpellier and Rotterdam in 1991." In *The passion and the Fashion: Football fandom in New Europe*, edited by Steve Redhead, 33–44. Aldershot: Avebury.

Brown, Adam. 2008. "Our Club, Our Rules: Fan Communities at FC United of Manchester." *Soccer & Society* 9 (3): 346–358. doi:10.1080/14660970802008967.

Castells, Manuel. 1996. *The Rise of the Network Society, The Information Age: Economy, Society and Culture Vol. 1*. Cambridge, MA: Blackwell.

Franičević, Vojmir. 2002. "Politička i moralna ekonomija u prvom desetljeću tranzicije u Hrvatskoj." [Political and moral economy in the first decade of the transition in Croatia.] *Politička misao* 39 (1): 3–34.

Giulianotti, Richard. 1991. "Scotland's Tartan Army in Italy: The Case for Carnivalesque." *The Sociological Review* 39 (3): 503–527. doi:10.1111/j.1467-954X.1991.tb00865.x.

Giulianotti, Richard. 1995. "Football and Politics of Carnival: An Ethnographic Study of Scottish Fans in Sweden." *International Review for the Sociology of Sport* 30 (2): 191–220. doi:10.1177/101269029503000205.

Gonda, Marcin. 2013. "Supporters' Movement 'Against Modern Football' and Sport Mega Events: European and Polish Contexts." *Przegląd Socjologiczny* 62 (3): 85–106.

Hodges, Andrew. 2016. "The Left and the Rest? Fan Cosmologies and Relationships Between Celtic's Green Brigade and Dinamo Zagreb's Bad Blue Boys." *Glasnik Etnografskog instituta SANU* 64 (2): 305–319.

Hodges, Andrew. 2016. "Violence and Masculinity Amongst Left-wing Ultras in Post-Yugoslav Space." *Sport in Society* 19 (2): 174–186. doi:10.1080/17430437.2015.1067771.

Hodkinson, Paul. 2002. *Goth: Identity, Style and Subculture*. Oxford: Berg.

Hughson, John. 2002. "Australian Soccer's 'Ethnic' Tribes: A New Case for the Carnivalesque." In *Fighting Fans: Footbal Hooliganism as a World Phenomenon*, edited by Eric Dunning, Patrcik Murphy, Ivan Waddington and Antonios Astrinakis, 37–48. Dublin: University College Dublin Press.

Kennedy, David. 2013. "A Contextual Analysis of Europe's Ultra Football Supporters Movement." *Soccer & Society* 14 (2): 132–153. doi:10.1080/14660970.2013.776464.

Kennedy, Peter, and David Kennedy, eds. 2012. *Football Supporters and the Commercialisation of Football: Comparative Responses Across Europe*. London: Routledge.

King, Anthony. 2003. *The European Ritual: Football in the New Europe*. Aldershot: Ashgate.

Lalić, Dražen. 1993. *Torcida – pogled iznutra* [Torcida – An Inside View]. Zagreb: AGM.

Maffesoli, Michel. 1996. *The Time of the Tribes*. London: Sage Publications.

Marsh, Peter, Elisabeth Rosser, and Rom Harré. 1978. *The Rules of Disorder*. London: Routledge; Kegan Paul.

Millward, Peter. 2011. *The Global Football League: Transnational Networks, Social Movements and Sport in the New Media Age*. New York: Palgrave Macmillan.

Muggleton, David. 2000. *Inside Subculture: The Postmodern Meaning of Style*. Oxford: Berg.

Muggleton, David. 2005. "From Classlessness to Clubculture: A Genealogy of Postwar British Cultural Analysis." *Research on youth and youth cultures* 13 (2): 205–219.

Numerato, Dino. 2015. "Who Says "No to Modern Football?" Italian Supporters, Reflexivity, and Neo-liberalism." *Journal of Sport and Social Issues* 39 (2): 120–138. doi:10.1177/0193723514530566.

Pearson, Geoff. 2012. *An Ethnography of Football Fans: Cans, Cops and Carnival. New Ethnographies*. Manchester: Manchester University Press.

Perasović, Benjamin. 1995. "Navijačko pleme: do nacije i natrag." [Football Supporters Tribe: Towards the Nation and Back.] *Erasmus* 3 (2): 61–67.

Perasović, Benjamin, and Marko Mustapić. 2013. "Football Supporters in the Context of Croatian Sociology: Research Perspectives 20 Years After." *Kinesiology* 45 (2): 262–275.

Perasović, Benjamin, and Marko Mustapić. 2014. "Football, Politics and Cultural Memory: The Case of HNK Hajduk Split." *Култура/Culture* 6: 51–61.

Pilkington, Hilary. 2004. "Youth Strategies for Global Living: Space, Power and Communication in Everyday Cultural Practice." In *After Subculture: Critical Studies in Contemporary Youth Culture*, edited by Andy Bennet and Keith Kahn-Harris, 118–134. New York: Palgrave Macmillan.

Pilkington, Hilary. 2010. "Introduction: Rethinking Skinhead Lives." In *Russia's Skinheads: Exploring and Rethinking Subcultural Lives*, edited by Hilary Pilkington, Elena Omel'Chenko, and Al'bina Garifzianova, 1–23. London: Routledge.

Porter, Christopher. 2011. *Culture of Resistance and Compliance: Football Fandom and Political Engagement in Manchester*. Manchester, NH: The Manchester Metropolitan University.

Redhead, Steve. 1990. *The End of the Century Party: Youth and Pop Towards 2000*. Manchester, NH: Manchester University Press.

Redhead, Steve. 1993. "The Politics of Ecstasy." In *Rave Off: Politics and Deviance in Contemporary Youth Culture*, edited by Steve Redhead, 7–29. Aldershot: Avebury.

Sandvoss, Cornel. 2003. *A Game of Two Halves: Football, Television, and Globalisation*. New York: Routledge.

Shafto, Cora. 2013. *An Examination of Social Activism in Contemporary Fan Owned Football Clubs: Investigating Football Club United of Manchester as a Case Study*. Liverpool: Liverpool John Moores University.

Spaaij, Ramón. 2006. *Understanding Football Hooliganism. A Comparison of Six Western European football Clubs*. Vossiuspers: Amsterdam University Press.

Stott, Clifford, and Geoff Pearson. 2007. *Football Hooliganism: Policing and the War on the 'English Disease'*. London: Pennant Books.

Testa, Alberto. 2009. "Ultras: An Emerging Social Movement." *Review of European Studies* 1 (2): 54–63.

Thornton, Sarah. 1995. *Club Cultures: Music, Media and Subcultural Capital*. Oxford: Polity Press.

Vrcan, Srđan. 2003. *Nogomet – politika – nasilje: ogledi iz sociologije nogometa*. [Football – Policy – Violence: Essays in Sociology of Football.] Zagreb: Naklada Jesenski i Turk; Hrvatsko sociološko društvo.

Vrcan, Srđan, and Dražen Lalić. 1999. "From Ends to Trenches, and Back: Football in the Former Yugoslavia." In *Football Cultures and Identities*, edited by Gary Armstrong and Richard Giulianotti, 176–185. London: Macmillan.

Webber, David. 2014. "No Longer the People's Game: Karl Polanyi and the Double-Movement 'Against Modern Football'." Whose Game Is It? FREE Project Conference on Supporters and Football Governance, Loughborough University, October 24–25. http://www.free-project.eu/documents-free/Working%20Papers/Webber%20No%20Longer%20the%20Peoples%20Game%20Karl%20Polanyi%20and%20the%20Double%20Movement%20Against%20Modern%20Football.pd.

Williams, John, Eric Dunning, and Patrick Murphy. 1989. *Hooligans abroad*. London: Routledge.

Županov, Josip. 1995. *Poslije potopa* [After the Deluge]. Zagreb: Nakladni zavod Globus.

Ethnography and the Italian Ultrà

Matthew Guschwan

ABSTRACT

I was enthralled by the energy at the stadium. I was captivated by the visual choreography and visceral energy of fans chanting, jumping and shouting together. For me, the anonymous individuals at the stadium were the spectacle. In graduate school, I learned systematic approaches to research, but the tools of analysis never interested me as much as the thing itself – the social life that occurs in and around a stadium. My goal was to get to the heart of football fandom in Rome, plain and simple. Ultimately, I tried to conceptualize the culture, and wrap my findings into an academic narrative that expresses how important fandom is to the people in the stands. Football fandom is about passion that transcends rationality, and makes life more meaningful for those who partake. The question of how to articulate that phenomenon is an open one. This essay grapples with that question.

Introduction

This essay is a meditation on my research into the ultrà culture in Rome, Italy and a reflection on the methods of doing such a study. I begin the essay with an exploration of the methodological process of ethnography and my perspective within this process. In the subsequent section, I use personal anecdotes from my time in the field to illustrate some of the unexpected experiences that made doing the research interesting and worthwhile. I conclude the essay with some commentary on the current state of the ultrà movement and the situation of fandom in Italy more generally. What I hope to provide is some 'behind the scenes' discussion on the joys and difficulties of doing this type of research. Furthermore, I want to ask how we can attempt to know Italy, the ultrà groups, and perhaps, social movements more generally.

Theory of ethnography

My approach to fandom in structured by my education. I was trained in the Department of Communication & Culture at Indiana University in Bloomington, Indiana. The department was an experimental combination of Rhetorical Studies, Media Studies and Performance & Ethnography. The impulse behind this departmental formation was to cross-fertilize complementary approaches to the study of culture. The department unified around the recognition that communication, and mediated communication in particular, is not transparent conduits between people, but, rather, that all forms of media structure communication, and ultimately, human relations, in ways that call for scrutiny. For the Rhetoricians, the formation of this department was an acknowledgement that media affects traditional understandings of public speech.[1] For the media scholar, the department symbolizes the understanding that the meaning of a media text needs to be understood as a negotiation with an audience situated within cultural bounds. This is opposed the outmoded notion of an idealized, unencumbered viewer or the notion that media are transparent texts that contain universal meanings that must be ratified by the scholarly expert.[2] Performance Studies focuses on public cultural performances, such as, but not limited to, those that take place on a theatrical stage (Bauman 1992). Performances communicate, reinforce or question communal values and identities. For the anthropologists who constituted the Performance and Ethnography contingent of this departmental experiment, they paid a greater attention to the ways that media makes and remakes culture, and the end to a preoccupation with the (fictional) isolated, pure, cultures uncontaminated by outside media.[3] The overlapping needs and strengths of these approaches spurred a bevvy of creative research rooted in a humanistic approach to communication in cultural context. With this goal in mind, the theory and practice of ethnography became a key methodological tool with which to investigate communication in context. My advisor is a Folklorist by training who conducted ethnographic fieldwork in many foreign and domestic locales. He came to understand that Folklore would benefit from strategic alliances with broader forms of communication in order to invigorate the research of folklore as well as to foster more student engagement in the undergraduate classroom.

All three elements of the department were invested in critical inquiry through qualitative study. One of outcomes of this department was to develop communication skills in undergraduate students that would enable them to critically evaluate public culture as engaged citizens. The department has since been dismantled[4] in order to form the nascent Media School that aims to place professionals in the media industries. It is unclear what the role of critical inquiry will be in this new department.

Within this now-dissolved department, my coursework was mostly in Performance & Ethnography and Media Studies while my minor was in Anthropology. I took two courses focused on the methodology of ethnography. Along with some basic skills such as note taking, these courses emphasized the practice of reflexivity (Bauman 1992, 46, 47). In Ethnography, this means the critical examination of one's own methodological approach. This essay is, in part, a product of this emphasis on self-critique. The emphasis on reflexivity is part of the post-colonial movement to atone for Anthropology's complicity in the colonial project.[5] There is now a greater attention to the power dynamics that often position the researcher and the research subject in unequal roles.[6] Well-meaning anthropologists could unwittingly[7] contribute to the dissemination of racial and cultural stereotypes at the same time that they were trying to appreciate the 'other' culture. The field has shifted to the extent that the young anthropologist might feel self-conscious or even guilty about saying anything about another culture, much less, making judgments.[8] One way to ease the burden of this situation is to critically consider one's own position in relation to those who are the subject of research. The idea is to expose one's own biases and cultural frameworks and hold them up for scrutiny. The anthropologist must let go of the illusion of omniscience or superiority or objectivity based in cultural and educational arrogance in favour of a position of cultural relativity wherein one's understanding is always rooted in one's particular, and limited, perspective. While this self-scrutiny can, in its extreme, be solipsistic, it is a step away from the sins of the past where the scholar had too much power to pass judgement on things he (and sometimes she) did not understand. The treacherous task of the anthropologist was to translate the ways of the unenlightened savage to his academic constituency back home in 'civilization'. This shift is an acknowledgement that many more ethnographies had been written by English speakers than by, say, Swahili or Tlingit speakers, even though those non-English speakers might have had quite a bit to say about the strange ways of the white academic interloper. My own self-disclosure in this essay is a way to try to position my work and my perspective in relation to those who hosted me and taught me about what they do – my so-called subjects.

The result of this training is my view on social life that might be best summarized by my advisor, Richard Bauman: 'Not only is communication socially constituted, but society is communicatively constituted' (Bauman 1992, xiv). This fundamental insight tuned my attention to the acts of communication that, I (we) believe, construct culture. In Rome, this included the fans' display of banners and songs at the stadium, along with the scarves, jerseys and other elements of personal appearance such as hairstyle and sunglasses that signify membership in a group. Outside the stadium, the walls of Rome literally speak through graffiti that makes claims of turf and declares expressions of pride. In cafes, I participated in small talk about the local team's predicaments. I surfed the net, read newspapers, listened to the radio and watched television. I interviewed fans of all types ranging from the casual to the hardcore. I rode on busses with ultràs to away matches. Consciously and subconsciously, I was constantly trying to arrange and connect the 'dots' gathered within this expansive conceptual net of 'acts of communication'. I was always asking: How does all of this communication simultaneously construct and reflect identity, agreed upon values, and cultural norms?

The academic context

One form of media that inevitably works its way into an ethnography is prior academic research. It is worth mentioning, even if obvious, that academic research is a social enterprise in which the researcher builds from previous research. It is the work of the graduate student to prepare to do original research by reading what others have done. The graduate student then (wittingly or not) internalizes some of the values and understandings of predecessors while developing criticisms and grudges against other values and understandings. After a certain period, the graduate student goes headlong into the field, perhaps with an axe to grind against the wrong-headed ideas of the past. Their findings become part of the academic conversation in which the new ideas are compared against the previous, ratified knowledge. Sometimes the new researcher is praised for innovation, sometimes criticized for misunderstanding or poor judgement, or worse, the work is barely acknowledged at all, much less read – at least until some new graduate student is doing her literature review.

The social process of the academy needs to be acknowledged by the ethnographer because new work is inevitably situated within this framework. Even if one of the goals of the ethnographer is to go into the field without corrupting preconceptions in order to collect 'unbiased data', one cannot escape the ideas of others (nor would it be a good idea to). I went into the field looking to see for myself – to document experiences and to dig up new data, but almost inevitably, an ethnographer needs to get acquainted with the history of a phenomenon that they were not present for. I would bet that the writing, recollections and documentation of others form the bulk of most ethnographies. It is out of necessity that we rely on the past. The collection of ethnographic information that any individual can reasonably obtain is quite limited in comparison to the historical record, (or any other documentation of a phenomenon). At the very least, the collection of data done by others guides the collection of new information – it gives a starting point and a set of questions to ask, re-ask and work against. This is true even if one is studying 'new' media as 'new' implies a contrast from the 'old' or 'not (as) new'. The same questions and understandings are used to situate the new. In ethnography, the stories that people keep telling themselves are always rich sources of information about what they embrace and what they reject, what they hold and what they forget. The tricky job of the ethnographer is to interpret what these long-standing stories and their repetition means.

Observation before interpretation

David Foster Wallace begins his commencement speech at Kenyon College with a joke.

> There are these two young fish swimming along, and they happen to meet an older fish swimming the other way, who nods at them and says, 'Morning, boys, how's the water?' And the two young fish swim on for a bit, and then eventually one of them looks over at the other and goes, 'What the hell is water?' (Wallace 2005)

When I taught interpersonal communication to first-year college students, the primary assignment of this course was to conduct an ethnography of a group of their choosing. Most students chose to do an ethnography of their friends. I would challenge these students to uncover what is 'special' or 'culturally specific' about the ways that their group communicates. I would prod them to consider: What topics are normal and which are off-limits? Does anybody dominate the group? What does it take to be part of the group? With few exceptions, students reported that their group could talk about anything, that their group is completely egalitarian and that anyone could join. After a semester working on this project, students would begin to recognize the social and cultural conditions and constraints of their context – features of the proverbial water in which they 'swim'.[9] We tend not to scrutinize that to which we are accustomed.

Additionally, in this course I was fighting against what seems to be the default cognitive process of people – the nearly automatic process of translating observation into interpretation. Our visual and other senses give us data that our minds compare with our warehouse of knowledge and experience in order to understand and interpret and extrapolate upon. It is challenge for an ethnographer, (or any observer) to disrupt this process by making it more transparent. This is at the root of bias. We fail to separate what we experience from what we interpret. Racism, fear, disgust, etc. creep into our interpretation of what we eventually recall as 'seeing' or 'hearing' (Crawford 2015). This effect is so strong that our memory of events is inevitably coloured by our interpretation even as we profess to tell only the facts. This is a long way of saying that ethnography is problematic and we need to pay attention to our biases and our shortcomings.

One of the guiding concepts of my perspective is that of culture. Culture is defined by the Cambridge English Dictionary as, 'the way of life, especially the general customs and beliefs, of a particular group of people at a particular time'.[10] Cultural knowledge enables us to participate in social life without overwhelming confusion and fear. Common customs allow us to the grocery store and exchange payment for sustaining food and clothing without too much friction. As water is imperceptible to a young fish, culture can be invisible to those who are in the midst of it, at least until they experience or imagine something different. When cultural rules are trespassed, they become evident – such as if one were to curse during a prayer ceremony, or wear the wrong scarf to a football match.[11]

The relationship between the individual and culture is another issue that needs to be addressed by the ethnographer. The ethnographer studies culture, but relies on the individual to gather information and to form an interpretation. In studying football fandom, I could spend a lifetime interviewing fans and come away feeling that I had not embraced the entire phenomenon. I had to ask myself: How do I bridge the gap between the individual and culture?[12] My practical solution is that I tried to carve out the contours of fan culture by focusing my interpretation of recurring themes, and interpretations that multiple informants or other sources had passed along. Of course, the elements of the culture that I found most interesting and that I was most likely to 'see' many instances of, were informed by my American-ness.[13] What intrigues me about Italian football fans and ultrà groups is how well-organized they are in comparison to American sport fans. Americans tend to have a radical sense of individual liberty, self-sufficiency and self-determination and so, seeing fans organized like armies and singing in unison caught my attention. Perhaps as an American in my non-native culture,[14] I was able to see the culture more than some. I had only my inherently biased position as an American male of European descent of fairly average height and weight, and good, but non-native speaking abilities. In some contexts, I could visually 'pass' as Italian,[15] though a verbal exchange of any length would reveal my imperfect accent. The best compliment I could garner was not that I sounded Italian, but that I did not sound American. My accent somehow took on a neutral tone. Sometimes being an outsider, people will show you things and explain them to you. They will not assume that you understand. Of course, sometimes informants lie or exaggerate because they think they can get away with it. Sometimes the informant is performing for the outsider. Going into the field, I was very conscious of my own shortcomings, but looking back, the process of learning and the state of being confused at times are useful in that I had to confirm things and ask lots of 'dumb' questions that could lead to quotable answers.

I was weary of grand social theories that programmatically explain the behaviour of groups and individuals. While I am also keenly aware of the limits of ethnography, I did not want to go into the field determined to either confirm or debunk a 'big' theory. I wanted any theoretical findings to arise organically out of the process of meeting people. I realize that the theories I have been exposed to implicitly orient how I understand things, but I tried to downplay theory in preference for messy data collection first. One relies on one's own discipline, one's own biases to try to make sense of things, but methodology has its limitations, and methodology steers the production of knowledge. As a communication scholar, I tended to focus on what is communicated, either intentionally or unintentionally, privately or publicly. While it is nearly impossible to avoid making interpretations about the psychic or emotional states that produced such messages, interpretations should be founded upon identifiable communicative acts. Communicative acts range from spoken words to explicit explanations and rationalizations, but all too often, come in the form of symbolic representations that leave at least a bit of ambiguity. The colours that people wear and the scarves that they wave at the stadium *mean* something, and the interpretation of communicative acts relies upon context. What I hope to have contributed to the field of communication is a study of identity through the communicative practices of fandom.

Practical methodology

The majority of my training in ethnography weighted theory over practice, but ethnography is a hands-on methodology. I wish I had been given a bit more practical advice and so, here I will map out a few anecdotes that illustrate the complexity and unpredictable nature of ethnographic research. The specific practices will inevitably vary by the social context, but in sharing a few anecdotes, I hope to demonstrate aspects of an ethnographic sensibility.

Funding it all

One member of the Core de Roma fan group asked me what I did during my days. It was a question I did not want to answer. I did not have a formal job as I did not have a work visa. For a while, I worked at a professional 'blog' about information technology, in the early days of that phenomenon and I taught English to a few clients. But I had a lot of free time. I used to joke that I should have learned how to fix small engines in order to fix the ubiquitous *motorino* motorbikes around Rome instead of spending countless hours on grant applications. Beyond the income, I probably could have written a second ethnography on underground labour if I had landed a job in a motorino repair garage.

In an interview for a prestigious grant that would have funded by fieldwork, I was asked by a non-ethnographer what the chapters of my dissertation would be. I fumbled to answer this question as I wanted to go into the field with an open mind as to what I would find. Surely, I had guiding questions, and there was information I had hoped to corral, but I had trouble indicating that my dissertation could not be formed before the research had been done. I did not get this grant. I would advise any would-be ethnographer to be prepared for this type of question, and to be prepared to educate others about the process of ethnography.

Social skills and tricks

An effective ethnographer relies on social skills. You have to develop relationships of trust and let (or subtly persuade) others to tell you things. You also have to interpret social cues, and perhaps, know when to speak up and know when to be quite; know when to laugh and know when to leave. One can start with etiquette and politeness guides, but more importantly, I would recommend trying to listen carefully and read non-verbal communication. One skill that might help an ethnographer is the ability to blend in. While spying and snooping are unethical and antisocial, sometimes your job is just to witness events or social meetings without drawing much attention to yourself. One hopes to capture 'real life' in these moments without interfering through one's corporeal presence. While I claim no expertise in the art and science of social relations, I think I presented myself as an affable and curious interlocutor. I hope the following anecdotes illustrate a few unpredictable social situations that convey some of the flavour of my ethnography.

One of the more successful practical tactics that I employed was to bring cigarettes when I went on trips with the ultràs. Many of the fans smoked, and they seemed to always be looking for a cigarette. Though I was not much of a smoker myself, I found sharing cigarettes to be an effective way to bond with strangers and ask some questions. Finding those little moments of down time is a key for building relationships. Sometimes, the ride to the event is much more productive than the event itself. Bus rides to and from away matches are some of the richest sites for learning about the ultrà culture. Enclosed in a small space for hours on end with little to do, the young men that I met revealed themselves.[16] They drank beer, they smoked marijuana, they shouted insults at each other and at the bus driver, they sang songs, they pleaded for more water. On the way to the match, cigarettes were in high demand, on the return, water was scarce as many of them had exhausted themselves shouting at the match, smoking, drinking and ingesting all sorts of substances. I have to admit that I did not want to know too much about hard drug use, and so I did not pry into that domain. On one of these bus trips, the Boys of A.S. Roma turned me into a sort of mascot by asking me in a theatrical blend of English and Italian, 'Tutt'okay, America?!'. As I was looking at them to tell me something about Italian culture, I became the embodiment of America to them. Looking back, I should have asked them directly what they thought about this American coming to hang out with them. I sense that the response to be a combination of pride in being studied and a sense of bewilderment of the same.

Some of the work of ethnography is social 'grunt work' as one must keep showing up and pestering people in order to meet people and to expand one's social network. Some contacts lead nowhere. At other times, good timing and luck lead to productive contacts. The internet has made some networking easier. I gained entry into one fan group simply by responding to an advertisement on their website that invited anyone interested to meet them for a banquet. Without much hesitation, I met one of the fan group members at the appointed place and time, and he drove me to the restaurant. I am still grateful for their openness and cheerfulness. Other times, prospective informants miss meetings, or just disappear. It can be difficult to start an ethnography as an unknown outsider. With persistence, networking gets easier. A prospective ethnographer would do well to contact people ahead of time, contact relevant organizations, and remember the most important question in networking: Do you know anyone else that I should talk to? (Followed by: Can you provide an introduction?)

One of the first people that I contacted in Rome was Valerio Marchi,[17] a Roman author and bookstore owner who wrote about youth counter-culture and the ultràs. After visiting the shop in the San Lorenzo neighbourhood, Valerio introduced me to the 'Boys' ultrà group. After some awkward small talk, I asked GianPaolo if I could join the bus trip to Livorno. He asked me if I was a communist. I said 'no'. I asked him if he was. He pointed to a statue of Mussolini holding a musket that was perched on a shelf behind me. After my initial meeting, I told Valerio that I was going on a trip with the Boys to the away match with Livorno, he warned me not to go. The Boys are a right-wing group and Livorno fans are staunchly left-wing. He said that the match would have nothing to do with football, and that I should choose another match to go to. I disregarded his advice, and had a memorable experience travelling in the bus, and seeing for myself the political symbolism, not to mention the massive police presence, in and around the stadium. Another time, I was warned by a friend not to go to a dinner with a group of fans that I did not know. In both instances, I am glad that I went. Of course, had I been stabbed outside the stadium or arrested, I might feel differently, but in both of those instances, things went well. I would not want to generalize too much, but I would say that taking risks is part of the experience of ethnography. One must read the situation carefully and listen fully to the locals, but ultimately, an ethnographer has to follow their own instincts, and hope that they take you to the right destination. I received some of the worst advice about ethnography during some preliminary research. I had made a new contact, but I had not done any 'fieldwork' yet. I was advised to push for permission to hang out with this group of friends, but I had not yet established a solid relationship. This approach backfired and I was never able to repair the trust with that contact. You have to trust your gut instinct in social settings, and strive to find the balance between persistence and nuisance, patience and assertiveness.

One of the most powerful ways to build trust in a relationship is by returning after a period of absence. Returning to the field signals an ongoing interest and commitment to the relationship, and, perhaps, it signals that the relationships that were built were not just for the sake of a study, but that there is a bond that transcends a particular project. It would take a psychologist to explain this, but I suspect that most of our relationships build through periods of presence and absence. A good relationship grows stronger upon return. For me, going back to the Roma Club Testaccio felt like a homecoming even though the club had been evicted from their previous clubhouse (the unfortunate effect of the gentrification of this historically working class neighbourhood). Testaccio's proximity to the central historic centre of Rome increases the real estate values and put pressure on old ways of life, but the Roma Club Testaccio endures under the sprightly leadership of Sergio Rosi. He and his son welcomed me back to the club, and they seemed genuinely happy to see me.

On the other hand, things change in one's absence, and some things cannot be recovered. In my absence, Lazio's ultrà group, the Irriducibili, essentially dissolved as the result of a scandalous rebellion involving threats against the owner, an alleged partnership with the now deceased Giorgio Chinaglia and alleged ties with the mafia. The former leaders of the Irriducibili served prison time, and their chain of stores selling Lazio merchandise has all but disintegrated. I had brought a gift to Rome for one of my contacts, but I could not track him down. Though my connection to the Lazio ultràs has gone away, it makes them easier to write about. That chapter has ended, and one need not speculate on their fate – it is now history. Of course, now there are new groups to fill the vacuum, providing an opportunity for a researcher to learn more. Online correspondence helps to maintain old relationships, but it does not replace being there.

Fear, luck or ignorance: the ethics of ethnography

One of my favourite aspects of the Italian football stadium is the clever homemade banners that appear in the stadium. I wanted to make one of my own banners in the spirit of admiration and experimentation. Could I create a banner that anyone would notice? I set about creating my banner by finding an old bed sheet and then visiting the local hardware store to purchase spray paint and plastic tubing with which to hold the banner. I briefly studied the distinctive fonts of other banners before sketching my design in pencil before committing to spray paint. I brought the banner to the stadium on the match day, and I had to show it to the security guards who wanted to make sure that I was not bringing in swastikas or any other offensive materials. Once in the stadium, I unfurled my banner and tried to get anyone to notice. Fortunately, I caught the attention of some of the photographers who were idle when the players returned to the locker room for pre-game coaching. A photo of the banner appeared in the online section of a major newspaper, and then shown briefly on national television. The banner referenced the transfer of the talented but tempestuous

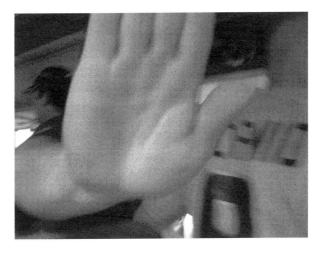

Figure 1. This is the only photo I was able to take on the Irriducibili bus.

player, Antonio Cassano[18] from Roma to Real Madrid. After Cassano left, Roma won a record 10 matches in a row. My banner thanked Real Madrid, for 'taking out the trash'.

On the theoretical level, the banner draws attention to the performative aspect of the football match, and the possibility for the average fan to gain visibility for their messages in the stadium. More directly, I gained credibility from other fans. I was asked to bring it to a banquet thrown by the Core de Roma fan group. They were bemused by the American who had pulled such a stunt. One of these fans also suggested that I correct the sign using a more Roman word for trash. The banner was a highlight of my experience doing participant-observation, and though the practice of banner making was not part of my methodology courses, I can assure you that it changed my status among the fans. Incidentally, recent police crackdowns on banners would make this display more difficult. Now fans need to get prior permission to display banners at the stadium.

I signed up to go with the Lazio ultrà group, the Irriducibili, to an away match at Siena. I had been acquainted with a few of the younger members of the Irriducibili and I thought the trip to Tuscany would be an easy trip. When I arrived at the appointed spot outside of their clubhouse at the proper time, I was surprised to see that the busses were already pretty fully loaded. The bus trips with Roma's ultràs, the Boys, were much less punctual. I stepped aboard the first bus that I saw. As I reached the top of the steps, I looked for a familiar face, and I saw none. Instead, I saw mirrored sunglasses, tattoos, and grizzled features. One of the passengers on that bus must have seen the confusion on my face before he blurted out, in English, 'Welcome to Hell!' It was a second that lasts an hour as my self-conscious embarrassment went into overdrive. On one hand, I knew he was trying to joke with me, but on the other hand, three hours on a bus with strangers doing who knows what kinds of drugs could have been a kind of hell. I scampered down the steps to get off of the bus, and somehow I wound up on the other bus that was filled with familiar faces – young men who looked like they were going on a field trip. Unfortunately, I have no photos to document the trip itself. One of their rules is that on the bus, there no photos are to be taken. I only learned this by taking out my camera (see Figure 1). Presumably, the bus ride is the private preparation for the public performance that will take place at the stadium. Photos of their antics inside the stadium are encouraged, and their newsletter, *La Voce della Nord,* captured and documented their banners and displays in the stadium, but not the bus.

Sometimes you cannot plan at all for the moments that can bring you into a group. When I travelled to Siena with the Lazio's ultrà group, the Irriducibili, we all got off the bus at one of the ubiquitous Autogrill roadside gas stations and convenience stores. A group of the Irriducibili started throwing around a rugby ball in the parking lot. Growing up, I would toss an American football around with friends, and so, throwing and catching a rugby ball was natural enough. I did not expect one of the Irriducibili to try to tackle me as I caught the ball. I instinctively moved out of the way, and he fell to the ground. I was worried for a moment that he would attack me or that I would be cast out, but instead, the others laughed at him, and congratulated me. His attempt to challenge me completely backfired. On the theoretical level, this incident draws attention to the physical body of the ethnographer. More practically, I gained status in the group accidentally. This was not something I learned about in graduate school, but in this male-dominated atmosphere, perhaps it should not be surprisingly that a bit of athleticism would be useful.

In Italy, and in Rome in particular, there is a degree of disdain for the official rules and a general mistrust of authorities. This meant that some fans that I met, and had good talks with, would not sign the research consent forms. They were happy to talk with me and they seemed delighted that I might use their ideas and words in a published work, but they would not put their signature on a form. A university's Institutional Review Board is a feature of the modern academy that, ostensibly, serves to protect the subject from cruel researchers, but in America, their more palpable role is to protect the university and its administrators from legal liability. No one would argue that medical researchers should have well documented consent in order to test new drugs and procedures, but the rules for the medical field seep into the form of the ethnographic consent form. As an American ethnographer from a legalistic culture, is it ethical to impose one's legal forms on those from other cultures? If I had waited for all parties to sign a form before I would listen, my ethnography would be impoverished.

When I met fans, I always stated, early in the conversation, that I was a student studying football fandom. Often, I would not say much more than that. I would adopt a position that had a bit of wiggle room. I was thirty years old during my longest stretch of research. I was roughly the same age of many of the people I was spending time with. I did not always say that I was completing a PhD and that I hoped to publish my findings. As a mere 'student', I felt it was somewhat ambiguous and non-threatening to the people that I was working with. I sensed that a formal, professorial stance would not sit well with these fans, and I have evidence to support that feeling: One of the leaders of the Boys asked me if was a journalist, and then indicated through gesture that if I was, he would slash my throat.

One Sunday afternoon, I was watching a Lazio match with an acquaintance and his friend. Both of them are dedicated Lazio fans who often travel to away matches, though they did not associate with the Irriducibili or any organized Ultràs group at the time. They were independent, but dedicated fans. We were seated in the Curva Nord (North Curve) several rows above the Irriducibili when they started singing one of their songs with anti-semitic lyrics. My new acquaintance told me that he is Jewish, and that these songs were the one *piccolo difetto* (the one 'little defect') in the otherwise glorious social phenomenon that is Lazio. He seemed ashamed of these other fans, but not particularly agitated. I got the sense that he had grown accustomed to this kind of thing. As an ethnographer, what do you do

Figure 2. This photo was taken from the visitor's section at the Siena-Lazio match, 9 April 2006. The barbed wire, and police with riot gear do not send a friendly message.

with this? The newspapers would claim that the racist Lazio fans were at it again. The *story* is that Lazio fans are a bunch of racists. So what does that make my acquaintance? A fool? A racist? A sell-out? A co-conspirator? Is he not a full Lazio fan because he does not share this conspicuous aspect of their identity? I do not believe him to be any of these things. In my view, he was trying to cope with a less than ideal situation. He was trying to convince me, and perhaps himself, that supporting Lazio was worth it even if it meant putting up with bullshit. Perhaps he was rationalizing and narrating his experience in order to retain his sense of personal integrity. This is what we do as fans, as ethnographers, as people.

These anecdotes bring me to one of the big lessons of ethnography – that we are storytelling. Often we are narrating stories about stories that were told to us. The most powerful of these stories orient us to verifiable facts in a particular way so that we gather evidence and data that support these views. It can seem like an impossible bind. Objective truth uncovered in controlled experiments with reproducible results – these are what science tells us can be the truth. We cannot do that in ethnography, so we try to verify information from multiple sources, we try to gather different opinions and perspectives, but it is hard to escape the notion that all of this 'data' are filtered in the mind of an individual. The shape of the narrative is determined by one's limited perspective.

Ultràs – Who are they after all?

After all of this methodological hand wringing, there is still the question of, who are the ultràs and what do they mean (to me)? I will try to capture what the ultrà movement means to me from my subjective viewpoint. I would define ultrà groups as well-organized hardcore fan groups that follow a common set of ideas that has developed over about five decades.[19] Their typical activities include meeting outside of the stadium to make banners for display at the stadium, to create and disseminate songs and choruses to be sung at the stadium and to organize travel arrangements to support the team at away matches. Ultrà groups developed a code of conduct or *la mentalità* (mentality) that includes a commitment to stand and sing throughout the match, to protect the pride of their team against enemies and to support the team home and away. Ultrà groups often criticize the administration of their team and the industry of football, and especially, the compromises it has made to business over sporting concerns. Many ultrà groups have political agendas that may or may not be separable from their football-related activities. Clashes between rival ultrà groups became commonplace, though for most groups, *la mentalità* regulated these clashes. Knives and other weapons were forbidden and there were rules of engagement to protect non-ultràs. These attempts at self-regulation were not always followed, and some tragic events have marked the history of Italian football (Mariottini 2004). In these times of crisis, ultrà groups have gathered together in attempts to organize and coordinate. In more recent times, these groups have found a shared enemy in the state and the perceived repression against them. They have put aside historical differences to coordinate their resistance against state oppression (Figure 2).

The distinction between ultràs and other dedicated fans can be complex. While the ultràs get a great deal of attention, they are part of a larger ecosystem of fandom that includes everyone from the casual to the dedicated. Some individual fans are completely committed to the team, but do not join ultrà groups. Some ultràs are probably involved for social reasons that have less to do with football and more to do with hanging out with friends and adopting a strong identity. Other fans are essential to the ultrà movement in that they provide the context and the audience for the ultràs. At the stadium, the ultràs banners are displayed outward to be viewed by those who are not sitting in the curved end of the stadium. The other fans respond to the ultràs, and the ultràs work to differentiate themselves from other fans.

One of the things that makes the ultràs so interesting is the tension between unity and division, cooperation and competition. While at a distance, one can discern and ultràs movement, the individual groups maintain heated rivalries with other groups. These rivalries can reflect regional or local identities mixed with socio-economic and political views. The most heated rivalries are often among those who are from the same place. Intra-city rivalries in Rome, Turin, Milan and Genoa are particularly intense. At various points, the ultràs have also cooperated with other fans, and other ultràs in order to support an initative or to formalize rules of engagement. Relationships between ultrà groups are always changing in one way or another.

Ultrà and ultras

In Italy, there is an important distinction between the terms 'ultrà' and 'ultras'. English speakers might assume that the 's' of 'ultras' simply indicates the plural of ultrà, but this is not the case in Italian usage (even though, to this point in the essay I have used the 's' to indicate the plural). A hardcore fan who is not part of an organized group might say, *[Io] sono un ultrà* (I am an ultrà) as a way of declaring their hardcore allegiance to a team. It would be like saying, 'I am a dedicated fan'. To say *[Io] sono un ultras* (I am an ultras) only makes sense for fan who is part of an established ultras group. 'Ultras' first developed with groups that had a strong political identity, though the name has since been used by less political groups. It is not completely clear how the distinction between ultrà and ultras arose and these distinctions can vary from team to team and region to region. This distinction in terminology speaks to the larger point that ultrà culture is untidy, variable, changing and sometimes contradictory. Perhaps like any social phenomenon, the closer you get, the more heterogeneity you see. There are rivalries and contradictions within even small groups. Members compete for power and authority within these groups and often try to change the reputation of the group. Some revolutions succeed, while failed coups reaffirm the status quo.

Unity vs. rivalry

One of the recurring themes of the broader ultrà culture is the movement between unity and rivalry. For example, the A.S. Roma ultrà groups formed the *Commando Ultrà Curva Sud* [Ultrà Command of the South Curve] (CUCS) in the late 1970s[20] in order to coordinate smaller groups that comprised the south end of the stadium. For a decade, the group succeeded in unifying the curve. Eventually, CUCS disintegrated because of opposing views over the signing of a former Lazio player. In contemporary times, there are competing groups and no overarching authority, but now, on occasion, the various ultrà groups come together to form one voice, particularly when their common interests are threatened. With internet communications and social media, the process of communicating within the group and to the public is, in some ways, easier and more efficient. The Roma ultrà groups periodically release announcements that state their position on keys issues. These statements are from the 'Curva Sud' though it is not completely clear who is included in the Curva, who drafts the statements and how widely they are adopted.[21] Nevertheless, these statements show a degree of unity in the curve.

The stadium affords a grand stage for the rivalries and pageantry of ultrà groups to play out in public. In addition to the tens of thousands of in-person spectators, there is massive media coverage in every imaginable form for every top-tier match. Organized fans are savvy at exploiting opportunities in order to float ideas in this media-surveilled space. These opportunities are intriguing, in part because of their rarity. As I have written elsewhere (Guschwan 2014), the stadium can represent a counter to the encroachment of homogenous gated communities and sterilized shopping malls that eradicate dissent. Semi-public spaces such as football stadiums can facilitate the visibility and acknowledgement of others and their divergent and inconvenient views. The Italian football stadium on Sunday survives as a space for vibrant dissent.

Not all face-to-face social aggregation is peaceful and democratic. The stadium can and does occasionally erupt in violence. While I have written in praise of the possibility for political resistance in the stadium, there have been events that seem to completely undermine the concept of the ultrà as engaged citizen. The death of Ciro Esposito is one of these instances. Esposito was fatally shot prior to the start of the final of the Italian Cup that was played between Napoli and Fiorentina on 3 May 2014. Esposito traveled to Rome with other Napoli fans in buses that parked about a mile from the stadium. As these Napoli fans were walking towards the stadium, they reportedly clashed with an infamous Rome ultrà, Danielle De Santis. Allegedly, De Santis provoked these fans by throwing flares at the buses. A group of Napoli fans, including Esposito, chased after De Santis, and possibly stabbed him. Lying on the ground, De Santis fired four shots, one of which ultimately killed Esposito. De Santis' trial has not begun at the time of writing, though his public statements claim his actions were in self-defence. De Santis was a well-known, radical right-wing ultrà. He was one of the fans who appeared on the field pleading with A.S. Rome captain, Francesco Totti, during the March, 2004 Roma-Lazio derby that was suspended mid-match (Marchi 2005). In the days after the shooting, images of De Santis adorned by right-wing paraphernalia surfaced online. He instantly became the face of the villainous ultrà movement, and a justification for crackdowns at the football stadium.

It is hard to reconcile De Santis' actions with the joy and vibrancy of football fandom. While the factual details of this situation are not completely clear, what is clear is that no one should be shot in the name of football. I have defended and promoted a version of active fandom that the ultrà groups embody – that of organization, strong identity, and political awareness. As an ethnographer, I focused my attention on the ideal of free speech and political resistance in the football stadium. I was witness to minor skirmishes and van-dalism, but I never directly witnessed serious violence or destruction of property – I have never seen anyone stabbed, or anything set on fire, though I have seen a police car already ablaze, and I was at matches where stabbings had occurred outside the stadium. I have seen fans running from police, and, from a distance, I have seen fans directly confront police. I did not focus my research on violence because others scholars have covered this aspect of fandom (Roversi 1992), and because mass media have covered, if not sensationalized, some of the violent acts that have occurred in and around the stadium. I was never afraid to go to the stadium. I tried to keep alert and to be aware of my surroundings, but I feel safer in an Italian stadium than I do on the Italian highway.[22] I felt my job was to put the violence in the context of a larger culture – a culture that I did not find to be particularly threatening.

Notes

1. See, for example, Medhurst and Benson (1991), for a view of the influence of media in Rhetorical Studies.
2. The Cultural Studies movement promoted this understanding of communication. In particular, Stuart Hall's ([1973] 1980) Encoding/Decoding altered the way that popular media texts would be studied.
3. See, for example, Askew and Wilk (2002).
4. All that remains is the website: http://www.indiana.edu/~cmcl/.
5. Said (1978) *Orientalism* is a widely acclaimed critique of academic racism.
6. I hesitate to use the term 'Research Subject' since it implies a position subordinate to the researcher. I would prefer terms such as co-conspirator, guide, participant, teacher, friend, host, allie, fan, or other terms that retain the agency of those being written about. At the same time, I must not overlook the fact that I am the one doing the writing about *them*, and that there is a power imbalance in that relationship, no matter how hard I might try to mitigate or hide it.
7. Miner's (1956) 'Body Ritual' critiques this power dynamic in a playful way.
8. Clifford's 'Writing Culture' remains controversial in asserting the aesthetic and narrative elements of Anthropology.
9. These were usually middle class white students at a big public university who tended to talk more about schoolwork than theology, more about sports than Proust.
10. 'Meaning of "culture"'. Cambridge English Dictionary. Accessed January 26, 2016.
11. Mariottini's *Ultràviolenza*, recounts the death of Vincenzo Spagnolo, a casual fan who fatally stabbed for being in the wrong place at the wrong time.
12. Ruth Benedict and Margaret Mead (1928) were some of the first Anthropologists to grapple with this question. Mead emphasized the power of cultural expectations in her work, *Coming of Age in Samoa*.

13. Themes of reflexivity are spurred in part by Said. For a more recent example, see Devisch and Nyamnjoh (2011).
14. I was, 'un americano a Roma' (an American in Rome), which is the title of a famous comedy starring Alberto Sordi, a young Roman man obsessed with American culture. I was basically the mirror image of Sordi's character, an American obsessed with Italian culture.
15. It was always fun to be asked for directions by Italian visitor to Rome. Romans somehow had a sense to not ask me for directions.
16. Tim Parks (2002), *A Season with Verona* tells his own tales of riding the bus.
17. I contacted Valerio on the advice of Ashley Green at the Progetto Ultrà, [Ultrà Project], an ultrà research and advocacy organization based in Bologna. Valerio died much too young from a heart attack in 2006. http://www.repubblica.it/2006/07/sezioni/spettacoli_e_cultura/morte-valerio-marchi/morte-valerio-marchi/morte-valerio-marchi.html.
18. In a somewhat sad postscript, Cassano publicly took responsibility for ruining his own career because of his attitude. http://www.espnfc.us/story/1450693/inter-milans-antonio-cassano-admits-career-regrets.
19. Podaliri and Balestri's (1998) essay on the ultras is the place to start for a definition.
20. The website, ASRoma Ultras website, which is maintained by a lawyer, and advocate of the ultras, is a marvelous repository of A.S. Roma fan history. http://www.asromaultras.org/2000.html.
21. For an example, see http://www.corederoma.it/online/wp-content/uploads/2015/10/comunicato_sud09102015.jpg.
22. In comparison to the neighbourhood I spent part of my upbringing in Chicago, I would feel much safer in the Italian stadium, and my neighbourhood was hardly the worst.

Disclosure statement

No potential conflict of interest was reported by the author.

References

Askew, K., and R. Wilk. 2002. *The Anthropology of Media*. London: Blackwell.
Bauman, R. 1992. *Folklore, Cultural Performances, and Popular Entertainments: A Communications-centered Handbook*. Oxford: Oxford University Press.
Crawford, M. 2015. *The World beyond Your Head: On Becoming an Individual in an Age of Distraction*. New York: Farrar, Straus & Giroux.
Devisch, R., and F. Nyamnjoh. 2011. *The Postcolonial Turn: Re-imagining Anthropology and Africa Publication*. Bamenda: Langaa Publishers.
Guschwan, M. 2014. "Stadium as Public Sphere." *Sport in Society* 17 (7): 884–900. doi:10.1080/17430437.2013.806036
Hall, S. [1973] 1980. "Encoding/Decoding." In *Culture, Media, Language: Working Papers in Cultural Studies, 1972–79*. Edited by S. Hall, D. Hobson, A. Lowe, and P. Willis, 128–138. London: Hutchinson.
Marchi, V. 2005. *Il derby del bambino morto: violenza e ordine pubblico nel calcio* [The Derby of the Dead Child: Violence and Public Order in Football]. Rome: DeriveApprodi.
Mariottini, D. 2004. *Ultràviolenza! storie di sangue del tifo italiano* [Ultrà-Violence! Stories of Blood in Italian Fandom]. Torino: Bradipolibri.
Mead, M. 1928. *Coming of Age in Samoa: A Psychological Study of Primitive Youth for Western Civilization*. New York: William Morrow.
Medhurst, M., and T. Benson. 1991. *Rhetorical Dimensions in Media: A Critical Casebook*. Dubuque, IA: Kendall/Hunt Publishing Company.
Miner, H. 1956. "Body Ritual among the Nacirema." *The American Anthropologist* 58: 503–507.
Parks, T. 2002. *A Season with Verona*. New York: Arcade.

Podaliri, C., and C. Balestri. 1998. "The Ultras, Racism, and Football Culture in Italy." In *Fanatics! Power, Identity and Fandom in Football*, edited by A. Brown, 88–100. London: Routledge.

Roversi, A. 1992. *Calcio, tifo e violenza: il teppismo calcistico in Italia* [Football, fandom and violence: football hooliganism in Italy]. Milan: Mulino.

Said, E. 1978. *Orientalism*. New York: Pantheon.

Wallace, D. 2005. "This is Water." Commencement Speech delivered at Kenyon College. Gambier, OH, May 21. http://bulletin.kenyon.edu/x4280.html.

Index

Note: Page numbers with 'n' denote notes.

3. Liga 54
1953 International 61, 62

AC Milan supporters 92
Adana Demirspor 39
AFC Wimbledon 130
Against Modern Football (AMF) movement 5,
129, 130–131; in Poland 142; and Torcida
136–139, 141–142
aggressive masculinity 10
Alexander, J. C. 25
AMF *see* Against Modern Football (AMF)
movement
Angel City Brigade 105
anti-communism, and Polish ultras 30–31
anti-modern football stance: Australia 115, 119,
122–123, 124; of Dynamo Dresden 59, 62;
Indonesia 87; United States 100, 101–102;
see also Against Modern Football (AMF)
movement
antisocial aspects of fan culture 1, 4
apolitical identity 4, 5, 46, 52, 58–62, 64, 102
Arab Spring 2
Arka fans 28
Arminia Bielefeld 52
Armstrong, Gary 44, 47, 102
Arseto Solo 90, 91
A.S Livorno 102
ASRoma Ultras 159n20
Australia *see* Red and Black Bloc (RBB); Western
Sydney; Western Sydney ultras
Austria Salzburg 108, 130
authenticity: Hapoel Katamon Jerusalem 71, 74,
75–76, 78–79; *Ultras Dynamo* 55
Azapović, Marko 137

B7 ultras of Pasoepati 88, 89, 91
Babelsberg 03 59
bâche 11, 12, 16
'background' people, of confrontational situations
4, 14–15
Bakhtin, Mikhail 131

Bakrie, Aburizal 91
Bakrie family 90–91
Barra Bravas 100, 103–104
Battini, Adrien 38–39
Bauman, Richard 147
BCS (Brigade Curva Sud) 95
Beitar Jerusalem 71, 77
Belözoğlu, Emre 43, 46
Benedict, Ruth 158n12
Berlusconi, Silvio 4
Beşiktaş and its fans 40–41, 43–44, 45, 48n1
Beşiktaş İnönü Stadium 41
BFC Dynamo Berlin 65n10
BJK 42; administrators 44; fans 43; Serdar Bilgili
administration 41
Bonek 1927 96–97
Bonek of Surabaya 96, 98
Bonek, ultras at 4
Boniek, Zbigniew 35n2
Borussia Dortmund ultras 2, 66n27
boycotts 130, 135, 137–138, 142n8
Brajamusti and its supporter group 92, 95, 98;
external rivalries 93–94; rivalry with The
Maident 93; rivalry with Pasoepati 93
Brigada Malcha 76
Bursaspor 38, 48n1

Calmund, Rainer 63
Canada 100, 101, 102, 110; supporters section in
soccer stadiums stands 104–105
çapulcu 42
çArşı 4, 40–41, 43, 45–46, 47, 48n6
Carlson, M. 25
Carl-Zeiss Jena 59
carnivalesque 5, 131, 140
Cassano, Antonio 159n18
casuals 3, 10, 11, 13, 18–19, 90, 98, 103–104
Catania, ultras of 1
Chinaglia, Giorgio 152
Ciamis fans 88, 89, 90, 94
Claussen, Detlev 110
Cohen, S. 52

INDEX

collective identity 119–120, 121
Collins, Randall 4, 12, 16–17
commercialization of football: in Australia 115,
    125; in Croatia 128, 130; in Israel 81–82
confrontational culture 10, 11–12, 19
confrontational situations 4, 12; beginners and
    women 14–15; discretion and avoidance
    strategies 18; equality of fighters 17–18; fighters'
    school 10–12; followers 15–16; 'good guys'
    and the 'first line' 16–17; hierarchy and role
    distribution 12–17; learning to fight 11; mock
    fights 12; no weapon rule 17; 'openers,' role of
    13; persons staying in the background
    14–15; search for adrenaline 19;
    witnesses 13–14
consumption and fandom 100–101
Cove, The 121
Cracovia club 28, 33
creative accommodation 82
Croatia and Croatia ultras 128–129, 129–130;
    'Against Modern Football' movement
    130–131; boycotts 130, 135, 137–138, 142n8;
    carnivalesque 131, 140; carnival supporters
    131; commercialization of football 128, 130;
    Dalmatia 132, 133; derby supporters 134,
    137; fight and self-defence 136; football
    establishment 133–134; hooligans 131; social
    class and subculturalization in 130; 'street'
    (ulica) 134–136, 140; street fight 136; Torcida
    see Torcida; violence as part of carnival 136,
    140; vs. Croatian Football Federation 133,
    137–138, 142n4; wealthy owner as solution for
    club's financial crisis 139
cultural forms of fandom 5
cultural pedagogies 115, 116, 117–118, 120;
    political nature of 115; practices 115
cultural sites 124
culture 148–149; as commodity, participants
    in 25–26
Cursed Soldiers (Żołnierze Wyklęci) 23,
    29–30, 35n1
customers, fandom as 110

Debord, Guy 45
derby supporters 134, 137
de-seriousization 57
deviant behaviour 53–54
DFB 54, 60
Dilmen, Rıdvan 46
Dinamo Zagreb 132, 135
dirigen 89
discretion and avoidance strategies 18
Djedović, Stjepan 133–134
Dresden ultras 3
Durkheim, Emile 117
Dynamo Dresden 51–52, 54; ban from European
    Cup 54; under Bundesliga 54; chaos club image
    54–55; modern football, anti-stance towards 62;
    relegations 54; reputation of 63

DynamofanTV 57–58
Dziedzic, Dawid 137

Eastern Germany 54, 56; Dynamo Dresden see
    Dynamo Dresden; football and fan activism
    59; symbolism 56; Ultras Dynamo see Ultras
    Dynamo (UD)
East-West opposition 121–122
Eko Satrio Pringgodani 93
Ekşi Sözlük 39, 48n4
Elbkaida TV 57
emotional domination 13–14, 17
Empire Supporters Club (ESC) 107–108
Engin, Tolga 42
equality of fighters 17–18
Erdoğan, Recep Tayyip 42
ethnic communities, and football 117
ethnography: ethics of 152–155; funding 150;
    practice 150–152; social skills and tricks
    150–152; theory of 145–147
Etzioni, Amitai 63
European Ultras 100
eyewitness, of confrontational situations 13–14

fanaticisms 43, 48
fandom: bonding and bridging 80; as community
    79–81; and exclusion 79; and responsibility 81–
    83; social dimension 82
fandom and culture studies 115–116;
    ethnographic venture 116; and theoretical
    approaches 116
fan-ownership 82, 84; see also Hapoel Katamon
    Jerusalem (HKJ)
Fans' Rights Association (Turkey) 39, 44, 45, 47
fanzines 9
fascination/fear discourse 4, 39–43, 44, 47, 48
Faust des Ostens 60–61
FC United of Manchester 82, 130, 139
female ultra fans 14–15, 19
Femen 61, 66n35
Fenerbahçe and its fans 40, 45, 46, 48n1
fight charisma 12, 13
Fight Club (movie) 19
fighters' school 10–12
'firm' 103
'first line' people, of confrontational situations
    4, 16–17
flares issue, in Australian football 123–124
folklore 146
followers, of confrontational situations 15–16
football hooliganism see hooliganism
football politics 5–6
Fortuna Köln 59
France, ultras in 9–10
Franičević, Vojmir 133
FSV Zwickau ultras 55

Galatama 91
Galatasaray and its fans 40, 45, 46, 48n1

GDR teams 3, 55, 64–65n5, 65n9
Geertz, Clifford 53
gender gap, in ultras study 6–7
Genny 'a Carogna 1
genuine support 75, 77, 78–79, 80, 83
Germany 102, 111n8, 111n9
Germany/German ultras; *see also* Dynamo
    Dresden; Eastern Germany; *Ultras
    Dynamo* (UD)
Gezi Uprising 39, 42, 45, 46
Giroux, Henry A. 116, 118, 124–125
Giulianotti, Richard 131
global–local conflict and influence 3–6
Glynis M. Breakwell 64
Golkar 91
Gonda, Marcin 142
'good guy' people, of confrontational situations 4,
    14, 16–17
Górnik Wałbrzych ultras 29
Green Angels 10
Green Nord 27 95–96, 96–97
'group identity' people, of confrontational
    situations 10

Hajduk 131, 132, 135, 137, 138, 142n8
Hajdučko Beer 137
Hall, Stuart 32, 42
Hamengkubuwono X, Sultan of Yogyakata 95
Hamsik, Marek 1
Hapoel Jerusalem (HJ) 71, 73, 85; and Hapoel
    Katamon Jerusalem, merger proposals 78–79;
    rejection of racism 77
Hapoel Katamon Jerusalem (HKJ) and fandom
    5–6, 70–72, 85; as an inclusive civil association
    83–84; authenticity 75–76, 78–79; banning of
    verbal violence and cursing, debate on 75–76;
    and Beitar Jerusalem 77; collective identity
    73, 77, 78; as community 79–81; community
    activity 71, 76; constitution 73; diversity versus
    authenticity 75–76; establishment of 71–72, 73;
    genuine support 75, 77, 78–79, 80, 83; identity
    of 76; inclusive strategy 75; legitimacy and
    authority 83–84; online forums 73–74, 75–76,
    78–79, 81; oral traditions and memories
    77–78; performance of 74–76; and
    responsibility 82–83; response to setting
    fire on Jerusalem's bilingual school 76; and
    symbolic definitions 72–74; violence against
    Arabs in Jerusalem, debate on 74; women
    supporters 75
hardcore fan 103
HNK Rijeka, supporters of 135
Hodkinson, Paul 130
'Homosexuality forbidden!' 31
Hong Kong 45
honour 4
hooliganism 5, 31, 53, 66n39; British hooliganism
    3, 4; in Croatia 129, 140; and fandom 81;
    hooligan and ultras groups, difference

between 56; in Poland 24, 31, 33–34; in United
    States 103
Hooltras 55–56
Hughson, John 140
hyper-commercialism 101
hyper-stylization, *Ultras Dynamo* 62

ideal fan 41
Independent Supporters Council (ISC) 105
Indonesia 4, 87, 97; Bakrie family 90–91; Bonek
    1927 96–97; Bonek of Surabaya 96, 98;
    Brajamusti supporter group 92–93; Eko Satrio
    Pringgodani 93; Galatama 91; Golkar 91;
    Green Nord 27 95–96, 96–97; Maident, The
    93, 95, 98; Pasoepati 90–91, 94, 97–98; PDI-P
    (Democratic Party of Struggle) 98; Pelita Bakrie
    (Pelita Bandung Raya) 90–91; post-New Order
    era 91–92; PPP (United Development Party)
    98; PSSI (Indonesian Football Association) 88,
    97; Suharto family 90
Indonesia ultras: AC Milan supporters 92; B7
    ultras of Pasoepati 88, 89, 91; Brajamusti
    and its supporter group 92–95, 98; Ciamis
    fans 88, 89, 90, 94; external rivalries 93–95;
    Juventus supporters 92; and Mayor Haristanto
    91; on modern football 87; performances
    qualities 88–90
industrialized football 44
inspiration of ultras culture 5
Irriducibili 152, 153–154, 154–155
Iskan, Dahlan 96
Israel *see* Hapoel Jerusalem (HJ); Hapoel Katamon
    Jerusalem (HKJ)
'Istanbul United' 46
Italy 6, 9; and culture 148–149; ethnographic
    ethics 152–155; ethnographic funding
    150; ethnographic practice 150–152;
    ethnographic theory 145–147; and folklore
    146; marginalization of ultras as a 'violent
    mob' 47; performances in 146; ultrà and ultras,
    distinction between 156–157

Jefferson, T. 32
'Jihad Legia' 31
Junaedi, Fajar 94
Juventus supporters 92

Kandang Menjangan 94
kapalı 40–41, 43
Kasapoğlu, Çağıl 46
Kennedy, David 39, 142
Kılıç, Suat 46
King, Anthony 31, 102, 109
Klopp, Jürgen 2
Kohl, Helmut 65n5
Kop of Boulogne 19
Koprivnica Brewery 137
Kurds 45, 48n9
Kusuma, Adnan D. 94

INDEX

Lazio fans 152, 153–154, 154–155
Lechia fans 28
Lechia Gdańsk ultras 30, 34–35
Lech Poznań ultras 33, 35n2
Lee, Francis 45
Legia Warsaw fans 28, 29–30, 33, 34, 35n2
Lehmann, Stefan 5, 55, 57, 58, 65n11
Leipzig 66n39, 108, 111n9
Lemert, Edwin M. 53
ŁKS club 33
lobbying for rights 105–106
local identity 10
looters 42
Los Angeles Galaxy 105
Lügenpresse 60

Maffesoli, Michel 142n1
Magic Fans 10, 133
Maident, The 93, 95, 98
Major League Soccer (MLS) 102, 105, 106, 111n7
Mamić, Zdravko 134
Mamić, Zoran 134
Manchester United supporters 109
Marchi, Valerio 151, 159n17
Marseille, groups from 17
Marsh, Peter 31
masculinity 4, 10, 31, 52, 53, 61
matos 10, 11, 15, 16
Mavi Şimşekler 39
Mead, Margaret 158n12
Meenzelmänner 66n27
mentalita ultras 6
metaphysics: of the ordinary people 117; on the stands 119–120
MetroStars 108
Meuser, Michael 61
mock fights 12
modern football, resistance to *see* Against Modern Football (AMF) movement; anti-modern football stance
Mosse, George 32
Mustapić, Marko 132
MYPLACE (Memory, Youth, Political Legacy and Civic Engagement) project 131–132

Naš Hajduk 138
national–Catholic ideology 23
neo-liberalization of soccer 102
New York Cosmos 105, 109
New York Red Bull 5
New York Red Bulls 105; and accountability 106–107; and supporters' limitations 107–109
Nice, groups from 17
No Name Boys (supporters of Benfica) 133
North America 102, 109
North American Soccer League (NASL) 110
'No To Modern Football' movement 5
Numerato, Dino 57, 102, 116, 122, 123–124, 142

Oberliga 54, 65n9
'openers,' in confrontational situations 4, 13
organized groups 26, 110, 156
Orientalism 42
OSP 135, 142n6
Özal, Turgut 39

Palermo, ultras of 1
Pasoepati 89–91, 94, 97–98
PDI-P (Democratic Party of Struggle) 98
Pearson, Geoff 130
Pegida movement 60, 62, 66n39
Pelita Bakrie (Pelita Bandung Raya) 90–91
Perasovic, Benjamin 132
performances 22–23; analysis of 24–26; and audience 25; display concepts 25; elements of 25; in Italy 146; and modernization 27; qualities of 88–90; stemming from rules of native local culture 26; theory of 24–26; *see also* Polish ultras
Persebaya 1927 96
Persebaya Surabaya 96
Persiba Bantul 95
Persijatim Solo FC 91
Persis Solo 4, 90
Petke, Michael 106–107, 109
Piast Żmigród fans 32
Pilkington, Hilary 130
Pilz, Gunter. A. 43
PKK (Kurdistan Workers' Party) 48n9
Plickert, Arnold 51
Poland 3; AMF movement in 142; anti-government slogan 23–24; conflict with the establishment 27; fifth-generation stadiums 26; football fans' response to raising issue of Islam in Europe 32; football stadiums, sociocultural activity and modernization of 23; institutionalization of ultras groups 27; and Lithuania 31; and Ukraine 31
Polish ultras 35; anti-communist performances 30–31; anti-modernization performances 34–35; anti-Semitic performances 32–33; choreographies 26–27, 28; Cursed Soldiers (*Żołnierze Wyklęci*) memoralization 23, 29–30, 35n1; extremist performances 32–33; gender gap 31, 35n4; history of 26–27; hooligan and prison-themed performances 33–34; Lechia and Arka rivalry 28; patriotic and historical performances 29–30; performance displays 25; performances as comment on current politics 31; performances expressing collective identity 28–29; resistance to modern football concept 32; social revolt and class system 22–24; support shows 27–35; and Tusk 23–24; unrealistic conflict 23
Polish Underground State (*Polskie Państwo Podziemne*) 23
political agency, in commodified modern football context 122–123

political identity 5–6
Porras 100
PPP (United Development Party) 98
Preussen Münster 61
primary deviance 53
PSIM 92–93, 94–95, 98
PSSI (Indonesian Football Association) 88, 97
PSS Sleman 94–95
Putnam, Robert D. 80

racism 42–43
RasenBallsport Leipzig 108, 111n9
rebellious' aspect of ultras culture 5
Red and Black Bloc (RBB) 3, 115; capo position in
    119; chants and choreographies 118, 119, 122;
    hierarchies and divisions in 119; and initiatives
    120; and modern football gatekeepers 122–123;
    and organic experiences 119; origins of 118;
    relationship with modern football gatekeepers
    122–123
Red Bull 111n9; *see also* New York Red Bull
#RedBullOut 106–107, 109
Red Bull Salzburg 108
Regionalliga 54
Reichstein, Mercedes 61
Resovia Rzeszów fans 32–33
Roma Club Testaccio 152
Roma ultras, attack on Napoli fans 1
rude culture 10
rule-breaking 53

Said, Edward 42
Saint-Etienne, ultra from 10–11, 19
Sandvoss, Cornel 100–101
Scalia, Vincenzo 47
Schwarz-Gelbe Hilfe 60
secondary deviance 53
self-defence 136
serious leisure communities 106
Širić, Željko 133, 134
Slemania fans 95
social agency 70, 116, 118
social aspects of fan culture 1–2
social class: differences in Polish stadiums
    25; othering of ultras, in Turkey 40; and
    subculturalization, in Croatia 130
social cohesion enhancement 116, 117, 120–121
social media 6; discipling ultras through 3
Solo-based ultras: rise of, and their incorporation
    into Pasoepati 91–92
South American Barra Bravas 100
Spain 102
spectacularization 39, 44–45, 48
Speziale, Antonio 1
stadium performances *see* performances
Stal Rzeszów fans 33
Standard Liege ultras 1
St Etienne ultras 4
St. Pauli 59

'street' *(ulica)* 134–136, 140
street fight 136
subculture 5, 129–130
Suharto family 90
supporters 109; accountability 106–107; fans
    engagement in collective action 105; limitations
    107–109; modes of expression 106; organized
    groups 105; privileges 105; section 103
Supporters Shield 111n7
Sydney Football Club (SFC) 120–121

Tal der Ahnungslosen 65n15
Taylor Report 42
Teksas ultras 38
Tek Yumruk 45, 46
temporary leaders 16
terrace displays 9, 10
Testa, Alberto 102
TFF 42
Thatcher, Margaret 142n2
Theweleit, Klause 32
tifos 9, 10, 14, 105, 118
Toledo, Luiz Henrique De 116
Topal, F. 39
Torcida 100, 132–133; and AMF 141–142; and
    the AMF movement 136–139; core members,
    carnival and hooligan 134–136; methods of
    struggle 137; OSP 135; stereotyping by media
    141; 'street' 134–136; supporters of
    Hajduk 131, 132; violence as part of the
    carnival 140
Torcida Górnik (Górnik Zabrze) 133
Tulus, Cak 96
Turkey: attempts to 'manage' ultras in 47;
    commercialization and legal restructuring of
    football in 44; fanaticisms 43, 48; fan groups
    and fellow ultras groups, lack coordination
    and cooperation among 39; Fans' Rights
    Association 39, 44, 45, 47; Law to Prevent
    Violence and Disorder in Sport (Violence Law)
    42, 44, 47; refraining the term ultras in 39
Turkish ultras 38–40; and branding 41–42;
    fascination/fear discourse 4, 39–43, 44, 47, 48;
    politics vs. culture 45–47; and racism 42–43;
    self-perception and agency 43–45
Tusk, Donald 23–24

Uhlig, Marcus 52, 55
ultras 9; ability to defend 11–12; activities of
    9–10; and branding 41–42; group's identity 5–6;
    history of 101–102; and hooligans, difference
    between 56; origination of 2; othering of 40;
    presentation of self 4; spread of 2, 3; subculture
    129–130
ultràs: definition of 155–156; and other dedicated
    fans, distinction between 156; and rivalries 156;
    and ultras, distinction between 156–157; unity
    vs. rivalry 157–158
Ultras 1923 92, 98

Ultras Dynamo (UD) 3, 5, 52, 54; and *1953 International* 61, 62; active scene 55, 57–58, 60, 61, 62, 64, 65n8; anti-media and anti-authority stances 60; apolitical, problematization of 58–62; banner of 55; collective identity 63; de-seriousization 57; discriminatory and exclusionary political activities 61–62; dress code 56–57; and Eastern German identity 55–56; and *Faust des Ostens* 60–61; folkloristic elements 53, 61–62, 66n33; football and fan activism 59–60; and hooliganism 55–56; hyper-stylization of themselves as the 'Other' 58; identity construction 62–63, 63–64; ideological political activities 60–61; media coverage 52; outsiders and stigmatized labelling 53; political attitude 62–63; right-wing extremism 55, 58–59, 60–61, 62, 65n10; *Schwarz-Gelbe Hilfe* 60; self-representation in the media 57–58; self-stylization 64; self-understanding 64; stylization of 55; YouTube channel of 57–58; *Zentralorgan* 55, 60–61
UltrAslan 38, 39, 41, 46
ultras tribe 142n1
Ulu, Sinan 41
Union Berlin 59
United States 100, 101, 102, 109, 110; Barra Bravas 100, 103–104; fans as consumers 104–106; markers of soccer-fandom 103; modern football in 100, 101–102; National Football League (NFL) 104; New York Red Bulls *see* New York Red Bulls; supporters in 107–109; supporters section in soccer stadiums stands 104–105
Universitas Sebelas Maret 94
Uygur, Mehmet 40, 41

Vamos Bien 45
Varteks Varaždin 130

violence 4, 10–12, 17, 53; limitations on 136; as part of carnival 140; *see also* confrontational culture; confrontational situations
Voce della Nord, La 154
Voorhees, Jason 1
Vrbanović, Damir 134

Wallace, David Foster 148
Warren, John 117
Warsaw Uprising of 1944 29
weapon, use of 17
Webber, David 142
Western Sydney 116–117; communal identification and involvement 116, 118, 125; region's profile 117; Sydney icons 117
Western Sydney ultras 114–115; cultural diversity in 120; immigrant population in 116; RBB *see* Red and Black Bloc (RBB); role in cultural panorama of Australian football 125; unity in 120
Western Sydney Wanderers FC (WSW) 3, 114–115, 120–121
West Java 94
Widzew club 33
Wisła, fans of 33
witnesses, of confrontational situations 4, 13–14
wogball 117
wogs 116–117
Wölki-Schumacher, Franciska 43
women, in confrontational situations 14–15, 19

Yılmaz, Hasan 42
Yogyakarta 92–93, 94–95, 96, 98n1
Young, Malcolm 44, 47

Zagreb 133
Zentralorgan 55, 60–61
Županov, Josip 133
Żyleta 26